The Corporate Paradox

Since the late 1970s the emergence of franchising arrangements has been a major part of the wider process of change taking place in the nature of modern business organization. The names of franchise companies are familiar to most people: Coca-Cola, McDonald's, Pepsi-Cola, Wimpy, Body Shop, ServiceMaster, to name but a few. But how many people realize that each such outlet is a separate legal entity, owned by a local franchisee? Franchising remains, at best, little understood.

This book is the first major, in-depth study of the franchise relationship and how it functions. While past debates have focused on the question: 'What do bosses do?', we are now being asked: 'Who really is the boss?'. Alan Felstead explores who controls what, why and how, setting his discussion within the context of the many current changes affecting traditional contractual bonds between employers and employees, producers and buyers, owners and managers.

The Corporate Paradox will appeal to all those who wish to understand more about the organizational structures of well-known companies – companies about which few details have been known until now. Offering a view forward, through the 1990s and into a new era of business transactions, it will be of seminal importance to students and teachers of management, organizational studies, marketing, industrial sociology and commercial law.

Alan Felstead is Research Associate at the Centre for Labour Market Studies, University of Leicester.

The Corporate Paradox

Power and control in the
business franchise

Alan Felstead

London and New York

First published 1993
by Routledge
11 New Fetter Lane, London EC4P 4EE

Simultaneously published in the USA and Canada
by Routledge
29 West 35th Street, New York, NY 10001

© 1993 Alan Felstead

Typeset in Times by
Ponting–Green Publishing Services, Chesham, Bucks

Printed and bound in Great Britain by
Mackays of Chatham PLC, Chatham, Kent

British Library Cataloguing in Publication Data

A catalogue record for this book is available from the
British Library

*Library of Congress Cataloging in Publication Data has been
applied for.*

ISBN 0–415–09983–8   0–415–09984–6

Contents

Figures

Tables

Preface

This book breaks entirely new ground in the study of the franchisor–franchisee relationship. Questions such as who controls what, how and why are posed, and some answers are offered. Variations between franchise systems are considered as well as how and why responsibilities might shift over time. But like so many other organizational issues, franchising opens up more than one avenue of research. Each warrants close investigation, and could no doubt justify a book in its own right. However, research requires quite specific objectives. The pursuit of several ends simultaneously puts in danger the construction of a coherent argument backed-up by solid empirical and theoretical evidence. In other words, one must be aware at all times of what to include and what to exclude. The primary aim of the book is to provide a serious investigation of the nature of the franchise relationship in order to assess whether or not firms who use franchising are relinquishing control over the actions of those on whom they rely for success or failure.

Franchising has had a enormous impact on the economies in which it has taken root. Not only have companies such as the Coca-Cola Company directly created around 20,000 jobs worldwide, but by using franchising many more jobs have been created by their franchisees (the Coca-Cola system, for example, is reckoned to account for the livelihoods of 650,000 people worldwide, *The Coca-Cola Company Annual Report 1991*: 10–11). Sharing their technical 'know-how' and marketing skills with franchisees has eased the difficulties associated with business start-up and raised their chances of survival. Once established, franchisees have stimulated suppliers such as bottle makers and cap producers. They, in turn, have taken on more labour, and in line with the multiplier principle, a further round of jobs has been created.

The published figures on the use of franchising in the major industrialized economies serve to indicate its magnitude. For the US, it is estimated that 35 per cent of all retail sales is generated by franchising

(International Franchise Association Educational Foundation, 1991: 7). While comparable figures are not available across Europe, there is evidence to suggest that franchising is being adopted by more and more companies (Euromonitor, 1987; European Franchise Federation, 1992). This book does not assess the economic impact of franchising, but instead discusses the evidence already available as a prelude to an assessment of the nature of the relationship.

Besides the macro-economic impact, franchising has had a significant impact on individuals. Many owe their jobs, and some their fortunes, to franchising. The trade press (e.g. *Franchise World*, the *Franchise Magazine* and *Business Franchise Magazine*) has many success stories and anecdotes to bear this out. Once again this book is not the place to find such an analysis.

The most recent books on franchising have come from a popular genre – offering advice on, and an introduction to, franchising. Most have been written for prospective franchisees. Attention is given to the advantages and disadvantages of franchising to the franchisor, franchisee and customer. Unlike the popular books on franchising, the present one does not weigh up the advantages and disadvantages to all the parties involved, and then offer a judgement or recommendation. Indeed, it is not the book's purpose to offer advice and encouragement *for or against* taking the franchise route either as a franchisee or a franchisor. That is for others to decide.

Instead, this book was written to inform a much wider debate about the changing nature of business organization. While past debates have centred around the question: what do bosses do? (Marglin, 1974; Landes, 1986), the break-up of today's large corporations prompts us to consider a question previously taken-for-granted: who really is the boss? The book provides evidence on how franchisors motivate, lead and control their franchisees' networks even though they do not formally hold stakes in their franchisees' businesses. It reveals how and why some of the credentials of an employer can be sustained even in the absence of a conventional employment relationship. As such, students and teachers of management studies, organizational behaviour, marketing, industrial sociology and commercial law will gain much from a thorough reading of this book; practitioners are likely to find the case study material of particular interest. The general reader, too, will find the book appealing since it deals with the organizational structures of well-known companies about which little detail has been known until now.

Alan Felstead
December 1992

Acknowledgements

No book, and certainly no research which underpins it, can be undertaken without the help and support of others. This book and the research on which it is based is no exception. A list of acknowledgements therefore allows the author to record publicly this help.

⟩ I am grateful first and foremost to the Edward Heath Charitable Trust for funding this research. Without this support franchising would have remained poorly understood despite its growing economic importance worldwide.

It is difficult to envisage a better place in which to conduct this kind of research than Nuffield College, Oxford; its research facilities and back-up are second to none. In addition, several Fellows of the College gave valuable support at one time or another: Chris Bliss, Michael Brock, Duncan Gallie, David Hendry, John Muellbauer and John Vickers. David Cox proved a constant source of advice and encouragement; his unswerving support is highly treasured. While all the research and the drafting of this book was conducted at Nuffield College, University of Oxford, the finishing touches were added during the first few months of my appointment at the Centre for Labour Market Studies, University of Leicester. I am most grateful for being allowed the time to complete unfinished business.

I would also like to thank collectively the hundreds of individuals who answered my questions and/or supplied me with materials about the way franchising worked in their organizations. Without them I would have nothing new to report. However, guarantees of confidentiality prevent me from naming even the most informative sources or those who eased my access into their franchise organizations.

Several individuals waded through the early drafts of the book, and offered helpful and constructive criticisms as to how the argument might be sharpened and improved. I am grateful to Patricia Leighton, Chris Rowley and Andrew Scott for undertaking this task and for doing so in a manner which did not pull any punches or spare any of my blushes. Finally, I would like to thank Lorraine Felstead for enduring the weekends I spent finishing the book; from now on, weekends will be for recreational purposes only, at least until another project nears a deadline!

Introduction

Most, if not all, of those who pick up this book will have dealt with a franchised business at one time or another, whether eating a McDonald's hamburger, drinking a can of Coca-Cola or calling out Dyno-Rod to unblock their drains. Yet, many people may not realize that they are, in fact, dealing with a locally run business operating in line with specifications set by the brand owner. While those who run individual hamburger restaurants, bottling plants or local drain cleaning operations (the franchisees) 'own' much of the physical apparatus of the business, the franchisor owns the brand name and has the right to determine how it is used. Many people are unaware of such subtleties. There are no obvious signs to distinguish one outlet from another; all do business in the same way and market themselves under a common (and often well-known) brand name. And yet, they are legally distinct businesses. This presents a paradox. On the one hand, a franchised business looks and acts like a branch of a much larger corporation, while on the other hand, it retains a distinct legal persona.

Until now, little has been done to unpack this paradox; questions such as who controls what, why and how, have remained unanswered, and franchising has, at best, remained poorly understood. The aim of this book is to fill the gap. Completion of such a task could not have been more timely. Franchising has grown significantly throughout the world during the last decade. Its growth has been rapid; more rapid than perhaps most people realize, until one looks at the names of those now offering franchise opportunities (see Appendices I, II and III for UK, US and Australian examples). Today, several of these examples can be found operating in almost every high street or shopping centre in the industrialized world. Moreover, there are several factors which will promote still wider use. For example, the growth of service industries, where franchising is most common, the growing number of American franchisors exporting their concepts to other parts of the globe, and the fact that one third of all retail sales in the US go through franchise channels, leaves little room for doubt that franchising will affect the lives of a growing number of people in the years ahead.

The purpose of these introductory remarks is to give the reader an outline of how the book investigates the franchise paradox. It therefore highlights chapters which may be of particular interest to the reader and the evidence upon which the book is based. Each chapter is designed to be more or less self-contained, so that chapters of particular interest can be read in isolation from the others without seriously diluting their impact.

OUTLINE OF THE BOOK

The production of goods and services is becoming increasingly fragmented. Across much of the industrialized world the nature of business is changing – large corporate entities are becoming more variegated and the number of small independent entrepreneurs appears to be growing. Does this mean that the long-established tendency towards the concentration and centralization of business interests within fewer and fewer hands is being reversed? Does this signal the development of a popular and broadly based capitalism in which an ever greater number of people can exercise meaningful control over their working lives? These broad questions inspired the research on which the book is based. Chapter 1 examines these questions and the evidence upon which one might draw. It illustrates that beneath an apparent diversification of business ownership, there lurks within franchising (as within other business relationships) less obvious but more important debates about who controls what, why and how. Indeed, the vertical disintegration of production and the rapid growth of 'independent' businesses, such as franchised ones, may conceal far more than it reveals about who really is in control.

Chapter 2 traces the historical development of franchising as a way of conducting business from its very beginnings up to its present-day practice. Particular attention is given to an analysis of those sectors where franchising has taken root, the entry costs for franchisees, and the form and level of on-going payments franchisees make to the franchisor. It also considers evidence of its growing significance across Europe, the US and Australia.

Why then has franchising become such a popular way of doing business? The conventional explanation is based on New Institutionalist economics, an explanation which has gone virtually unchallenged until now. Chapter 3 develops an alternative. The assumed equality between franchisee and franchisor is rejected in favour of an explanation based on franchisees being more dependent on their franchisor than the franchisor is on them. Franchisors therefore remain in strategic control of franchisees' business, and take some of the value they produce. Franchisees, on the other hand, have a greater financial incentive to work themselves and their workforce harder than would be the case if they were 'employed'. The asymmetry of dependence is further underlined by results of a survey of 199 UK franchisees which shows that existing franchisees had few ideas of their own on which to base a business.

The franchise contract plays a major role in determining the relationship between franchisor and franchisee; a contractual analysis is central to an assessment of what makes franchising work. What does a franchise contract actually contain? Under what circumstances are franchisees held to abide by its clauses? Chapter 4 examines both of these questions. The first question is answered by scrutinizing 83 UK franchise contracts provided to the author on request. Each contract is analysed with three subsidiary questions in mind: where does the operational control of the business reside; what are the financial linkages between franchisor and franchisee; and who holds the ownership title to, and control of, the tangible and intangible business assets. On each, franchisees are found to occupy an ambiguous position – to be neither fully in control nor fully controlled. The degree of control formally bestowed on franchisors by contract varies significantly from franchise to franchise; some are 'harder' than others. The chapter also considers the question of when and why the terms of the contract are enforced. Although more difficult to gauge, the chapter argues that their use is determined by the state of the market for franchisees and their product, as well as the nature of the product market franchisees face.

The effects of change on the nature of the franchise relationship are the subject of Chapters 5 and 6. Chapter 5 considers the repercussions which might follow a change in franchisor ownership. It tracks the consequences of just such an eventuality in one case study company: the shift towards a 'harder' franchise relationship, the reaction of franchisees and the attempts to enforce a weak franchise agreement. Changes in the commercial environment franchisees face may also reveal the divergent interests of franchisor and franchisee. For example, the large economies gained from concentrating production in fewer plants coupled with the rise in the buying power of those to whom Coca-Cola franchisees sell, have served to reveal the divergent interests of the Coca-Cola Company and its franchisees. Chapter 6 follows this process in Germany and explains why the franchise structure was reshaped in the way it was. Consideration is also given to the reshaping of the Coca-Cola Company's franchise structure worldwide.

The book ends by synthesizing the argument of the book and tracing its implications. For many disciplines, the firm has been taken to refer unquestionably to the legal institution. However, this book forms part of the growing recognition (e.g. Handy, 1984; Amin and Dietrich, 1990) that businesses are able to exercise control far beyond their narrow legal boundaries. This book provides evidence of how franchisors organize their networks, and how they motivate, lead and control their franchisees. Other inter-firm relationships will require similar treatment in order to assess who really controls what, why and how.

SOURCES OF EVIDENCE

The book's task is to reconcile the apparently contradictory marketing techniques and slogans used by franchisors in different contexts. When addressing an audience of prospective franchisees great stress is placed on franchising as a 'chance to be your own boss', an opportunity to 'mind your own business' and so on. This is at odds with the corporate image portrayed by a common trade mark/format/idea which is used to attract business for the franchisee. Both marketing strategies reflect different aspects of the franchise relationship. They also reflect the tension at the heart of the relationship: who's really in control of which aspects of the franchisee's business, why are these controls considered necessary, and how and when are these powers exercised. To investigate these questions, one has to go beyond the superficialities of franchise brochures and company accounts (issued free of charge if quoted on the stock market) to an examination of franchising at work. This immediately presents problems. First, the data for the analysis are relatively inaccessible. There is no public record of the terms on which franchises are offered or subsequently changed; they remain private agreements between legally independent entities. Without the co-operation of the parties involved the workings of franchising remain hidden from view. Second, 'those who sit among the mighty do not [readily] invite sociologists to watch them make their decisions about how to control the behavior of others' (Kahl, 1957: 10, quoted in Zeitlin, 1974: 1085). Evidence for this book has therefore been drawn from a wide variety of sources. Broadly speaking, the data were collected at two levels: general level and specific/case study level. The bulk of the fieldwork was carried out between June 1988 and June 1991. This section details the methods and analytical tools used in collecting the data at each level.

General level

Research conducted at the general level comprised: keeping the trade and financial press under constant review; conducting interviews with a range of people who had an interest in franchising; regular attendance at the relevant franchise exhibitions; and a systematic analysis of franchise contracts.

The number of franchise-specific magazines now available in high street shops, such as W.H. Smith, bears ample testimony to the growth of franchising in the UK. They also provide researchers with valuable information on current developments within UK franchising. The three magazines (*Franchise World* founded in 1978; *Franchise Magazine* launched in 1985; and *Business Franchise Magazine* first on sale in 1987) were therefore monitored on a regular basis. This was supplemented by reports on the financial state of franchise companies as reported by journalists writing for the *Financial Times*. The relevant specialist trade publications were also consulted whenever interviews were conducted with franchisors or franchisees who operated in sectors with which the author was unfamiliar. So publications such as *Motor Trader*, *Popular Food Service* (now *Restaurateur*), *Inplant and Instant Printer* and *The Grocer* were on occasion consulted. Other press reports were also used, and are referred to in the text, but were collected in a more ad hoc manner. For example, some interviewees cited certain press reports which were followed up and then used, where relevant, in the analysis (e.g. *Wall Street Journal*, *Atlanta Constitution*).

Franchising has a host of professional services supporting its development: bankers, accountants, lawyers and consultants. Like the franchise press, their numbers have swelled as franchising has grown. For example, in 1981 the National Westminster Bank appointed a franchise manager to co-ordinate the bank's lending policy to franchisees. The other major high street banks in the UK quickly followed suit: Barclays appointed a franchise manager soon after the National Westminster, Lloyds put a franchise manager in place in 1982 and the Midland had a manager with special responsibility for franchising in post by the end of 1983 (Stern and Stanworth, 1988). The growth of franchising also offered more work for other professionals: accountants called upon to scrutinize pro forma accounts provided by franchisors to prospective franchisees; lawyers asked to draw up franchise contracts, commissioned by prospective franchisees to check their legality as well as engaged to offer advice, arbitrate or act as advocates in dispute resolution. Interviews were therefore conducted with 15 high profile bankers, accountants, lawyers and consultants (all, but one, were listed as affiliates of the British Franchise Association, a listing widely replicated in many 'source' books: e.g. Barrow and Golzen, 1991; Stanworth and Smith, 1991). Each interview was structured around the interviewee's specialism and how it was used in the context of franchising.

Interviews were also conducted with those operating at the sharp end of the franchise relationship: franchisors and franchisees. Thirty-five were interviewed: of these 19 were franchisors and 16 were franchisees. Franchisors were selected mainly on the grounds of their size (i.e. number of franchised establishments), while the franchisees were selected mainly as the result of their being in dispute with their franchisor (some of which were unsolicited, i.e. they contacted the author). Both sets of interviews were designed to elicit the nature of the franchise relationship as practised by different systems. The interviews with franchisees in dispute were also motivated by the need to assess under what circumstances the legally binding franchise contract was used. Written documentation was also collected (e.g. offer documents, correspondence, lists and affidavits). In addition, 12 'industry' officials and observers (e.g. franchise journalists) were interviewed. All in all, 62 interviews were conducted at this general level of analysis. Copious field notes were taken during interviews and then written up either that evening or the day after. Some of the evidence collected during these interviews is used in Chapter 4.

Franchisors now have the opportunity to display their franchises at the twice-yearly franchise exhibitions (typically held in London and Birmingham). For example, the 1991 National Franchise Exhibition held in the Autumn attracted the highest number of visitors in the event's eight-year history – a total of 13,098 people attended over a three-day period. This represented a 10 per cent increase over the previous year's Autumn exhibition, and was notched up in spite of depressed trading conditions throughout the economy. Around 100 franchise systems were on show. Four of these exhibitions were visited, because they enabled the researcher to gather the franchise prospectuses made freely available to visitors to the exhibition. A total of 130 were collected in this way.

The general level interviews consistently emphasized the centrality of the franchise contract to the nature of the franchise relationship. An assessment of franchise contracts was therefore called for. Requests were made of 325 business format franchisors listed in the UK's *Franchise World Directory 1990* to supply copies of: (a) the franchise prospectus they would send to a prospective franchisee; and (b) the franchise contract that would govern the relationship once a franchisee had been recruited. From a single mailing, 117 supplied a copy of their franchise prospectus, 83 of whom also provided a copy of their franchise contract. This added 86 franchise prospectuses to the 130 already collected (i.e. there were 31 duplicates). More significantly, around one in four of the business format franchises available in the UK at the time supplied their contracts for analysis. All those who did so were supplied with a brief summary of the findings. Each contract was analysed with respect to 23 key clauses: duration; renewal conditions; exclusive territories; management services fees; advertising fees; franchisee advertising expenditure; ordering operating supplies; use of approved supplies only; unilateral changes to operations manual; franchisor's ownership of telephone/rights to transfer telephone number; minimum sales and/or targets; expansion triggers; approval for changes in the voting capital of the franchisee and/or specifications on its composition; restrictions on business activities of franchisee; non-competition clause at expiry/termination of contract; non-solicitation clause at expiry/termination of contract; franchisor's right to assign; franchisee's right to assign only to an approved buyer; commission/fees paid to franchisor on sale of business; franchisee's right to terminate; opening/working hours specified; and prior approval for holidays. The results of the analysis are reported in Chapter 4.

Specific case studies

Issues identified at the general level of analysis were investigated in more detail in a series of case studies. The workings of four business format franchisors in the UK were therefore investigated. Research was also conducted on the reshaping of the Coca-Cola Company's franchise network in Germany (and elsewhere), and some interviews were conducted with corporate managers of McDonald's and several of their US franchisees. This part of the research was carried out as follows.

Unlike in the US, there is no legal obligation in the UK on the part of franchisors to supply would-be franchisees with a complete listing of their franchisees. Prospective franchisees therefore have no way of knowing whether any list they are given is complete. The only other alternative is to construct a listing from telephone directories such as the *Yellow Pages*. Much the same can be said for the franchise researcher. However, asking franchisees to fill in a postal questionnaire without involving the franchisor was rejected for two reasons. First, the aim of the case studies was to compare franchisors' views with those of their franchisees. Interviews therefore had to take place with both parties to the relationship. Secondly, it was felt important to be able to approach franchisees by name and to be able to show that the research had the co-operation of (but that it was not commissioned by) the franchisor.

Interviews were therefore conducted with the franchisor's personnel. Copious field notes were taken, and were then subsequently written up either that evening or the day after. A postal questionnaire was then developed and tailored to the particular franchise (although most questions were common). The questions covered their occupational background, their motivations for becoming a franchisee and how the franchise operated in practice. A covering letter from the franchisor, drafted by the author, but written on the franchisor's notepaper accompanied the questionnaire on its first mailing (a stamped addressed envelope was also included). Two subsequent mail-outs were made to non-respondents within 10–14 days of the previous mail-out (the first was simply a reminder, the second contained another questionnaire and a stamped addressed envelope). Out of 251 franchisees drawn from four franchise companies, 199 usable replies were returned (i.e. a response rate of 79 per cent). Of those respondents, 32 were also interviewed on a face-to-face basis in order to flesh out some of the quantitative material and provide the research with illustrative quotations. The quantitative data was processed using a conventional computing package. The results of this analysis are reported in Chapters 3 and 4.

One of the case study companies provided a striking illustration of what can happen when a franchise changes hands, since it consisted (entirely at the time) of franchisees who had broken away from their original franchisor shortly after it had been taken over and a new franchise contract issued. It is therefore the subject of a separate chapter (see Chapter 5). The response rate in this case was 82 per cent (i.e. 61 usable replies from 74). A further 11 follow-up interviews were also conducted on a face-to-face basis to flesh out the quantitative data obtained from survey returns. Interviewees were selected so as to yield a cross-section of franchisees. They ranged from relative newcomers to the more experienced operator, and from the relatively low to the relatively high performers. This added greater depth to the results, enabling the citation of specific examples and providing a wealth of illustrative quotes. Initially, the intention was to make a comparison of the views of franchisees who had broken away with those who remained. However, the original franchisor refused to supply a list of current franchisees, without assurance that an approach would not be made to the break-away group. These conditions could not be met since approaches to the break-away fleet were already well advanced. Given the bad feeling and suspicion generated by the take-over and the break-away, independent approaches to those who remained with the original franchisor were rejected. Nevertheless, a few franchisees who remained under the new regime for a time, but who had since left, were tracked down and interviewed on a face-to-face basis. A wealth of court proceedings, sworn affidavits, franchise agreements (old and new) and correspondence was also collected.

Two of the most internationally renowned users of the franchise system were the subject of a more internationally oriented phase of the research: the Coca-Cola Company and McDonald's. The research on the Coca-Cola Company's franchise structure sought to examine why the Company's original franchised bottler structure in Germany had by the 1980s outlived its usefulness, and why a reshaped franchise structure was put in its place. It also considered the reshaping of the Coca-Cola Company's franchise structure worldwide. Two main research techniques were adopted: the collection of documentary evidence, both of a historical and contemporary nature; and a series of semi-structured interviews designed to tease out the whys and wherefores of change as well as its consequences. The latter were conducted at three levels: the corporate level (Atlanta), where 24 top executives of the company were interviewed (through 26 interviews); the division responsible for Coca-Cola operations in Germany (Essen), where 19 personnel were interviewed (through 25 interviews); and at the level of the German franchised bottler, where 9 current (10 interviews) and 4 former bottlers were selected and interviewed, in order to yield a representative sample of the entire network. Where appropriate, the German interviews were conducted through a translator. Chapter 6 is based on the analysis of this data.

A further set of revealing interviews was conducted with McDonald's. In this case, nine corporate level (Chicago) managers were interviewed, three franchisees (with many more met during a Chicagoland Operators' meeting) and a former McDonald's franchisee. Documentary evidence and the rulings of reported legal cases were also collected. The insights gained from this case study figure at various points in the book.

Throughout the research, and the subsequent writing of this book, the attempt has been to knit together a picture of franchising from a rich patchwork of data sources. In this way, it is hoped that justice has been given to the quality and quantity of data amassed, and that a credible (and, I hope, interesting) 'story' has been told in the process.

1 Binding 'firms' together

I was once in the habit of telling pupils that firms might be envisaged as islands of planned co-ordination in a sea of market relations. This now seems to me a highly misleading account of the way in which industry is in fact organised.

(Richardson, 1972: 883)

The owners of fast food and gas station franchises could be seen as occupying a contradictory location between the petty bourgeoisie or small employers and managers. While they maintain some of the characteristics of self-employed independent producers, they also become much more like functionaries for large capitalist corporations.

(Wright, 1976: 37–38)

'The defendant [franchisee] is a kind of 'cross-breed' – he is neither employee, strictly, nor a purchaser, strictly. It may well be that he is like a labrador 'with a touch of white' – he may have had an ancestor who was a pointer, and therefore cannot be called a true labrador.'

(Lawton LJ in *Office Overload Ltd v. Gunn* [1977] FSR 39 CA
at page 43)

INTRODUCTION

Where are the boundaries of the firm? How can we identify its frontiers? Indeed, what do we mean by 'the firm'? These questions are of perennial interest and importance to social scientists drawn from the disciplines of economics, sociology, business history and law. Not only do the answers given have significant theoretical implications, they can have far-reaching practical effects too. Assessing the nature of the franchise relationship forces one to tackle these questions head-on.

For many years, economists saw a reasonably sharp dividing line between transactions *within* and transactions *between* firms (Coase,

1937). Where the dividing line actually fell rested on relative costs; the boundaries of the firm extended up to the point at which the costs of organizing an extra transaction within the firm were equal to the costs of carrying out the transaction on the open market. Accordingly, the frontiers of the firm were easy to identify. However, recent economic literature (as reflected in the first quotation at the top of the chapter) has recognized that business relationships are more complicated than a simple 'make or buy' distinction; products need not be wholly made or bought, but can instead take the form of a blend of the 'make or buy' distinction (Williamson, 1975, 1979, 1980, 1981a, 1981b, 1986). As a result, spot purchases on the open market (markets) and complete production from raw materials to finished product (hierarchies) are viewed as alternative systems of economic government standing at polar extremes along a continuum of alternative organizational structures. In between lies a range of 'mixed modes' – franchising, subcontracting, long-term service contracts, technology transfer agreements, patents and so on.

Business historians, too, have based much of their analysis on the presumption of a sharp dividing line between firms and the market. Chandler (1977: 1), for example, argues: 'modern business enterprise took the place of market mechanisms in co-ordinating the activities of the economy and allocating its resources. In many sectors of the economy the visible hand of management replaced what Adam Smith referred to as the invisible hand of market forces.' Implicitly, the visible and invisible hands were considered separable, and the division between the two distinct. However, several writers on business organization have recently noted the growth of 'organisational modes which overlay market-contracting relations with various integrative arrangements' (Child, 1987: 12). The identification of similar developments are central to the alleged emergence of the 'flexible firm'. Although these firms are alleged to roll back their frontiers to include only a narrow 'core' of workers, it is acknowledged that they can still exercise various degrees of control over those operating on the 'periphery' (Atkinson, 1984; Atkinson and Meager, 1986; Pollert, 1991). This extends to those with whom the 'flexible firm' appears to have a commercial rather than employment relationship – franchisees, subcontractors and self-employed workers. In other words, even in organizational relationships where invisible forces (markets) *appear* to hold sway, the visible hand (hierarchies) can still exert considerable influence, and vice versa. For example, Benetton – the manufacturer and retailer of fashion clothing – insists that all its suppliers produce for no other retailer. This allows Benetton to control the volume of work its suppliers receive. It is therefore able to influence the profitability and work intensity of its suppliers without jeopardizing their legal independence (Belussi, 1987). Similarly, ownership of a significant, but minority, shareholding in a company, though insufficient to provide legal control, can often suffice to ensure effective managerial control in practice (Collins, 1990a).

For sociologists, too, the identification of the boundaries of the firm has important implications for one of their central concerns: the definition of who is placed in which class and why. This is not just a question of esoteric academic interest, but a question that matters a great deal to our understanding of how social actors relate to one another. The answer has developed from the crude suggestion that classes can be ordered into a hierarchy on the basis of wealth, with no attempt to explain why the dividing lines fall where they do, to the more sophisticated analysis of writers such as Wright (1976, 1978). He suggests that a person's class is determined by their relationships at work: whether they can set their own pace of work and working time, and do the same for others; whether they have control over the entire business apparatus; and whether they can direct where investments are made as well as reap the rewards of these decisions. The two major class categories – workers and capitalists – are polarized on each of these dimensions: the capitalist class has control over the entire apparatus of production, over the authority structure as a whole and over the overall investment process; the working class has none of these attributes. However, not each and everyone's relationships at work perfectly correspond to this dichotomous structure. Some fall between the two. For example, the author of this book was unable to exercise control over the work of others (since there were no research assistants), yet he was able to enjoy considerable autonomy over his own conditions of work such as choosing when, where and for how long he would work, albeit within the loose parameters set by an Oxford University college. There are many others, not the least of which are franchisees, who are neither fully-fledged workers nor capitalists according to Wright's criteria (as revealed by the second quotation at the top of this chapter). Drawing a neat dividing line between capitalists and workers is not possible, since some people occupy positions in which they simultaneously have one foot in the capitalist camp and one foot in the working class. These 'contradictory class locations' bear testimony to the ambiguous divide.

The dividing line between markets and firms is also of crucial importance for lawyers. If one is deemed to be buying the product or service of someone's labour as opposed to setting someone to work, then quite different laws apply. For example, the employment of others carries legal responsibilities: protection for health and safety at work, redundancy pay, minimum notice of termination, guaranteed lay off pay, maternity pay and maternity leave, protection from unfair dismissal, time off for trade union duties, and several others. Those found not to be 'employees' fall through the safety-net provided by legislation (Dickens, 1988). Crucially, therefore, both the employer and the employee need to be clearly identified in order that responsibilities be properly shouldered and appropriate protection given. Only those identified as 'employees' working under a contract of employment/ service are eligible for many of the statutory rights created in the UK since the 1960s; but how does one decide whether a particular worker is an employee or not? Claims to determine vicarious liability, the assertion of statutory employment rights and the collection of appropriate social security contributions and tax revenues rest, in the first instance, on the answer to this question. The development, interpretation and re-interpretation of various legal tests have been used to deliver a verdict on this preliminary question (Felstead, 1992). Resulting case law has produced an uneven, conflicting and often contradictory set of guidelines. This has led one leading authority to note that:

> To the uninitiated it may be difficult to understand why a bass player, who worked regularly for 13 years in an orchestra was 'self-employed', while musicians working for a 16-week summer season at a holiday camp were 'employees', or why a bar steward and a television researcher working on an avowedly 'self-employed' basis were held to be employees under contracts of employment, while an architect working alongside other employed architects was held to be self-employed under a contract for services.
>
> (Hepple, 1986: 70)

Such confusion is reflective of the ambiguous position in which many self-employed people work (as reflected in the third quotation at the top of this chapter). Although their work may be characterized by a significant element of investment, risk and independence, research (Leighton, 1983; Kneppers-Heynert, 1992; Allen *et al.*, 1992) suggests that working conditions and practices can differ little, if at all, from those classified as employees.[1]

Many branches of social science have for several years commonly focused upon two distinct modes of organizing production: internal organization through vertical integration, or external organization through arm's length transactions between firms. Sheard succinctly summarizes this position and its limitations:

> For any input to the production process a firm has two options – to produce the input in its own factories or purchase it from other firms

via the free market. Profit maximising firms are presumed to choose the least cost method of these two alternatives. However, between the two extremes of internal organization (in house production) and free market transactions lies a spectrum of intermediate interfirm arrangements including production through a subsidiary or affiliate, subcontracting, and monopsonistic power over suppliers. Most of these intermediate modes are not treated explicitly by economic theory but may in fact be more typical than the polar modes of internal organization and free market transactions.

(Sheard, 1983: 51, quoted in Holmes, 1986: 83)

Until recently, much the same could be said of sociology, business history and law.

The long-held belief behind much of this theorizing was that there was an inexorable trend towards vertical integration, market concentration and the growing power of the large corporation. It was only a matter of time before relationships betwixt and between the two extremes would become relics of the past, and so, for the purposes of analysis, they could safely be ignored. The facts seemed to be in line with this belief, at least until the early 1970s. Most studies revealed that capital ownership was continuously concentrating, and enterprises and establishments were growing in size. However, a dramatic turnaround occurred in the mid to late 1970s across much of the industrialized world. By hiving off parts of their sprawling empires companies have returned 'to their knitting' (Peters and Waterman, 1982: 293), the remaining parts have been divided into quasi-independent operating divisions or businesses in an attempt to shift from 'management by task' to 'management by performance' (Drucker, 1977), and aspects of production have been increasingly rearranged through franchising, subcontracting and external sourcing. The post-war trend of ever-increasing size has been reversed; average plant sizes have diminished, new firm formation rates have leapt and there has been a rise in the number of small businesses. Similar developments have been replicated in the public sector through privatization, the local management of schools, fund-holding general practitioners, compulsory competitive tendering for local authority services and the introduction of trust status hospitals (cf. Bach, 1989; Ferner, 1989).

This chapter reviews the empirical evidence underlying these changes. It then considers some of the theoretical work which seeks to understand and interpret the way in which today's businesses are organized and its implications. Contrary to a number of writers (e.g. Piore and Sabel, 1984; Loveman and Sengenberger, 1990) and the political rhetoric of the 'enterprise culture', the chapter argues that empirical evidence of vertical disintegration need not necessarily be associated with the decentralization of economic power. The nature of inter-firm relationships act as the key intervening variable which can just as easily represent a strengthening, as much as a weakening, of corporate control.[2] One must look beyond the legal boundaries of the firm in order to assess how and on what basis a firm can exercise control, if at all, over others. Against this backdrop, the bulk of the book offers an assessment of the relatively neglected franchise relationship. It provides an analysis of who controls what, why and how. Variations between franchise systems are considered as well as how and why responsibilities might shift over time. The chapter ends by summarizing the academic debates which prompted the research and made franchising an appropriate area for academic enquiry.

DISINTEGRATION OF AND DECENTRALIZATION WITHIN 'THE FIRM'

> It is a commonplace that in the course of the present century British industry has witnessed a transformation from a disaggregated structure of predominantly small, competing firms to a concentrated structure dominated by large, and often monopolistic, corporations . . . These developments were not, of course, confined to the United Kingdom; indeed, the tendency to increasing industrial concentration is one of the better attested facts of the recent economic history of most economically advanced Western countries.
>
> (Hannah, 1976: 1–2)

This 'commonplace' observation was widely shared both across social science disciplines and between theoretical traditions. Industrial economists saw the tendency to large-scale production as the inevitable consequence of the economies wrought by specialization and economies of scale. The explanation rested on the principles underlying Adam Smith's pin-making example: working alongside others, but specializing in one stage of the production process, workers in a pin-making factory could each make 4,800 pins in a day compared to, at best, 20 if they worked alone. While writers adopting a Marxist approach (e.g. Marglin, 1974; Braverman, 1974: 62–64) did not dispute the *conclusions* of orthodox economists, they offered a very different *explanation*. According to them, the trend towards larger and larger enterprises was not so much a product of their technical efficiencies as part and parcel of the process of growing capital concentration and centralization driven by capitalists' need to overcome worker resistance. Small enterprises would only remain in pockets of the economy 'which modern industry has only sporadically or incompletely got hold of' (Marx, 1934: 5, 7, 8, quoted in Loveman and Sengenberger, 1990: 2) and would be 'always on the point of extinction' (History Workshop Editorial Collective, 1977: 2).

Snap-shot evidence of the structure of European corporate capital *appears* to bear this out (Sisson *et al.*, 1992). Of 92.4 million people employed across the European Community (EC), nearly 26 million (28.1 per cent) were employed in enterprises employing 500 or more employees.[3] And yet, they only accounted for 0.1 per cent of the total number of enterprises. On the other hand, there were more than 900 times as many enterprises employing less than 10 workers, but they only managed to provide a similar number of jobs (see Table 1.1).

Table 1.1 Size distribution of enterprises and employment in the European Community

Size group (Number of employees)	Number of enterprises	Percentage	Number of employees (millions)	Percentage
0–9	12,265,066	91.34	24.85	26.89
10–99	1,076,920	8.02	41.60	45.02
100–499	72,511	0.54		
500 +	13,428	0.10	25.96	28.10
Total	13,427,925		92.40	

Source: Commission of the European Communities (1990), figures reworked by Sisson, Waddington and Whitson (1992), Table 1.

Static evidence of this type fails to reveal the direction and pace of corporate change, however. Has the transformation from small to large enterprises – identified by Hannah over the past century – quickened, slowed or has it been put into reverse? To answer this question, it is necessary to consider the empirical evidence, which indicates that there has been a revival of small enterprises across the industrialized world in addition to evidence which suggests that there have been moves towards decentralization *within* firms as well.

Re-emergence of the small enterprise

The widely held belief that small enterprises were the anachronistic relics of the past has been severely challenged by events. Their predicted demise has not come to pass. Instead, their numbers have actually swelled throughout all industrialized economies regardless of whether they grew from a small or large base.[4] Time series data covering nine industrialized economies (United States, Japan, France, Germany, Norway, Switzerland, Italy, Hungary and the United Kingdom) show a common 'V' shaped pattern among them all – a fall in the employment share of small units, dating back to the time when records began, being halted and then reversed in the mid-1970s through to the 1980s (Loveman and Sengenberger, 1990: 8–20; Granovetter, 1984). The 'V' shaped pattern applies to both enterprises and establishments as well as to the total economy and manufacturing. The fall and rise of the small unit is a feature which persists across a wide range of countries, sectors, size distributions and institutions.

Furthermore, in six EC countries for which there are data, companies with a staff of fewer than ten can be held largely accountable for the growth in the total number of businesses registered during the mid-1980s (see Table 1.2). In all of these cases, it was the service sector that grew the fastest. In two countries, Italy and Belgium, the growth of the service sector was accompanied by declines in other sectors, as can be seen from its share exceeding 100 per cent. A similar pattern can be observed in the different growth rates experienced by micro businesses (employing fewer than 10), small businesses (10–199 employees), medium-sized businesses (200–499 employees) and large enterprises (employing more than 500). In Italy, Belgium and France, the growth of micro businesses exceeded the growth in the total number of businesses registered, implying that the number of business in other size categories

Table 1.2 Net growth in the stock of enterprises by main sector and size class, selected countries, 1983–1986

Country	Years	Growth (absolute)	Growth (%)	Sector	Share (%)	Class	Share (%)
Germany	3	111,481	6.8	Services	96.6	Micro	99.6
France	3	116,451	6.1	Services	89.3	Micro	103.3
United Kingdom	3	279,120	14.6	Services	70.1	Micro	96.8
Italy	3	86,282	2.8	Services	162.2	Micro	107.5
Netherlands	2	35,759	7.1	Services	84.9	Micro	98.9
Belgium	3	4,641	1.1	Services	106.6	Micro	102.9

Key:
micro business = 0–9 employees
small = 10–199 employees
medium = 200–499 employees
large = 500 or more employees
Source: Commission of the European Communities (1990), p.16.8.

Table 1.3 Self-employment across the European Community, 1979–1990 (as a percentage of the total labour force)

Year	EURO10	EURO12	B	D	DK	E	F	GR	I	IRL	L	NL	P	UK
1979	NA	NA	14.6	8.8	12.8	NA	12.5	NA	22.7	23.1	10.9	10.2	NA	7.4
1981	13.7	NA	14.8	8.6	12.1	NA	12.5	38.2	23.6	21.7	NA	10.6	NA	9.3
1983	14.2	NA	14.7	9.0	11.6	NA	12.8	36.5	23.9	21.3	9.7	9.5	NA	10.2
1984	14.7	NA	15.8	9.3	10.3	NA	13.0	35.8	24.6	21.7	9.8	11.8	NA	11.3
1985	14.5	NA	15.9	9.2	9.9	NA	12.6	36.0	24.1	21.6	9.4	9.1	NA	11.4
1986	14.4	15.5	15.6	9.1	9.4	22.6	12.7	35.3	23.9	21.6	9.0	10.7	26.2	11.5
1987	14.7	15.9	15.3	9.2	9.2	23.5	12.7	35.4	24.4	21.8	9.2	10.1	27.2	12.5
1988	14.7	15.9	15.2	9.0	8.8	22.6	12.8	35.2	24.6	22.5	9.2	10.0	26.7	12.7
1989	14.8	15.8	16.1	9.1	9.2	21.7	12.5	34.3	24.6	22.2	9.3	10.0	26.3	13.4
1990	14.8	15.7	16.1	8.9	9.5	20.9	12.9	34.8	24.3	22.6	9.3	10.0	25.8	13.4

Key:
B = Belgium
D = Germany
DK = Denmark
E = Spain
F = France
GR = Greece
I = Italy
IRL = Ireland
L = Luxembourg
NL = Netherlands
P = Portugal
UK = United Kingdom
NA = not available

Source: Eurostat Labour Force Surveys 1979–1990.

was falling. Finally, in Germany, the UK and the Netherlands both the services sector and micro enterprises were growing fast, but other sectors and size categories were growing too, albeit at a much slower pace.

The re-emergence of the small firm has also been reflected in the growth of self-employment across the European Community (see Table 1.3). However, the aggregate figures mask important country variations. On the figures available up to 1990, five out of twelve EC states recorded rises in the number recorded as self-employed and seven registered falls.

Trends evident in the European economies and the other industrialized countries of the world were particularly pronounced in the UK. The post-war trend towards ever-increasing size was halted and then reversed in the mid to late 1970s. Until then, the dominant trend was for the largest enterprises to multiply at the expense of the small, for enterprise ownership to spread to more establishments, and for a greater and greater proportion of the workforce to be employed in the largest enterprises and establishments. Policy makers, too, had taken the position that 'bigger was better'. Successive governments, partly in response to the perceived success of restructuring and planning measures in other countries such as France and Italy, placed emphasis on the need to take advantage of economies of scale to succeed in world markets, thereby marginalizing and dismissing the role of the small firm.

However, this long-established trend was abruptly put into reverse during the 1970s – the number of large enterprises fell, they owned fewer and fewer establishments, and the proportion of the workforce employed by the largest enterprises and establishments declined (see Tables 1.4 and 1.5). Mounting unemployment and evidence of the job-generating potential of small firms (Birch, 1979; OECD, 1985; Storey and Johnson, 1987; Daly *et al.*, 1991) coupled with the political inclination towards individual self-help prompted policy makers to switch their allegiance. Attention shifted from the promotion of industrial concentration to active encouragement and financial support for small firms. They were considered to offer benefits both to the individuals involved and to society at large:

> Self-employment and work in small firms offer individuals the opportunity in a very direct way to take *control of their working lives and assert their independence*. A healthy and growing small firms sector is good for the country too. It acts as a well-spring of new ideas, new products and *new jobs*, and increases the economy's ability to respond flexibly to change.
>
> (Employment Department, 1992: 47, my emphasis)

Table 1.4 Enterprise size in UK manufacturing industry, 1958–1990

Enterprise size (Number of employees)	Year	2,000+	5,000+	10,000+	20,000+	50,000+
Number of enterprises	1958	469	180	74	32	8
	1979	406	174	83	34	9
	1986	276	114	52	20	4
	1990	294	111	42	16	4
Number of	1958	5,805	3,788	2,224	1,398	467
establishments under	1979	7,911	5,242	3,446	1,995	720
enterprise ownership	1986	5,985	3,810	2,269	1,313	295
and control	1990	4,656	2,784	1,523	820	135
Percentage of	1958	45.8	34.3	24.8	17.3	7.3
employees working	1979	55.6	44.7	34.9	24.4	12.7
for these	1986	45.1	34.9	25.4	16.1	5.9
enterprises	1990	42.7	31.3	21.0	13.6	6.5

Source: Sisson (1989), Table 2.2; updated with figures from *Business Monitor: Report on the Census of Production Summary Volume*, 1990, PA 1002 (HMSO: London, 1992), Table 12.

Table 1.5 Establishment size in UK manufacturing industry, 1951–1990

Percentage of employees working in establishments with:	1951	1979	1990
500 or more employees	44.3	54.1	41.0
1,000 or more employees	30.8	40.9	27.5
1,500 or more employees	23.9	32.9	21.7

Source: Sisson (1989), Table 2.1; updated with figures from *Business Monitor: Report on the Census of Production Summary Volume*, 1990, PA 1002 (HMSO: London, 1992), Table 6.

Leaving aside the question of their job-generating role, there is no doubt that small firms and self-employment have leapt significantly in the UK during the last decade.[5] For example, the overall number of businesses in the UK rose by two-thirds between 1979 and 1989 – an average of nearly 500 additional firms every working day – the overwhelming majority of which were 'small' by any reasonable definition (Daly and McCann, 1992: 48; see Table 1.6). Self-employment, too, has risen dramatically over the decade: from around 8 per cent of the workforce at the beginning of the decade to 13 per cent at the end (see Figure 1.1).

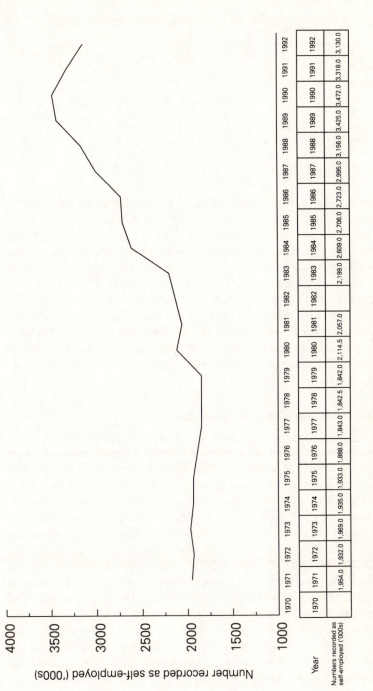

Year	1970	1971	1972	1973	1974	1975	1976	1977	1978	1979	1980	1981	1982	1983	1984	1985	1986	1987	1988	1989	1990	1991	1992
Numbers recorded as self-employed ('000s)		1,954.0	1,932.0	1,969.0	1,935.0	1,933.0	1,888.0	1,843.0	1,842.5	1,842.0	2,114.5	2,057.0		2,199.0	2,609.0	2,706.0	2,723.0	2,995.0	3,156.0	3,425.0	3,472.0	3,318.0	3,130.0

Figure 1.1 Growth of self-employment in the United Kingdom, 1971–1992
Sources: Labour Force Surveys, 1971–1991, as reported in the *Employment Gazette,* and *Labour Force Quarterly Bulletin,* September 1992 (Department of Employment: London), p.4.

Table 1.6 Size distribution of enterprises and employment in the United Kingdom, 1979–1989

Size group (number of employees)	Percentage of enterprises			Percentage of employment		
	1979	1986	1989	1979	1986	1989
1–10	89.1	93.0	93.8	19.1	27.8	28.7
11–199	10.4	6.7	5.9	30.0	27.4	26.5
200–499	0.3	0.2	0.2	8.2	9.5	10.6
500–999	0.1	0.1	0.1	7.4	6.5	6.7
1000+	0.1	–	–	35.3	28.8	27.5

Source: reworked figures from Daly and McCann (1992), Table 4.

While there is little dispute about the technical nature of the trend towards smaller units of production, the interpretation of events is the subject of a more vigorous debate. In the main, this centres on the nature of the relationships small units forge with others, whether they be co-operative relations with similarly placed enterprises or the relationships they form with those with whom they do business (Pyke, 1988). An assessment of these relationships has an important bearing on whether the large firm is really 'giving up any idea of *controlling* the small company' (Clutterbuck, 1985: 10, his emphasis). This question is examined later in this chapter. Before doing so, however, the chapter appraises the evidence of a parallel movement towards decentralization *within* firms.

Decentralization within the enterprise

Despite the declining importance of the large enterprise since the mid- to late 1970s, this type of enterprise still holds a significant place in the economic landscape of the industralized economies. Yet here, too, there have been apparent moves to decentralize economic decision-making. The sheer diversity of the large enterprise's interests, both in terms of markets and locations, has continually posed an organizational problem: will those in control of the modern corporation be willing and able to operate it in the interests of shareholders? Initially, this problem was negligible; enterprises were large, single-product, multi-functioned entities. They were structured around the main departmental functions of the business: sales and marketing, finance, research and development, personnel, production and so on, with each department handling the complete range of the firm's products or services. This organizational structure is commonly referred to as the 'unitary' or 'U-form' enterprise. The lines of communication and pattern of accountability were reasonably clear-cut.

The addition of different products and the opening-up of new markets, however, blurred things considerably; head office management found it more difficult to keep in touch with day-to-day developments in each and every product area, and it became increasingly difficult to monitor their performance (Chandler, 1962: chapter 7; Williamson, 1975: chapter 8; Marginson *et al.*, 1988b). Faced with these problems the Du Pont Company and General Motors devised what Chandler (1962: 229–314) calls the 'multi-divisional' or 'M-form' enterprise in the early 1920s in the US. It involved substituting quasi-autonomous operating divisions (organized along product or geographic lines) for the functional divisions of the 'U-form'.[6] Inasmuch as each of these operating divisions was subsequently divided along functional lines, we can characterize these operating divisions as scaled-down 'U-forms', i.e. the creation of firms within firms. By the 1960s many of the large enterprises in the US were operating with 'M-form' style structures (Marginson, 1985).

UK organizations were much slower to change. Nevertheless, by the early 1980s Hill and Pickering (1986) found that 82.6 per cent of 144 companies they surveyed (all of which were among the largest 500 companies listed in *The Times 1000*) were using a divisional structure. The most popular method of division was by product (38.2 per cent), division by geography accounted for 9.7 per cent, a mixture of the two was the second most popular (20.1 per cent), and 11.8 per cent were split into product divisions but with a separate international division as well. Only a tiny minority (1.4 per cent) were still operating on functional lines, all of which had little, if any, product diversity, e.g. companies such as Marks and Spencer and Ford (Hill and Pickering, 1986: 29–30; Francis, 1989). The remainder (16.0 per cent) were organized on holding company lines, i.e. 'H-form'. But given that the holding company structure is also decentralized, it can be inferred from these results that most of the UK's large companies operate along decentralized lines.

The M-form organization acts to divide strategic decisions from operating ones – the former being the preserve of head office or corporate management and the latter being the responsibility of those in the divisions.[7] Four advantages are claimed for the multi-divisional firm. First, operating decisions are assigned to divisions and they are made profit or cost responsible for their actions. Secondly, head office staff perform an advisory and monitoring role, ensuring greater control over the behaviour of their operating divisions. Thirdly, the head office is solely in charge of strategic decisions, such as where and when to expand (contract) and how to allocate the profits generated by the divisions. Finally, head office staff are able to identify more easily with the overall performance of the organization rather than being distracted by functional concerns (Williamson, 1975: 137).

While Hill and Pickering (1986) found that large UK companies were operating, almost unanimously, on a multi-divisional basis, their survey had a 'sting in its tail'. They also found that the divisions themselves had become too diverse and that the enterprise performance was suffering as a result (ibid: 42–49). A further round of decentralization was called for, so that operating decisions are taken on the ground not at divisional headquarters. Ten years earlier a similar cry was made: 'successful big corporations should devolve into becoming "confederations of entrepreneurs"' (Macrae, 1976: 42).

Several writers have questioned the presumption that decentralization can automatically be equated with the delegation of certain decision-making activities to the operating division. For example, the appearance of decentralized pay bargaining structures conveys the impression that pay is *decided* at this level, but this may be nothing more than an illusion.[8] Plant management may be free to negotiate, but only within limits set by higher-level management, or they may have to check with divisional or corporate headquarters before making a settlement. A survey of management at different levels in 143 enterprises in the UK (Marginson *et al.*, 1988a) showed that only 10 per cent of head office managers were *not* involved (either giving instructions, offering their approval, issuing guidelines or convening pay policy meetings) in establishment-level negotiations (Edwards and Marginson, 1988: 151). The same goes for a range of non-pay personnel and industrial relations decisions such as union recognition, closed shop agreements, the number employed, redundancy terms, holiday entitlement and so on. On all these matters (except patterns of work, e.g. shift working), the majority issued their establishments with instructions. In other words, operating units had virtually no autonomy in deciding these matters 'off their own bat' (Marginson, 1986a: 55).

Even where establishments did have decision-making powers, corporate management still claimed to issue policy initiatives. For example, non-management personnel were recruited by establishments without the need to seek the approval of higher-level managers (Marginson and Sisson, 1988: 92). Yet many corporate managers claimed to have changed their policy on the employment of temporary workers, subcontractors and outworkers. In spite of this, there was little evidence of higher-level policy decisions being instrumental in guiding establishment practice. Where the direction of change matched corporate aims this was far more likely to be the result of initiatives taken on the ground than the result of a policy decision taken at a higher level within the enterprise (Marginson, 1989: 107–108).

Devolution of responsibility to operating units conceals as much as it reveals. This is borne out in the private sector as much as in newly privatized companies such as British Telecom, British Gas, the water companies, the electricity distributors, and the electricity generators (privatized in 1984, 1986, 1989, 1990 and 1991 respectively). Subject for some time to the criticism of being too highly centralized and unresponsive, their switch from public to private sector has supposedly pushed them into a world of competitive markets and profit-centres. In practice, however, the change has been far less dramatic (Colling and Ferner, 1992: 213–214). The creation of profit-centres has been more of a symbolic gesture than indicating any practical change. Revenues continue to be determined by centralized pricing decisions, and there is a wide range of costs over which operating managers have no control (e.g. pay determination continues to be centralized).

Overall, the mere existence of decentralized corporate structure is not a sufficient indicator of devolved decision-making. There is clear evidence, for example, that operating units do not have a free rein over industrial relations and personnel matters. Despite appearances to the contrary, managers in operational charge are not completely free agents even in their acknowledged spheres of influence. The limits on their actions can vary, and are subject to change. Much the same can be said of the *apparent* decline in the economic significance of the large enterprise, and the concomitant rise of the 'independent' small enterprise. The identification of empirical trends says nothing about the nature of the inter-connections between 'firms' and the consequent distribution of economic power. For this, a more qualitative assessment is called for. It is to this that we now turn.

FORGING LINKS BETWEEN 'FIRMS'

For some time social scientists treated firms as distinct economic units, only connected to each other indirectly through the buying and selling of their wares. However, interest in the nature of inter-firm relationships has grown considerably following the suggestion that some will do more than others to promote economic success. Hirst and Zeitlin (1989), for example, argue that in Britain 'an emphasis on price competition and the absence of a supportive inter-firm culture encourages openness to foreign competition at the upper end of the market on the basis of superior design and quality and at the lower end from low-cost products from NICs [newly industrializing countries]' (ibid: 8).

One can identify four ideal types of inter-firm relationship which might be forged: satellite production; active engagements; subordinate co-operation; and independent co-operation (this typology is taken from Penn, 1991: 5–8). The first two relate to vertical relationships between buyers and suppliers, while the third and fourth concern relationships forged between competing firms.

Satellite production

The classic relationship between firms is that which is regulated by the market mechanism alone. Such relationships are established whenever the goods or services produced by one party (the supplier) are bought by another (the buyer). The goods or services may be standardized (i.e. off-the-shelf) or customized according to buyers' specifications. Furthermore, they may involve a prime contractor commissioning work to a subcontractor with or without the necessary machinery and materials (i.e. subcontracting or labour-only subcontracting, see Evans, 1990). Either way, the relationship between buyer and supplier is co-ordinated and regulated by the market as a commercial transaction. As a result, it has often been treated as an arm's length relationship carrying 'the common-sense view that businessmen [*sic*] dealing with each other at arm's length should not be responsible for each other's economic and physical security to any greater extent than provided for by their contractual agreement' (Collins, 1990b: 354).

The importance of satellite production has been underlined by the debate surrounding the now familiar construct of the 'flexible firm' (Atkinson, 1984; Atkinson and Meager, 1986). These firms are reckoned to divide their workforces into 'core' and 'peripheral' groupings. This two-tier employment structure separates full-time workers from those who work under a range of non-conventional employment contracts, such as part-time work, homeworking and temporary work, on the one hand, and the 'displacement of employment contracts by commercial contracts' (Atkinson and Meager, 1986: 9), as exemplified by subcontracting, self-employment and agency working, on the other. Three contrasting types of flexibility flow from this employment structure. First, the 'peripheral' workforce offers numerical flexibility. This enables the employing firm to adjust the number of hours worked and/or the number of workers to meet fluctuations in product demand. Secondly, the 'core' group of workers provides functional flexibility. This allows the employer to deploy workers across a wider range of tasks, thereby enhancing their versatility and polyvalence. Thirdly, financial flexibility cuts across the 'core'–'periphery' divide to provide a structure of pay which 'encourages and supports the numerical and functional flexibility which the firm seeks' (Atkinson, 1985: 26). Applied to the 'core' workforce this aspect of flexibility gives firms the ability 'to adjust pay structures to encourage functional flexibility, match market rates for scarce skills and/or reward individual performance' (Atkinson and Meager, 1986: 9). When applied to the 'periphery' it allows employers to hire labour as cheaply as possible by ensuring that 'pay and other employment costs reflect the state of supply and demand in the external labour market' (Atkinson, 1984: 28).

The 'flexible firm' has assumed an important place in academic and policy-making circles. Yet, it is not without its critics (Pollert, 1988a, 1988b, 1991; MacInnes, 1987a: 113–124, 1987b; Marginson, 1989). For our purposes, however, the importance of the 'flexible firm' debate is the way in which it has served to highlight the linkages 'firms' might forge between themselves. The concept of 'distancing', whereby employment contracts are replaced by commercial contracts, is particularly noteworthy. Despite evidence which suggests, for instance, that 'the direct re-employment of the *same individuals* in nominal self-employment within *identical jobs* is apparently rare' (Creigh *et al.*, 1986: 193, my emphasis), those who supply the 'flexible firm' are cast in a dependent role. They appear to remain in, but not of, 'the firm'. They provide the 'flexible firm' with numerical and financial flexibility in much the same way as 'peripheral' workers do; suppliers can be chopped and changed according to the lowest tender and short-term requirements, and price negotiation can involve playing-off one supplier against another (Rainnie, 1984). Yet not all supplier–buyer relations are based on subservience (Blackburn, 1992). Suppliers may have scarce skills, they may have a range of customers to serve and/or they may be in a position to offer their clients important design advice (Morris and Imrie, 1992: 36). Even so, the very concept of 'distancing' may be something of a misnomer since the market mechanism may be laden with integrative elements. For example, the label 'self-employment' covers a range of levels of autonomy, yet labour law's two-fold classification is ill-equipped to cope with this fact. Even so, case law and the development of the legal tests to determine whether one is working under a commercial or an employment contract serve to illustrate that 'distancing' is a relative concept. Moreover, each of the three legal tests have been variously adapted to allow market transactions to carry more and more hierarchical elements without redefining their legal status. In fact, the 'distance' between legally separate businesses may be very small indeed.

Take the 'control' test, for example. For many years the distinction between the employee in a master–servant employment relationship (to use Drake's (1968) terminology, the 'wage slave') and the independent entrepreneur was based on the concept of control (*Yewens v. Noakes* (1880) 6 QBD 530). This meant that the employer of direct labour was one who could 'not only tell you what to do, but also how to do it'. However, current case law has dismissed the notion that this feature is an exclusive characteristic of being an employee (*Ready Mixed Concrete (South East) Ltd v. Minister of Pensions and National Insurance* [1968] 2 QB 497). Instead, an obligation to do work subject to another's control is regarded as a necessary, though not always a sufficient, condition for a contract of service. In other words, the self-employed contractor can allow himself or herself to be controlled by the hirer, without in any way compromising their independent status. Self-employment need not therefore be equated with freedom from another party's control in performance of the task or even in the selection of plant, equipment and materials. At its extreme, a system of payment by results has been interpreted as giving an independent contractor sufficient scope for independence in the performance of tasks to be considered self-employed (cf. Lawton LJ dissenting in *Ferguson v. John Dawson and Partners (Contractors) Ltd* [1976] IRLR 346 CA).

On the other hand, the absence of direct, physical control in performance of tasks can be taken as strong evidence of the existence of a contract for services (i.e. self-employment). In other words, this can be taken as being inconsistent with a contract of service, and can tip the balance towards being defined as an independent contractor of services. This has been of particular significance in determining the employment status of highly skilled, professional workers who have something to offer on the open market, and whose tasks defy detailed instruction by their 'employer'. For example, aside from the minimal requirement that musicians in an orchestra assemble together to fulfil an engagement, their 'employer' has no control over the manner in which they carry out their work. The absence of such control may therefore give the courts sufficient grounds for sustaining the self-employed 'label' under which such professionals work (*Midland Sinfonia Concert Society Ltd v. Secretary of State for Social Services* [1981] ICR 454 QBD).

By reconciling the tight controls that might govern the contractual relationship between an independent contractor and their client with the contractor's legal independence, the 'control' test has given legal recognition to the concept of 'distance' even though it may be quite small in practice. On the other hand, the absence of direct, physical control (as opposed to that which is delegated) might be considered sufficient to define a relationship as one of self-employment (compare

Construction Industry Training Board v. Labour Force Ltd [1970] 3 All ER 220 QBD with *Global Plant Ltd v. Secretary of State for Heath and Social Security* [1971] 3 All ER 385 QBD). In both of these ways, the 'control' test has widened the legal definition of self-employment, and has revealed that the level of autonomy varies widely within the group.

The second test adopted by labour courts – 'in business on your own account' – is designed to give legal expression to the economic independence self-employment is reckoned to provide (first articulated in *Market Investigations Ltd v. Minister of Social Security* [1969] 2 QB 173). The test has three main limbs. The first is the question of who owns the equipment necessary for the performance of the task, whether it be a truck for carriage, a sewing machine for garment assembly or a licensed bar for the sale of alcoholic beverages. The second is the question of who bears the risk and who may profit from the venture. And the third component is whether the person engaged under a self-employed label does so in the course of an already established business. Though not a decisive factor, the third limb of the 'in business on your own account' test is of considerable importance to the book's assessment of franchising at work.

Whereas the 'control' test has lowered the threshold of self-employment, the 'in business on your own account' test raises the threshold quite markedly. Take the case of two former employees of a textile firm engaged on a self-employed basis as outworkers (*Nethermere (St Neots) Ltd v. Taverna and Gardiner* [1984] IRLR 240 EAT). Each was supplied with a sewing machine, garments were delivered for machining on a daily basis, and payment was made on task completion. While applying the 'control' test (the absence of direct control, and the freedom to choose how and when to work) pointed towards self-employment, the 'in business on your own account' test (the economic dependence of the machinists on a single client in terms of custom, tools of the trade and skill acquisition) pointed in the opposite direction. In this particular case, the 'in business on your own account' test helped to persuade the court that these outworkers were employees. However, despite encapsulating many of the commercial features of 'being one's own boss', the 'in business on your own account' test has been inconsistently applied, and has often been set aside and given relatively little weight where elements of autonomy can also be identified (e.g. *Wickens v. Champion Employment* [1984] ICR 365 EAT).[9] Even the apparently contradictory finding that a group of self-employed driving instructors were 'not really [in] business on their own account' has been explained away (*Cronin v. Customs and Excise Commissioners* [1991] STC 333 QBD).

Testing for 'mutuality of obligation' is the third test which might be applied in order to determine whether a person is self-employed or not. Its absence is taken to signal self-employment, its presence the status of the conventional employee. In practice, it has made employee status more difficult to sustain (achieve), particularly for who already have difficulty in establishing their continuity of employment (e.g. casual, temporary and agency workers). The test refers to the obligation on the part of the 'employer' to provide work, and the obligation of the part of the 'worker' to accept. Its absence has been enough to take regular casuals and agency workers outside the legal definition of employees and into the ranks of the self-employed in a number of recent cases. It is notable that in each of these cases the failure to discover mutuality of obligation has been sufficient to overturn the finding that these persons are *not* 'in business on their own account' (*O'Kelly and others v. Trusthouse Forte Plc* [1983] IRLR 369 EAT; *Wickens v. Champion Employment* [1984] ICR 365 EAT; *Ironmonger v. Movefield Ltd t/a Deering Appointments* [1988] IRLR 461 EAT).

However, the 'mutuality of obligation' test can itself be diluted by interpreting this at its minimum. In other words, courts may seek to uncover whether an irreducible minimum obligation on both parties is in evidence. For example, the fact that it was up to homeworkers to decide how much work they wanted to take but subject to the condition that their chosen workload is worthwhile for the van driver to call, could be read as an obligation on the part of homeworkers to take a reasonable amount of work. Conversely, the fact that it was the van drivers' duty to ensure that each homeworker was supplied with a fair allocation of the available work, could be taken as an indication that the company was obliged to supply each homeworker with a reasonable amount of work (*Nethermere (St Neots) Ltd v. Taverna and Gardiner* [1984] IRLR 240 EAT).[10] However, when the dividing line is finely drawn it is unusual for a judge to come down on the side of a finding of employee status. Its practice appears to be instrumental, and is consequently adopted only when a finding of self-employment would leave a badly injured building worker uncompensated or a long-serving homeworker unprotected from dismissal (Leighton, 1985).

The self-employed tag denotes a commercial, as opposed to an employment, relationship. However, the 'distance' between the two may be no more than a legal artefact. This further confirms the blurring of the dividing line between 'firms' and does much to caution against their separateness in practice. Only by examining the inter-connections between 'firms' can one fully appreciate that the ability to exercise control over production may stretch beyond a firm's legal borders. Such power can be exercised through the market via subcontracting or, as this book will argue, franchising.

Active engagements

Rather than relying on market exchange and commercial contracts to forge close links between firms with whom one does business, firms may take up more active positions in each other's business. This involves shifting the nature of the buyer–supplier relationship from one based on the asymmetrical dependence of the supplier on the buyer to one of mutual dependency. The former has been labelled 'arm's length contractual relations (ACR)' and the latter 'obligational contractual relations (OCR)' (Sako, 1990). The hallmarks of ACR-type relations are reckoned to characterize much of British industry's inter-firm relations, notwithstanding their alleged 'transformation' of late (Morris and Imrie, 1992). By contrast, the use of OCR-type relations is said to be a pillar of the Japanese economy's success (Hirst and Zeitlin, 1989). It is therefore in the context of the 'Japanization' debate that the nature of inter-firm relationships has also come to the fore (Turnbull, 1986; Sako, 1987; Oliver and Wilkinson, 1988; Ackroyd *et al.*, 1988; Morris, 1988; Crowther and Garrahan, 1988; Dickens and Savage, 1988; Wood, 1991).

A host of features distinguish 'arm's length' relationships from those of a more 'obligational' kind (Sako, 1990: 192–249). These will be briefly discussed (see Table 1.7). Under OCR, suppliers and buyers are locked into a state of dependency: suppliers have a narrow customer base, while buyers have only a single-source of supply; the reverse applies under conditions of ACR. Tendering for new orders is open and determined on the basis of price under ACR, whereas buyers commission a single supplier under OCR. Production of orders only takes place on receipt of written confirmation of the order under ACR, whereas only tacit, oral confirmation is needed for production to take place prior to receipt of written confirmation under OCR. The contractual terms of the exchange are closely and strictly adhered to under conditions of ACR trading compared with the enforcement of more lenient remedies under OCR. The supplier is trusted to produce goods of the required quality without it being necessary to make checks on delivery (it may even feed directly into the buyer's production process), whereas under ACR complete or sample checks are made on each batch delivered. Channels of communication are narrow and formal under ACR compared with the much wider, less formal and more frequent channels which typify OCR trading. The same goes for technology transfer: rare under ACR, more common under OCR. Finally, ACR trading is typified by the buyer's desire to 'make a quick buck' thereby shifting risk onto the supplier wherever possible, whereas OCR traders share the risk to which either is exposed.

Table 1.7 Comparing the features of arm's length contractual relationships (ACR) with obligational contractual relationships (OCR)

Arm's length contracting	Obligational contracting
Low transational dependence – wide customer base and multi-sourcing	High transational dependence – narrow customer base and single sourcing
Competitive tendering – tenders won or lost on price	Commissioned orders
Written confirmation of orders	Only tacit, oral confirmation of orders
Strict and closely adhered to contractual terms	Few, if any, formal contractual terms
Sample checks on quality of incoming products	Quality assurance on outgoing products
Formal, narrow channels of communication	Informal, wide and frequent channels of communication
Technology transfer rare	Technology transfer common
No risk sharing	Risk sharing

Source: derived from Sako (1990: 249).

'Obligational contracting' is reinforced, indeed prompted, by a distinct pattern of inter-firm shareholding. Shares are held not to obtain dividends and capital gains (as they are in the UK, for example), but as an expression of some other business relationship (as in Japan, for example). Japanese 'firms rely more on bank capital, and a lot of their equity is in the hands of their banks, their suppliers, their insurers – *more interested in the business they do with the firm than in the returns on their stock holding*' (Dore, 1989: 429, my emphasis). Over a quarter of Japanese shares, for example, are held by industrial and commercial companies, most of whom are either the firm's suppliers or its customers. The pattern is often reciprocated by the other side, so that if Nissan owns several million shares in Hitachi, then Hitachi will seek to own several million of theirs (Dore, 1987: 108–124). These arrangements lock firms together; on the one hand, buyers will be less likely to withdraw their custom from suppliers in which they have a stake, while on the other, suppliers will find it more difficult to sever their links with buyers once they have received training, advice and technological guidance. In other words, the bonds are strengthened by simultaneously raising the incentives to stick together and the disincentives to breaking up (Campbell and Harris, 1990: 37–38).

As yet there is only fragmentary evidence on whether or not British buyer–supplier relations are being transformed along Japanese lines. What evidence there is, however, points towards an affirmative answer, with the most notable transformers being Japanese companies themselves. Nissan, for example, is reported to have a policy of gaining a 20 per cent stake in companies supplying its Sunderland plant (Oliver and Wilkinson, 1988: 64).[11] This is designed to cement the creation of 'obligational contractual relations' between the two. For the supplier, a valuable trading contract is secured and the demand for its product is guaranteed over a lengthy period. For Nissan, the supplier becomes dependent upon them, thereby allowing 'the latter to exert a controlling influence on product development, pricing, *and* employment relations' (Crowther and Garrahan, 1988: 55, emphasis in original). So much so, that a Nissan supplier has been reported as saying: 'If Nissan says shit's toffee, we chew it' (*Independent*, 12 September 1992).

The prospect of active engagements in firms with whom a firm might do business has highlighted a further dimension to the apparent breakup of the large firm: large enterprises may have many legally independent subsidiaries in addition to others in which they have a minority stake (cf. Collins, 1990a: 733–734). While subsidiaries are *de jure* independent, they are *de facto* part of the holding company's empire and should be accounted for accordingly. For example, Bade (1983: 317) found that 31 of the largest manufacturing enterprises operating in the Federal Republic of Germany spawned a further 1,033 subsidiaries in 1981, almost double the number ten years earlier. If this phenomenon extends internationally (and the move towards 'Japanese-style' buyer-supplier relations would seem to provide a further push in this direction), then the rise in the number of small enterprises may be no more than a statistical quirk.

Subordinate co-operation

Subordinate co-operation relates to the relations forged between firms producing similar products or services, often for the same narrow set of customers. It is subordinate in the sense that horizontal co-operation arises out of a common dependency on a few customers. This makes for a relationship which is characterized by a mixture of competition and co-operation, so that those involved are 'conceived as competitors in one breath and then "friends" or collaborators in the next' (Pyke, 1988: 360).

Firms involved in subordinate co-operation have an interest in maintaining the communal interchanges rather than rejoicing when rivals go out of business. For example, Pyke (1988: 353) cites a case of competitors rallying around to provide a rival firm whose factory had been gutted by fire with the necessary machinery and floor space to minimize the disruption to its production. However, this is not purely altruistic behaviour; much can be gained by helping each other out. Being part of a network has its advantages. First, orders are passed between members in the network if those commissioned cannot complete the order owing to capacity constraints or because they lack the technical specialities required. They may even recommend customers to one another. Second, the spirit of helping one another acts as an insurance policy against hard times – the owner of the burnt-out factory referred to above can be viewed as cashing in on the times he/she helped others out in the past. Third, certain firms may be known to have specialized labour or machinery which could be borrowed or engaged on a subcontract basis from time to time. Finally, the subcontracting of work between competitors transforms them into customers, and with it rivals for work are transformed into work providers.

While empirical evidence for subordinate co-operation is very patchy, it has important implications for the nature of the inter-firm relationship. Crucially, it still underlines the principle of '*customer* sovereignty' which means that co-operative relations are forged under their auspices. The same cannot be said for 'independent co-operation' which is reckoned to signal the end for large-scale corporate capital, and its concentrating and centralizing influences.

Independent co-operation

The final type of inter-firm relationship is that formed by clusters of craft-based firms catering for a differentiated market with which mass production techniques and organization can no longer cope. The growth of independent co-operation (typified by industrial districts) and the decline of mass production is judged by some to bear testimony to this fact (Murray, 1985, 1988). At a theoretical level, this is taken to mean that a fundamental and irrevocable shift has taken place, with 'flexible specialization' replacing the once-dominant Fordist methods of production (Piore and Sabel, 1984).

The foundations on which Fordism was based are allegedly withering away. Products which were once standardized are becoming customized, labour and purpose-built machinery are becoming more versatile, once fragmented work tasks are becoming more consolidated and production centred around the conveyor belt is giving way to craft-based production. Mass/Fordist production could only be sustained with mass markets, or so the 'flexible specialization' theorists argue. Dedicated plant was expensive as well as task-specific, ensuring that only high volume production would be worthwhile (high fixed, low variable costs). As soon as mass-produced goods became acceptable, Fordism spread from sector to sector like wildfire, costs and prices fell further and mass-produced goods became more acceptable still. However, from about the 1960s consumer tastes have begun to change: demand for standardized, mass-produced commodities has declined, while the demand for high quality, specialized products has grown (Piore and Sabel: 184–193). Instead of keeping up with the Joneses there has been a move to be different from the Joneses – the 'yuppie' phenomenon has spread. Changes in how production is organized have followed. The main beneficiaries are small craft-based firms who are best placed to step in and serve the fragmented markets which Fordist producers have vacated. Two, now highly familiar, examples tend be cited: the Marshallian, small firm, craft industrial districts of the Third Italy (i.e. Emilia-Romagna, The Marches, Tuscany and Umbria); and high technology complexes such as Silicon Valley in California and Route 128 in Massachusetts.

The 'flexible specialization' debate has sparked a voluminous litera-ture. While a full and comprehensive survey of this literature is outside the scope of the book, three aspects of the debate can be noted in passing. First, there is much controversy surrounding the claim that a significant break with the past has taken, and is taking, place (Pollert, 1988a; Smith, 1989). Second, the claim that 'flexible specialization' represents a 'high road' for small enterprises characterized in the past by relatively low pay and poor working conditions is hotly debated (GLC, 1985; Murray, 1987; Nolan and O'Donnell, 1987; Loveman and Sengenberger, 1990; Amin, 1991; Rainnie, 1991). Third, the extent to which local authorities can intervene to 'restructure for labour' (i.e. to provide better pay, improved conditions and equality at work) is a moot point (Murray, 1985; Best, 1986; Gough, 1986).

The possibility, though, of a network of craft/artisan-based firms acting in concert to serve niche markets cannot be ignored; some inter-firm relations may indeed resemble networks of independent co-operation. According to Piore and Sabel (1984) these networks are communally based with no dominant firm among them nor a firm on which they are dependent. A horizontal trading pattern is thereby created, distinguishing it from the vertical relations of satellite pro-duction and active engagements as well as the mixed horizontal/vertical relations of subordinate co-operation discussed above. However, in later formulations of 'flexible specialization' its proponents (Sabel, 1989: 31–40; Hirst and Zeitlin, 1991) claim that large firms are now pursuing survival strategies designed 'to recreate among their subsidiaries and subcontractors the collaborative relationships characteristic of the industrial districts' (Hirst and Zeitlin: 4). Much emphasis is placed on Japanese-style subcontracting relationships and the benefits of closer integration. This brings us back once again to active engagements which bind firms together vertically rather than horizontally. This conflation aside, the 'flexible specialization' debate has raised the prospect of firms relating to one another via independent co-operation. It therefore offers the researcher another ideal type of inter-firm relationship to be on the lookout for when analysing the nature of the relationships firms forge with one another.

CONCLUSION

The fact that a long-standing trend towards larger units has been reversed across much of the industrialized world suggests that something quite important and fundamental has taken place. The legal decomposition of capital and the growth of legally independent businesses is reckoned by some to signal the death of the large, ever-growing corporation. However, such an assessment overlooks a host of other less overt methods of integration. Firms can be bound together by buyers taking ownership stakes in suppliers or vice versa, firms may be economic-reliant on others, or contractual ties such as franchising may bind firms together. Either way:

> The plant of 1999 will be a 'flotilla', consisting of modules centered either around a stage in the production process or around a number of closely related operations. Though *overall command and control will still exist*, each module will have its own command and control.
>
> (Drucker, 1990: 98–99, my emphasis)

The purpose of this book is to provide an assessment of the overall command and control structures present in the franchise relationship. In so doing the issue of where the boundaries of the firm lie constitutes its unifying theme.

Existing debates have already shown that the *appearance* of market exchanges taking place between legally independent firms does little to reveal their true *nature* (Cowling and Sugden, 1987). Delving into published company accounts will similarly fail to enlighten, since they will only report activities which the company carries out directly, even though many more may be co-ordinated through the market. Against such a background, franchising appeared a fruitful area for serious academic enquiry. On the face of it, franchisees are legally independent from both their franchisor and others within the chain, yet they trade in much the same way and under a common brand name as those from whom they are supposed to be autonomous. How can we explain this paradox? Do the forces of autonomy or control have the upper hand? In what circumstances are these forces strengthened or weakened? The following chapters explore these issues.

2 Defining what franchising is, its development and scope

INTRODUCTION

Most, if not all, readers of this book will be familiar with the most successful companies in which franchising is at work: Coca-Cola, Pepsi-Cola, Seven-Up, McDonald's, Kentucky Fried Chicken, Burger King, Wimpy, Prontaprint, Tie Rack, Body Shop, Dyno-Rod and Service-Master, to name but a few. Yet, there are many other less well-known firms in which franchising is at work. Only when one looks at the lengthy lists of firms using franchising (such as those given for the UK, US and Australia in the Appendices) does one become aware that franchising is big business. It is a fair bet that armed with such a list almost *every* local high street or shopping centre can boast several franchise operations. Some will be newly formed; others will be nationally, even internationally, well-known.

However, only a few people will know that franchising is being used. Many more will be unaware of this fact and unclear about what it means for the way in which these businesses are, in fact, organized. Even for those with some idea of how franchised businesses are organized, the widespread use of the term 'franchise' in different contexts can have a confusing effect. For example, during discussions regarding the right to vote in elections, whether it be for governments, clubs, trade unions or whatever, reference is frequently made to the 'franchise' to vote, that is, the right or privilege to cast a vote in the ballot. Similarly, the right to broadcast TV programmes, the allocation of airline routes to particular operators and a team's right to play American football, baseball or basketball in a particular city in the relevant American professional sports' league are all referred to as 'franchises' (Lewis, 1975; Sturgess, 1983; Domberger and Middleton, 1985; Domberger, 1986; Veljanovski, 1987). Yet these uses of the term have little in common with the

businesses cited above and the type of relationships which are the subject
of this book.

In this chapter, we start by discussing the origins of franchising and
its early commercial uses. The chapter then moves from definition by
example to review a variety of formal definitions which have been put
forward by researchers and 'industry' associations. Attention is also
paid to the pattern of franchising's growth in the UK, Europe, the US
and Australia, and the typologies commonly adopted to identify its
newer and more novel elements. The chapter ends by spelling out what
is meant by franchising for the purposes of this book.

ORIGINS

It is a commonly held belief that franchising is a very recent phenomenon imported from the US, where it began to take root in the 1950s.
However, its origins, in one form or another, can be traced as far back
as the Middle Ages. Today's standard dictionary definition of franchising still reflects this historical heritage, 'a privilege granted by the
sovereign power to any person or body of persons' (*The Shorter Oxford
English Dictionary*, Oxford University Press: Oxford, 1983). In this
context, a franchise referred to the granting of various rights and
obligations from the sovereign which would otherwise be reserved for
the Crown. For example, in Norman England, barons were granted
territories by the King in return for the payment of royalties and
provided they met many other requests made by the monarch. Similarly,
later on in the Middle Ages, it was accepted practice for local
governments to offer important persons, who might also be high church
officials, a franchise. This granted them the right to maintain civil order,
determine and collect taxes, and levy special taxes in their area. The
franchisee paid the franchisor a specified sum from the tax revenues
collected, in order to receive military or other forms of protection. In
this way, the monarch could control the lands within its sphere of
influence by providing protection to its tax collectors. Although this
system of tax collection came to an end in the middle of the sixteenth
century, the sovereign's use of franchising re-emerged two centuries
later. These arrangements often called for a pledge of allegiance to the
monarchy in return for the right to develop one's personal wealth by
exercising managerial authority over a specified geographical territory.

Franchise relationships have also existed for some time in private
business and commerce. In Japan, for example, the *Norenkai* system,
whereby a former employee opens an independent branch operation in
return for a royalty, has operated since the early sixteenth century

(Abell, 1989). However, the brewers in the UK are often credited with the accolade of being the first widespread commercial users of franchising (Izraeli, 1972: 67). Its use was prompted by the stricter licensing laws introduced towards the end of the eighteenth century. The end of the Civil War of 1642 brought to a close a period of harsh licensing laws and ushered in a period of no-restraint. Ale-house licences were freely issued, coffee-houses diversified into the sale of liquor, and spirit consumption leapt. Only piecemeal attempts were made to regulate and restrain the number of licences issued until, in 1787, a royal proclamation was made against vice and immorality. This, together with the public outcry against the excessive level of drinking and of the large number of retail outlets, prompted magistrates to refuse to renew a great number of licences, to remove licences from others on the grounds of misconduct and to insist on raised standards in those licensed premises which remained. All this served to increase the value of the remaining licensed premises, often beyond the reach of licensees, and put the added obligation on publicans that they must adhere to higher standards if they wished to keep their licence. Brewing companies, anxious to secure outlets for their products, and fearing competition, bought some premises outright, and gave loans to others on the condition that the publican would sell no beer other than the brewer's (Hawkins and Radcliffe, 1971; Housden, 1976: 6–7). In this way, the 'tied' pub was born.

Just over 200 years later, the UK government sought to dilute the 'tie' significantly on the grounds that it limited competition by 'tying' tenants to the brands of one brewer. The government ordered that brewers owning more than 2,000 pubs had to free at least 50 per cent of licensed premises above that ceiling from the 'tie', and that tenanted publicans and recipients of 'tied' loans must be free to choose and sell at least one cask-conditioned guest beer. That meant that the top five brewers had to get rid of 11,000 pubs by November 1992, or give up their brewing interests altogether (Monopolies and Mergers Commission, 1989; *Financial Times*, 11 July 1989). Despite the much reduced importance of franchising in shaping the brewery–tenant relationship, its imprint as a forerunner of modern day franchising arrangements still remains.

As far as actual *companies* are concerned, the Singer Sewing Machine Company is often credited as being the first to use a franchise method of distribution, albeit briefly. During the 1850s, Singer experienced difficulty in marketing its new product across the US. Since the sewing machine was an innovative product, Singer first needed to educate the consumer about its uses, its versatility, and its superiority over traditional hand sewing techniques and other competing machines on the market. The company believed that the best way of doing this was to display it in impressive showrooms where its successful operation could be demonstrated and new users instructed in its operation. However, Singer did not have the capital resources to hire a large sales staff or open a large number of branch offices. As the product was untried and without a track record, securing the necessary capital from a fledgling capital market was impossible. Singer, therefore, turned to commission agents who were given the right (i.e. franchise) to supply consumers with machines within a designated territory. The Company tried to secure agents who could invest in business – setting up showrooms, keeping an adequate stock of demonstration models and staffed with a female operator offering on-the-spot demonstrations. Agents made their money through the difference between the price at which Singer supplied them with machines and the price at which they were sold. However, once the sewing machine caught on, carving up the country into territories in which Singer agents had the exclusive right to supply Singer sewing machines proved expensive – the commission was too large, the machines were becoming easier to sell and yet pockets of franchisees' territories were not being catered for to their fullest extent. Faced with these problems, the Company switched to selling its machines through company-owned offices during the 1860s. Nevertheless, franchising had proved its worth in terms of accelerating the market penetration of an innovative product (Jack, 1957).

Although the commercial use of franchising declined before the turn of the century, its advantages were not lost on those in car distribution and soft drink bottling. The use of franchising in both of these pioneering sectors proved so successful that its application spread to other sectors – drug stores, the sale of car parts, petrol distribution and then to the companies which we most readily associate with franchising today, e.g. McDonald's, Prontaprint, Dyno-Rod, Service-Master, and so on.

Coca-Cola was conceived in 1886 as a non-alcoholic alternative to 'hard' drinks such as beers and spirits. It was said to be invigorating, to cure hangovers, and to have the properties of an aphrodisiac (Watters, 1978: 14–15). However, since it was dispensed at soda fountains by mixing a specified amount of syrup with carbonated water, it was not portable and could only be sold from static sites. This seriously limited the size of its market and hampered its growth. However, the idea of bottling Coca-Cola was to change all that. The rights to bottle and sell Coca-Cola everywhere in the US (apart from New England, Mississippi and Texas, where prior distribution arrangements had already been concluded) were granted to two franchisees – Thomas and Whitehead – in 1899. The contract granted Thomas and Whitehead the rights to make up and bottle Coca-Cola from syrup provided; the Coca-Cola Company granted them sole use of the trade mark on their bottles, and furnished them with labels and advertising matter. The franchise is reputed to have cost $1.

Soon after the agreement had been concluded, Thomas and Whitehead parted company; and Whitehead, realizing that he did not have the $5,000 needed to set up his own bottling operation, formed a partnership with another Chattanooga businessman, John Thomas Lupton. The capital resources required to set up bottling plants across the entire US were still beyond their reach. Therefore, both 'parent bottlers' began to franchise their bottling rights for well-defined geographical territories to others. They ceased to be bottlers themselves and instead became wholesalers of Coca-Cola syrup to a network of 'actual bottlers' (Tedlow, 1990: 22–68). Parent bottlers remained in the US until 1975, but the franchise system still remains, albeit in a modified form, the linchpin of the Coca-Cola Company's business in the US and elsewhere (see Chapter 6). Indeed, the Company's worldwide expansion was based on granting indigenous businesspeople the rights to bottle and sell Coca-Cola in their native country. For example, the Hawaiian Soda Works in Honolulu was the first to be granted an overseas franchise in 1907. Others were granted shortly afterwards – Puerto Rico (1911), Panama and Manilla (1912), Nicaragua (1914), Guatemala (1915), Guam (1917), and Paris (1919) (Giebelhaus, 1988). Subsequent years saw Coca-Cola franchises being granted all over the world, thereby helping, sustaining and promoting the Coca-Cola Company's presence in more than 185 of today's national markets.

Coca-Cola's arch-rival, Pepsi-Cola, also adopted the franchise method. However, it franchised to bottlers directly rather than relying upon 'parent bottlers' as go-betweens. By 1910, Pepsi-Cola had 280 bottlers operating in 24 states. Although it was declared bankrupt twice within 10 years – in 1922 and then again in 1931 – it remained committed to franchising and, like the Coca-Cola Company, has used the franchise method successfully to penetrate markets worldwide (Tedlow, 1990: 69–106).

Also at the turn of the century, car manufacturers began to use franchising to distribute their product more widely. Until 1910, most cars were sold directly by manufacturers to customers from plants at which they were assembled (Justis and Judd, 1989). However, the advent of mass production required mass sales. Making assembly-line production profitable required that what was produced was sold. Several selling methods were tried: mail order campaigns, agencies were established on a consignment basis, door-to-door salespeople were engaged and large department stores were used as outlets by some manufacturers. Only the use of agents on a consignment basis proved successful. It was therefore on this basis that car dealership networks were established. Since car manufacturers lacked the capital resources to set up retail outlets of their own, they appointed dealers for particular areas. Cars were supplied to them at discounted prices, allowing the dealer a margin between purchase and selling price to pay their running costs and allow them to make a profit. Dealers were allocated exclusive territories within which to work and in return they agreed to sell only those cars manufactured by the parent company. Today, franchised dealer networks for car distribution exist in all countries where cars are freely bought and sold (Kessler, 1957; Macaulay, 1973; Monopolies and Mergers Commission, 1992a: 73).

Several reasons have been advanced as to why the franchised dealer system became so widespread and popular with car manufacturers. First, early car makers regarded themselves, first and foremost, as experts in engineering and production; selling was for others. A franchised dealer network reflected this division of skills: it allowed manufacturers to concentrate, without distraction, on making technical improvements to their products and recouping the economies of large-scale production, while a network of 'independent' entrepreneurial units operating on a commission basis would heighten the incentive to maximize sales volumes and provide a more widespread service than would be the case in a company-run chain.

Secondly, a small locally based business can tap into, develop and maintain its contacts with the local community. Personal involvement and the commitment of their own capital strengthens dealers' incentives to maintain a high reputation and develop customer loyalty.

A further factor, which may originally (but not now) have influenced car manufacturers to contract out their retail operations, was that it was not easy to raise capital for what was then considered a risky business venture. By contracting out, they were absolved from finding the additional capital required to set up the retail network and finance the stocks of new cars in the showrooms. The capital cost of the premises and stock was provided by the dealer; these overheads can be spread over other business activities the dealer might conduct from the site, such as second-hand car selling, and car servicing and repairs.

These factors not only summarize the reasons for the continuance of the franchise system in car distribution, but they also cover the advantages of franchising as practised in many other fields. For example, until about 1930, the large oil companies owned most of their service stations worldwide. However, few were profitable. Price wars with independents were putting sales under pressure. The oil companies responded by leasing sites to once-salaried managers for 'independent' operation. Petrol was supplied at a discount, allowing franchisees a retail margin from which to cover their operating costs and allowing them to make a profit. Sales increased, since the franchised retailer had a greater incentive to work longer hours, often drawing on the help of family members. Personal attention to detail was also thought to be much greater under franchise ownership when compared with company ownership. Since the oil companies already owned the service station properties, they continued to exercise control over the site while also benefiting from the advantages of 'independent' ownership.[1] The franchise system was thus cemented into the petrol distribution industry; it remains largely intact today (Rehbinder, 1973; Vaughn, 1979; Monopolies and Mergers Commission, 1990).

The 1930s also saw the growth of franchising among already established small retailers, whereby retailers would combine to strengthen their collective buying power and co-ordinate marketing and mechandising campaigns under a single brand name. This was largely in response to heavy discounting by the major multiples, the growth of the large chain and the exclusion of small independents from shopping centres (Hall, 1964). This form of franchising took root in American drug stores, the sale of car parts and hardware stores. Walgreen, Western Auto, Valu Stores and Ace Hardware are some of the widely-cited US examples. UK chains such as VG and Mace, as well as European ones such as Spar, are further examples.

Other companies such as McDonald's, Prontaprint and Dyno-Rod, which have more recently brought franchising to the fore, have been conspicuous in a number of respects. First, they are based not on the supply of a tangible product to their franchisees, but on supply of a way of doing business. Second, they are not confined to a particular business sector such as car distribution or soft drink bottling as previous users of franchising have tended to be, but are instead located in sectors far and wide. Several authors have attempted to capture these differences by advancing a franchise typology. Before considering this, however, we need to review the formal definitions commonly used to separate franchising from other forms of business organization.

FORMAL DEFINITIONS

Much confusion surrounds what is actually meant by franchising. This stems in part from the variety of business arrangements that closely resemble franchising proper, and in part from the widespread use of the term in a wide range of contexts (see Housden, 1984). Sharpening up the definition of franchising is important for three reasons. First, a clearer definition will enable would-be franchisees to assess with a greater level of confidence whether a business proposition is all that it appears to be. Second, it is important that precise definitions are established and widely used, so that franchising statistics are comparable (differing definitions make international comparisons exceedingly difficult, see pp.53–56). Third, a sharper definition will make it easier to identify those schemes (such as pyramid selling in the 1960s) which are, at best, ill-conceived and, at worst, organized by fraudulent operators. This section therefore begins by reviewing past attempts to provide a workable definition of franchising. It then considers a two-fold typology which is designed to tease out the nuances and novelties of franchising as practised by private capital.

Reviewing past attempts

Some of the broadest definitions of franchising cast their net so wide that they include several activities on which this book has little to say. For example, Housden (1984: 31) quotes the following early definition of franchising: 'In modern commercial usage a franchise is a right to do or use something which is granted by one party (the franchisor) to another party (the franchisee) for a consideration'. This would cover the auctioning of the Independent Television Network's 16 regional commercial television companies, which grabbed the headlines when the winners and losers for the ten-year franchises were announced (*Financial Times*, 19 December 1991). It would also cover the suggestion that franchising be extended to the sale of publicly-owned 'natural' monopolies such as electricity generation and now the railways (cf. Sharpe, 1983; Domberger, 1986; Conservative Central Office, 1992: 35; *Financial Times*, 20 January 1992). Such a strategy appears to acknowledge one of the major criticisms levelled at the UK government's privatization programme, namely that transferring ownership from the public to the private sector will do little to promote competition which, ostensibly at least, is the overriding policy objective (Kay and Silberston, 1984: 16). In contrast, franchising is said to combine the desirable elements of competition – through franchise bidding – with a regulatory framework which may be essential for the prevention of monopolistic and other 'inefficiencies'. These types of franchise, although falling within the definition outlined above, are beyond the scope of this book.

Thompson's (1971) definition provides a more promising starting point as to what type of relationships this book is focused upon. Even so, it still leaves certain aspects of the relationship unspecified. It runs as follows:

> Franchising is a contractual bond of interest in which an organization, the franchisor, which has developed a pattern or formula for the manufacture and/or sale of a product or service, extends to other firms, the franchisees, the right to carry on the business, subject to a number of restrictions and controls. In almost all cases of significance, the franchisee operates using the franchisor's name as a trade name.
>
> (quoted in Housden, 1984: 31–32)

Although this definition captures much of the franchise relationship, it fails to mention one important ingredient: the on-going payments made by the franchisee to the franchisor. In some franchise systems these payments are direct by way of a royalty on turnover, in others they are more indirect since they are contained in the wholesale margin of goods supplied.[2] Other definitions which have followed have largely plugged this gap. Mendelsohn (1985: 1–2), for example, identifies four basic features common to franchises awarded by *private* capital. The first is that the franchisor is the owner of a name, an idea, a secret process, a product, or a specialized piece of equipment and the goodwill associated with it. The second is the issuing of a franchise specified by contract, permitting the franchisee to use the name, idea, process, product, or equipment and goodwill associated with it. The third is the inclusion in the franchise contract of regulations and controls relating to the operation of the business in the conduct of which the franchisee exercises his/her rights. Finally, the payment by the franchisee of a royalty or some other consideration, such as payments for franchisor-produced supplies, in return for the rights obtained and franchisor services provided. Several 'industry' bodies have based their definitions on these four points. According to the European Franchise Federation,[3] for example:

> Franchising is a system of marketing goods and/or services and/or technology, which is based upon a close and on-going collaboration between legally and financially separate and independent under-takings, the franchisor and its individual franchisees, whereby the Franchisor grants its individual franchisees the right, and imposes the

obligation, to conduct a business in accordance with the franchisor's concept. The right entitles and compels the individual franchisee, in exchange for a direct or indirect financial consideration, to use the franchisor's trade name, and/or trade mark and/or service mark, know-how, business and technical methods, procedural system, and other industrial and/or intellectual property rights, supported by continuing provision of commercial and technical assistance, within the framework and for the term of a written franchise agreement, concluded between parties for this purpose.

(European Franchise Federation, 1990: 2)

This study is confined to how and why private capital uses franchising as formally defined in this way. However, this definition still embraces a wide variety of franchising forms. Establishing a two-fold typology helps to reveal some of the most important differences and the uneven pattern of growth within franchising itself.

Establishing typologies

From much of the discussion so far, two main types of franchise arrangement can be readily identified.[4] The first is known as product or trade mark franchising and refers to the situation where the franchisor is typically either a manufacturer seeking outlets for its branded products, or a product component manufacturer seeking someone else to make-up the finished product and distribute the branded product to retailers. Under this arrangement the franchisor may provide some advertising, management assistance and training, but the franchisee generally conducts business as an independent distributor acquiring the identity of the franchisor through the product/trade mark. This type has a long commercial heritage and for this reason is often referred to as 'first generation' franchising. The arrangement between a manufacturer of soft drink flavouring syrup (or concentrate) and a franchised bottler, whereby the latter is given exclusive production and distribution rights for the syrup (concentrate) manufacturer's soft drink brands within a designated territory, is a classic example (see Chapter 6). Other examples include 'tied' pubs, car dealerships and service station retailers.

The second broad type of franchise arrangement, and the one around which much of the more recent growth has centred (see pp.52–53), is known as the business format franchise. Under this system, the franchisee not only sells the franchisor's product and/or service, but does so in accordance with a set of precisely laid-down procedures or 'format'. This type of franchise is most commonly offered by an operating retailer who has experienced a level of success sufficient to suggest that if other retailer franchisees were to reproduce the franchisor's formula and systems in similar locations, they would also succeed. As in product or trade mark systems, it is franchisees who provide most, if not all, of the capital outlay required for each individual business set up under the franchisor's auspices. On-going payments are also made under both – often a percentage of franchisee turnover in the case of business format franchises, but more commonly a mark-up on the products supplied by the franchisor in the case of product or trade mark systems. In addition to these payments, business format franchisees usually pay a one-off franchise fee on entry. In return, the franchisor provides the franchisee with assistance in carrying on the business. This includes training in the operation and methods of the business prior to opening, in addition to continuing advice and assistance in the areas of staff training, management, marketing, advertising, research and development, and so on. Clearly, some of these elements are to be found in many of the franchise arrangements discussed above. However, the business format franchise involves the use of not merely goods and services identified by a trade mark or invention, but a package or 'blueprint' containing *all the elements necessary* to establish the business and run it profitably on a predetermined basis. The package or blueprint is carefully prepared from the company's wholly-owned and/ or pilot operations, thereby minimizing the risks involved in setting up a conventional small business.

What constitutes business format franchising may be made clearer still if we briefly consider other types of contractual arrangements commonly confused with it. One such arrangement is the situation in which a retailer is given the right to sell a particular product or range of products in a department store. These are known as in-store concessions. These arrangements range widely; from the concessionaire being merely a tenant paying a fixed rent for the privilege of operating in the premises, to the concessionaire being paid by the department store for services rendered. In between these extremes are arrangements in which the concessionaire pays a fee calculated as a percentage of turnover for the right to operate within the store, and arrangements where both parties jointly participate in the trading outcome of the venture. However, in-store concessions differ from business format franchising in a number of respects. They are not 'turnkey' operations (i.e. ready-made businesses) offered to business entrants, the organizational and marketing back-up they offer extends little beyond that normally expected of suppliers, and they are often in competition with similar products sold in the same store.

Pyramid or multi-level selling (known in the American literature as direct selling organizations) has also frequently been confused with business format franchising. This type of arrangement refers to a system of distribution which involves a pyramid-like structure of distributors. The manufacturer or supplier appoints distributors who sell products and services directly to consumers through personal demonstrations, primarily in private homes. Demonstrations are either 'one-on-one' or, more often, in 'parties' such as those made by Tupperware, for example.[5] Distributors profit by selling at retail prices products which they purchase at wholesale cost from the manufacturer/supplier or from another distributor. As independent contractors, they purchase the products they sell and pay for the cost of promotional materials. Members of the network also recruit or 'sponsor' new members into the organization. Members usually receive financial incentives, often a percentage of a recruit's sales, to do so. It is this recruitment element that gives multi-selling organizations their pyramid-like structure. Each distributor is encouraged to 'sponsor' others, each of whom is encouraged to do likewise (see Biggart, 1988a, 1988b).

The essential difference between business format franchising and multi-level selling is the sponsorship structure. In business format franchising, franchisees *cannot* recruit others into the organization, although master franchisees can recruit a second tier of franchisees. Secondly, in business format franchising, no franchisee can simply buy their way into the organization, but instead must go through an often rigorous vetting procedure administered by the franchisor. Thirdly, whereas the business format franchisee is given continuous on-going support by the franchisor, in the case of multi-level selling the relationship between the manufacturer/supplier and distributor (and hence 'downline' to others in the chain) is essentially one of supplier and wholesaler (Housden, 1984).

Many businesses are currently operating and offering franchises on a business format basis. They span such sectors as the provision of cleaning services, building maintenance and repair, vehicle services, quick printing, fast food, and the retailing of a variety of products and services. The investment costs and franchise fees required to enter business as a franchisee as well as the on-going royalty payments (usually expressed as a percentage of turnover) display a similarly wide degree of variation. In the case of the catering and hotels category, for example, an average investment of around £260,000 is called for, compared with around £16,000 for a franchise providing cleaning services such as upholstery or carpet cleaning (see Table 2.1). Differences can also be found in the level of on-going royalty payments and

Table 2.1 Investment costs, franchise fees and on-going royalties associated with becoming a business format franchisee in the United Kingdom

Business sector[1]	Examples	Average investment costs (set-up costs, franchise fees and working capital)	Average franchise fees	Average royalties[2] (management services fee plus advertising levy)
Cleaning services (n=19)	ServiceMaster, Safeclean	£16,664 (n=11)	£7,144 (n=9)	8.8% (n=9)
Commercial and industrial services (n=42)	Recognition Express, National Vacuum Cleaner Services	£24,765 (n=20)	£5,514 (n=11)	11.4% (n=17)
Employment and recruitment agencies (n=14)	Alfred Marks, Travail	£21,167 (n=6)	£8,092 (n=6)	7.4% (n=4)
Domestic and personal services (n=42)	British School of Motoring, Kwik Strip	£19,290 (n=16)	£5,920 (n=17)	9.7% (n=13)
Distribution (n=23)	Unigate Dairies, Snap-On-Tools	£24,420 (n=15)	£6,491 (n=9)	5.0% (n=7)
Building services (n=69)	Dyno-Rod, Dampcure-Woodcure 30	£26,240 (n=29)	£9,085 (n=26)	10.4% (n=28)
Vehicle services (n=37)	Budget-Rent-A-Car, HomeTune	£26,444 (n=17)	£6,788 (n=16)	12.3% (n=15)

Business sector	Examples			
Parcel/courier/taxi chauffeur/removal services (n=17)	Interlink, Amtrak	£32,200 (n=5)	£11,400 (n=5)	23.0% (n=2)
Estate agencies/business transfer agencies (n=20)	Seekers, Century 21	£42,545 (n=11)	£6,345 (n=10)	10.0% (n=11)
Retailing (n=131)	Tie Rack, Body Shop	£58,633 (n=30)	£8,745 (n=38)	7.3% (n=33)
Quick printing/ graphic design (n=8)	Prontaprint, Kall-Kwik	£123,250 (n=8)	£11,813 (n=8)	9.9% (n=8)
Catering and hotels (n=55)	Holiday Inn, Kentucky Fried Chicken	£260,609 (n=29)	£9,471 (n=29)	7.4% (n=25)
Overall average		£69,125 (n=197)	£8,148 (n=184)	9.3% (n=172)

Notes:
1. Not all 477 of those listed in the *Franchise World Directory 1992* provide information on their investment costs, franchise fees and royalties. The calculations are therefore based only on those franchisors who supplied the relevant details. Below each average is the number of observations on which the calculation is based. These should be compared with the total number listed in each business sector. These are shown in the left-hand column.
2. Royalties refer to management services fees plus advertising levies. Most franchisors levy these as a percentage of franchisee turnover. However, 19 per cent *also* make a flat rate charge or mark-up the materials they supply to franchisees. A minority of franchisors (9 per cent of those on which there is data) link their income to the fluctuations in franchisee sales by marking-up the materials they supply to franchisees (either alone or in addition to flat rate payments). For example, Wimpy collects revenue from its franchisees by marking-up the goods it supplies to franchisees. It is reckoned that this equates to about 8.5 per cent of turnover. Only 5 per cent of franchisors (on which there are data) gain (lose) nothing no matter how well (badly) a franchisee does since they levy a flat rate charge unrelated to franchisee turnover.
Source: calculated from data contained in the *Franchise World Directory 1992* (Franchise World Publications: London, 1991).

the franchise fee payable on entry. The overall average as well as the business sector averages are just that, and as such they conceal wide variations.

The establishment of a two-fold typology of franchising serves to provide a barometer with which to track the uneven development of franchising in recent years. In the US, for example, it is estimated that 35 per cent of total retail sales in 1991 occurred through franchise company outlets and that, all told, franchise company sales of goods and services were running at about $750 billion (International Franchise Association Educational Foundation, 1991: 7). Sales in real terms rose by 65 per cent over the 1972–1991 period while the number of establishments increased by one-fifth in the same period. However, these aggregate figures conceal an uneven pattern of development. While the sales generated by both product or trade mark and business format franchisors increased in real terms, the rate of increase was more rapid in the case of the latter. Consequently, business format franchising made up one-fifth of the total sales generated in 1972 whereas almost 20 years later this proportion had risen to about a third (see Table 2.2). The shift in terms of establishments was more dramatic. Business format franchising's proportion rose from 42 per cent in 1972 to 65 per cent in 1991 (see Table 2.2). While the number of outlets set up by business format franchisors leapt, the number of establishments operated by product/trade mark franchisors *fell* (see Figure 2.1). For example, the number of soft drink bottlers was halved from 1984 to 1990 as the two major players, Coca-Cola Company and PepsiCo Incorporated, began to rationalize their US networks (US Department of Commerce, 1988: 93; International Franchise Association Educational Foundation, 1990: 96; see also Chapter 6).

Unfortunately, in the UK no systematic evidence has been collected on the growth of franchising as a whole. Instead, efforts have been made to track the development of business format franchising only. Nevertheless, by piecing together fragmentary evidence an overall picture can be derived. This mirrors the US pattern remarkably well. For example, the number of establishments operated by product/trade mark franchisors is on the decline. Some of the major business categories which make up the product or trade mark variety of franchising have seen their networks, sometimes dramatically, reduced. Following the UK government's investigation into the competition effects of the brewer–tenant relationship, 11,000 previously 'tied' outlets have been sold off or closed (Monopolies and Mergers Commission, 1989). The long-term decline in the number of petrol stations has continued apace. Petrol companies owned fewer sites in 1988 than in 1977, although as a

Table 2.2 Distribution of franchising by franchise type in the United States, 1972–1991

Year	Establishments as proportion of total number		Sales as proportion of total	
	Product/ trade mark	*Business format*	*Product/ trade mark*	*Business format*
1972	58.0	42.0	80.0	20.0
1973	55.4	44.6	80.0	20.0
1974	52.4	47.5	77.9	22.1
1975	51.5	48.5	78.0	22.0
1976	49.8	50.2	78.6	21.4
1977	46.8	53.2	74.9	25.1
1978	45.8	54.2	77.2	22.8
1979	44.2	55.8	76.9	23.1
1980	42.9	57.1	75.0	25.0
1981	41.1	58.9	74.3	25.7
1982	39.4	60.6	73.7	26.3
1983	37.4	62.6	73.9	26.1
1984	36.2	63.8	75.1	24.9
1985	33.7	66.3	74.0	26.0
1986	32.5	67.5	68.0	32.0
1987	30.2	69.8	71.7	28.3
1988	29.5	70.5	72.5	27.5
1989	28.3	71.7	71.5	28.5
1990	25.9	64.1	70.1	29.9
1991	24.8	65.2	69.4	30.6

Source: calculated from *Franchising in the Economy 1991* (International Franchise Association Education Foundation: Washington DC, 1991), pp. 8, 64.

proportion the petrol companies owned more rather than less of those petrol stations trading at the end of the period (Monopolies and Mergers Commission, 1990: 37–42). During the 1982–1991 period the number of car dealerships has fallen by almost 1,000 with the large networks of Rover and Ford among the hardest hit (Monopolies and Mergers Commission, 1992b: 67).

Quite a different picture emerges when one considers the fate of business format franchising in the UK in recent times. Unlike the US, however, there is no *officially inspired* data on which to draw (cf. note 4). Instead one has to rely on an annual survey commissioned by the British Franchise Association and sponsored by the National Westminster Bank. This charts the quite staggering growth of business format franchising since the mid-1980s. For example, within eight years real sales have risen almost four-fold while the number of franchised outlets, franchise systems and the employment franchising

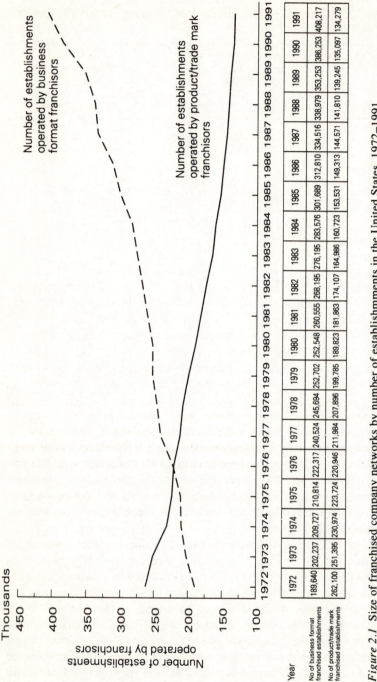

Thousands

Number of establishments operated by business format franchisors

Number of establishments operated by product/trade mark franchisors

Number of establishments operated by franchisors

Year	1972	1973	1974	1975	1976	1977	1978	1979	1980	1981	1982	1983	1984	1985	1986	1987	1988	1989	1990	1991
No of business format franchised establishments	189,640	202,237	209,727	210,814	222,317	240,524	245,694	252,702	252,548	260,555	288,195	276,195	283,576	301,689	312,810	334,516	338,979	353,253	386,253	408,217
No of product/trade mark franchised establishments	262,100	251,395	230,974	223,724	220,946	211,984	207,896	199,785	189,823	181,863	174,107	164,986	160,723	153,531	149,313	144,571	141,810	139,245	135,097	134,279

Figure 2.1 Size of franchised company networks by number of establishmments in the United States, 1972–1991
Source: Franchising in the Economy 1991 (International Franchise Association Education Foundation: Washington DC, 1991) pp. 8, 64.

Table 2.3 Extent of business format franchising in the United Kingdom, 1984–1991

Year (mid)	Annual turnover (£bn at current prices)	Annual turnover (£bn at 1991 prices)	Number of franchised outlets	Number of franchised systems	Employment generated
1984	0.85	1.27	7,900	170	72,000
1985	1.30	1.85	9,000	NA	93,000
1986	1.90	2.57	10,900	NA	126,000
1987	3.10	4.03	15,000	253	169,000
1988	3.80	4.79	16,000	244	181,000
1989	4.73	5.55	16,600	295	185,000
1990	5.24	5.71	18,260	379	184,000
1991	4.80	4.80	18,600	432	189,500

Sources: BFA/NatWest Franchise Surveys, 1984–1991; Retail Prices, 1914–1990 (HMSO: London, 1991), Table 1.

generates has risen by a factor of two-and-a-half (see Table 2.3). Each indicator points in the same direction: business format franchising has grown by leaps and bounds. Though, expressed as a proportion of total retail sales, business format franchising is reckoned to account for just 3 per cent (International Franchise Association Educational Foundation, 1991: 7–8, 72). This appears meagre compared with the figure of 35 per cent so often claimed for franchising in the US. However, comparing such raw data is meaningless, because the UK estimate relates to business format franchising only, while the US estimate embraces franchising as a whole. A more accurate comparison can be made by excluding from the US figures the sales made by product or trade mark franchisors (i.e. sales of cars and petrol). This exercise reveals US and UK franchise penetration to be far narrower than a straight comparison of the raw statistics might first imply – 8 per cent of retail sales in the US compared with 3 per cent in the UK. Even so, ample room for expansion in the UK still apparently exists, with US franchisors viewing the UK as a popular destination for international expansion (Walker and Cross, 1989).

Evidence for the rest of Europe is also patchy. Nonetheless, business format franchising appears to be well established (see Table 2.4), and its roots have been strengthened as it has become more widespread (Euromonitor, 1987: 7–10). The same is true of Australia: estimates put the growth of business format franchising between 1988 and 1991 at around 17 per cent a year as measured by outlets and turnover (see Table 2.5). This is reckoned to represent 30 per cent of Australian

Table 2.4 Extent of business format franchising across Europe, 1991

Country	Number of franchisors	Number of franchised outlets	Franchisee sales (ECU billions)
Austria	80	2,500	NA
Belgium	90	3,200	3.3
Denmark	42	500	0.5
Federal Republic of Germany	265	9,950	4.0
France	600	30,000	21.0
Ireland	20	NA	0.1
Italy	318	16,100	8.5
Netherlands	309	11,005	6.3
Norway	125	3,500	3.0
Portugal	50	800	NA
Spain	117	14,500	2.1
Sweden	200	9,000	6.0
United Kingdom	432	18,600	6.8
Total	2,648	119,655	61.6

Source: figures supplied by the European Franchise Federation, 1992.

Table 2.5 Extent of business format franchising in Australia, 1988–1991

Year	Number of franchisors	Number of outlets	Total turnover (A$ billion)
1988	250	11,000	5.5
1989	275	12,800	6.4
1990	305	15,000	7.5
1991	340	17,200	8.8

Source: taken from *Franchising in the Economy 1991* (International Franchise Association Educational Foundation: Washington DC, 1991), p. 110.

franchising, the remainder comprising car dealerships and petrol stations, i.e. franchises of the product or trade mark variety.

The distinction between product or trade mark franchising and business format franchising also serves to capture some of the newer and more novel elements of how franchising is practised today. Business format franchising is broadly different from its product or trade mark counterpart in at least four respects. First, business format franchising is growing at a faster rate, offering more opportunities for aspiring entrepreneurs seeking to 'be their own boss'.

Secondly, the concentration among product or trade mark franchise networks is raising the capital required to become a franchisee, sometimes considerably. For example, the Coca-Cola Company appears to be establishing a network of large cornerstone bottlers throughout the world. This is taking place through a variety of mechanisms: encouraging franchisees to merge, taking equity in bottlers and buying bottlers outright (see Chapter 6).

Thirdly, recent evidence suggests that the number of potential franchisees may be on the increase. A poll conducted for the BBC and the *Independent* found that 40 per cent of young people hoped to run their own company as opposed to some 35 per cent content to work for others (reported in *Economic Progress Report*, October 1989). Where these hopefuls lack a specific business idea to put into practice, business format franchisors can provide a complete, tried and tested business package. Supplying this *and* the ability become 'one's own boss' is more questionable. The franchise relates to the entire business, not just the product. A step-by-step approach to how to run the business is provided and the franchise is geared towards helping aspiring entrepreneurs in start-up situations. Little, if any, experience is called for. In general, experience is more likely to be sought by product or trade mark franchisors such as car manufacturers and soft drink syrup (concentrate) producers, since they are more concerned with the distribution of the products they make than with the supply of 'off-the-peg' businesses.

Lastly, a franchise based on the intangible assets of a ready-made business is more likely to be protective of its 'know-how' than one based on the supply of a branded product. For example, car dealership as well as soft drink bottling agreements do not impose restrictions on franchisees once they leave the network (cf. Monopolies and Mergers Commission, 1992a; Chapter 6 in this book), whereas business format franchise agreements invariably do (see Chapter 4).

However, despite the apparent clarity in the franchise literature (e.g. Vaughn, 1979: 4–20; US Department of Commerce, 1988: 1–5) as well as in the discussion so far, the distinction between product and business format franchising is becoming increasingly difficult to detect in practice. Some franchisors, who might at one time have been classified as product franchisors by virtue of the fact that they granted independent operators the right to retail products manufactured by the franchisor, have since provided more intensive support to their retail franchisees. Petrol companies such as Shell and Esso, for example, now provide some of their filling station franchisees with comprehensive and detailed manuals covering the operation of forecourt shops (cf. Monopolies and Mergers Commission, 1990: 367–371; *Motor Trader*, 11 February 1989). By the same token, a number of those classified as business format franchisors have since vertically integrated backwards into the manufacture of the products they supply to franchisees. The

Body Shop, a retailer of natural cosmetics, for example, originally supplied products to franchisees on a wholesale basis, but has recently begun to manufacture an increasing proportion of the products it supplies to franchisees (*The Body Shop International Plc Annual Report and Accounts 1991*: 4). Such problems typify the establishment of typologies which attempt to characterize different empirical tendencies. Rather than relying on them providing hard and fast distinctions, one should value the insights they provide in terms of the pattern of franchising's development, and the identification of its newer and more novel elements.

CONCLUSION

A good deal of time and effort has already been expended by others in the search for a definitive definition of franchising. It has not been the purpose here to add another variant to those already on offer. Instead, the definition provided by the European Franchise Federation is sufficient for our purposes. This is based on four elements: the franchisor's ownership of a name, an idea, a secret process, a product, or a specialized piece of equipment; the issuing of a contract permitting the franchisee to use it; regulations on the way it is used; and payments made by the franchisee for its use.

Even within this definition there are variations – some grant franchisees the right to sell franchisor-branded products, while others provide franchisees with a complete 'blueprint' of how to run a business as part of the franchisor's network. Two varieties of franchise can therefore be identified: product/trade mark franchisors and ones based on a business format. Dividing franchising in this way serves to reveal the contours of its growth. The empirical evidence suggests that most of the recent growth is concentrated among the business format variety – sales, outlets and employment generation are all rising. This pattern is common for much of the industrialized world. The growth of product/trade mark franchising is less clear-cut – sales are rising, but the number of outlets is shrinking and there is some evidence of franchisors taking up ownership positions in their franchisees. In these cases, questions of who really is in control is most visible. However, even where franchisors do not own any of the equity of their franchisees the notion of independence may be oversold. In the words of a franchisor, franchisee applicants are told that they can expect to 'work like hell, put in long hours, follow every rule – and make a lot of money' (quoted by Burck, 1970: 120). The assessment which follows aims to test this claim.

3 Explaining how and why franchising works

INTRODUCTION

During most of this century the tendency has been towards the vertical integration of more and more areas of production. This movement has taken place in both directions; backward via the takeover of suppliers and subcontractors, and forward through the acquisition of those selling the final product. Many branches of the social sciences have almost taken for granted the inevitability of this process, and have built their theories accordingly. Industrial sociology has mainly focused on the employment relationship in large firms (cf. Granovetter, 1984), economics and business history on providing a justification for the emergence of the large corporation (Williamson, 1981b; Chandler, 1977), and law has concerned itself with the protection of those working for the large corporation (Collins, 1990b). As outlined in Chapter 1, all have been challenged by the vertical disintegration of production (Murray, 1983), the growth of self-employment and small businesses (Leighton and Felstead, 1992), and the movement towards apparently more market-based business relationships (Child, 1987).

Nowhere has the challenge been greater than for orthodox neo-classical economics. Indeed, until relatively recently, orthodox neo-classical economists had little to say about the organization of the firm, whether towards vertical integration or disintegration: 'most economic theorists treated the organization as an entrepreneur in a field of entrepreneurs, and saw little need to inquire into the nature of the organization itself' (Perrow, 1986: 11); 'conventional theory ignores how and why work is organized within the firm and establishment in the way that it is' (Gordon, 1976: 3). Instead, their attention was focused on how the firm maximizes profit within the boundaries of its own production function. Matters of internal organization (hierarchical structure, internal control processes) were ignored.

However, two closely related theories in economics – agency theory and transaction cost analysis – have shifted attention to the organizational structure and shape of the firm. Agency theory focuses on the problem the 'principal' has in making sure that 'agents' act on its behalf (Alchian and Demsetz, 1972; Jensen and Meckling, 1976; Fama and Jensen, 1983a, 1983b), and transaction cost analysis focuses on the advantages of eliminating market contracts by incorporating suppliers and distributors into one's own firm – the replacement of markets by hierarchy (Williamson, 1975). Both were mainly developed in response to the power theorists' (Marglin, 1974; Edwards, 1979) claim that the role of management, and the growth of the firm of which it is a part, derive from power rather than efficiency considerations (cf. McPherson, 1983; Francis *et al.*, 1983). In short, power theorists argue that capitalists are able to coerce more labour from workers in the factory than those workers would willingly provide in home or cottage production (Drago, 1986).

Yet, the growth of franchising as an organizational form is the exact opposite of what agency cost and transaction cost theories aim to explain, and power theorists predict. Agency cost theory seeks to answer the question: what is the role of management, and what are the consequences of the sale of the firm, or part of it, *by owner-managers* to outsiders who then simply hold equity interest in the firm? Franchising turns this question on its head, since it involves the sale of a notional firm *to owner-managers* (franchisees) by those who hold a brand/idea/format (franchisors). Transaction cost theory faces a similar challenge. It seeks to answer the question: under what circumstances is the takeover of suppliers and subcontractors advantageous? Again, franchising reverses the roles, since suppliers (of a brand/idea/format) partly take over those they supply. Nevertheless, several authors – known collectively as the New Institutionalists – have claimed that the theoretical frameworks of agency cost and transaction cost theory are adaptable enough to explain the growth of franchising (Caves and Murphy II, 1976; Rubin, 1978; Higson and Orhnial, 1985; Brickley and Dark, 1987; Krueger, 1991; Brickley, Dark and Weisbach, 1991).

The purpose of this chapter is to evaluate the contribution these theorists make to an explanation of franchising. Three main criticisms are levelled at the approach. First, identifying the quest for greater efficiency as the main determinant of the organizational structure and shape of the firm is contentious. The New Institutionalists measure 'efficiency' solely in terms of a franchisor's profit maximization without considering whether the improvement is, wholly or partly, at someone else's expense. Secondly, the role of power as the driving force of franchising is ignored. Historical evidence suggests that employers (franchisors) *actively* select forms and legal structures of work organization which most effectively serve their own interests. Yet, the New Institutionalists depict employers (franchisors) as *passively* accepting the verdict of the 'invisible hand' (cf. Rubery, 1988). Thirdly, by simply comparing the costs of one form of organization with another, the New Institutionalists fail to identify how an increase in 'efficiency' might be at someone else's expense, and why one party's interests might be privileged over another's.

On the basis of these criticisms, and an examination of power or control models of the firm from which they stem, an alternative explanation of franchising is built. The chapter then discusses the results of a survey of 199 franchisees. It suggests that most are attracted to franchising by the business idea, format and brand name it provides. This is further reinforced (though not always) by franchisors' preference for novices or 'rookies' in relation to the specific operational area. The final section summarizes the argument, leaving subsequent chapters to trace the consequences this has for claims that franchising offers franchisees 'a chance to be their own boss'.

NEW INSTITUTIONALIST MODEL

Sensitive to the long-standing interest that the organization and structure of the firm elicits and mindful of the silence of neoclassical theory on these issues, the so-called 'transaction cost' approach first suggested by Commons (1934) and Coase (1937) has since been rediscovered (Williamson, 1975, 1979, 1980, 1981a, 1981b, 1986). This rediscovery was first prompted by the growing importance of giant corporations in many sectors of the economy until the mid to late 1970s, and fears that they would distort the allocative process. The theory provided reassurance; the shift from many organizations to a few larger ones was put down to efficiency enhancing, not debilitating, considerations. Not only was this conclusion at odds with orthodox neoclassical theory, but it also represented a denial of the power theorists' claim that the expanding boundaries of the firm were inspired by the desire to control when and how much workers exert themselves *without* enhancing efficiency (Marglin, 1974: 81, 84).

Transaction/agency cost theorists regard the buying of products and services on the spot market (markets), and the production of these products and services in-house (hierarchies) as alternative modes of economic organization. Moreover, markets and hierarchies are reckoned to stand at opposite ends of a continuum of alternative modes of economic organization. In between lies a range of 'mixed modes' with franchising often singled out as offering a fitting example of just such a mode (Williamson, 1981b: 1544). Not only do the New Institutionalists claim to provide an explanation for the growth of the giant corporation, but they claim to be able to account for its subsequent demise and the growth of the mixed modes which are now taking its place (cf. Chapter 1). Several authors have therefore sought to explain franchising using the tools provided by the New Institutionalists (Caves and Murphy II, 1976; Rubin, 1978; Higson and Orhnial, 1985; Brickley and Dark, 1987; Krueger, 1991; Brickley, Dark and Weisbach, 1991).

Components of the New Institutionalist model

The central tenet of New Institutionalist theory is the extension of the notion of cost minimizing behaviour used to explain the allocation of resources within production to an explanation of 'why co-ordination is the work of the price mechanism in one case and of the entrepreneur in another' (Coase, 1937: 389). A transaction is assumed to occur whenever a good or service is passed across a technologically separable interface. The resources consumed in the process either before, during or after the exchange has taken place are referred to as transaction costs. According to New Institutionalists the decision to use one organizational mode instead of another is determined by the relative transaction costs involved. For example, the decline of the putting-out system of production and the rise of the factory system as its replacement is explained in terms of relative transaction costs. Putting-out suffered from three basic transaction costs drawbacks: 'embezzlement and like deceits', work flow and quality control deficiencies, and weak incentive structures. Dispersed work stations made chronic theft and the substitution of lower quality supplies difficult to counter. Merchants were often reliant on the work pace and product quality supplied by a small number of outworkers. This made it difficult for merchants to respond quickly to fluctuations and changes in the composition of product demand. To cap it all, outworkers had little incentive to act differently – for the most part they could get away with it. The factory system economized on each of these transaction costs; leakages were prevented, work flow and product quality were controlled, and workers could be dismissed for 'malingering' (Williamson, 1980: 21–30).

The existence of transaction costs rests on the combination of certain human attributes and the presence of certain environmental factors. The behavioural factors are bounded rationality and opportunism, and the environmental factors are uncertainty/complexity and small numbers exchange. Bounded rationality replaces the more restrictive and stronger assumption of hyperrationality common to most neoclassical writing. It specifies a state in which economic agents have limited analytical and data processing powers compared with hyperrationality, which assumes that economic actors are capable of processing, without error, an infinite quantity of information. Such limited competences do not, however, imply irrationality. Instead, although boundedly rational agents experience limits in formulating and solving complex problems and in processing information, their behaviour is 'intendedly rational' (Williamson, 1981a: 553–554). Were it not for bounded rationality, all economic exchange could be organized through contracts written for each and every contingency (an idea first developed by Debreu, 1959). However, the costs of bounded rationality would only be reduced, not eliminated, in a more certain/uncomplicated world. In this way, the concept of bounded rationality and the condition of an uncertain and complex world reinforce one another.

The environmental condition of small numbers exchange and the behavioural assumption of opportunism are similarly inter-related. The former refers to the problems and costs associated with bilateral monopoly trading, while the latter points to the possibility that some (not necessarily all) individuals may exploit such situations for their own personal gain. Small numbers exchange raises the costs of opportunism; larger numbers may reduce, but not eliminate, these costs. The pursuit of self-interest is central to neoclassical economics; that individuals are prepared to cheat, lie, cut corners and so on, is not. Thus, whereas bounded rationality suggests that decision-making is less complex than the usual assumption of hyperrationality, opportunism suggests calculating behaviour more sophisticated than the usual assumption of self-interest. In both these respects, transaction cost theory records a break with the neoclassical tradition.

Accordingly, it is on the key concepts of bounded rationality and opportunism that an understanding of the internal organization of the firm must rest: 'But for the *simultaneous* existence of both bounded rationality and opportunism, all economic contracting problems are trivial and the study of economic institutions is unimportant' (Williamson 1981b: 1545, emphasis in original). The presence of bounded rationality precludes complete *ex ante* contracting, thereby rendering all contracts incomplete, while opportunism necessitates various institutional devices to deter malpractice during the life of the contract. Of itself, bounded rationality is not sufficient to prohibit autonomous market contracting, since if *all* individuals could be relied upon to adhere to the spirit and letter of the contract, contracts could be adapted *ex post* to circumstances as and when they arise. New Institutionalists, however, believe opportunism and bounded rationality to be pervasive. As a result, an assessment of efficient organization rests on the capabilities of alternative contracting modes to economize on bounded rationality while simultaneously safeguarding those transactions against the hazards of opportunism. Greater levels of uncertainty/complexity and a smaller number of actors with which to trade serve to raise transaction costs – only those organizational structures which are able to minimize these costs will be able to out-compete less efficient ones. With these concepts in mind, New Institutionalists claim to provide a theory robust enough to be applied to a wide variety of issues previously considered off-limits to conventional economics – the move towards franchising is one.

Applying the New Institutional Model to Franchising

Economists applying the New Institutionalist tradition to the growth of franchising begin their analyses by observing the sort of economic activities in which franchising is prevalent. The most striking characteristic of franchised operations is that advertising and promotion of the 'brand' are undertaken centrally while the franchised good or service is supplied locally. As Caves and Murphy II put it:

> The franchisor typically advertises and promotes his [*sic*] trademark or brand identity at least on a regional basis, if not a national or international one. On the other hand, the hamburger, the motel room, the car rental carrying the trademark must be supplied to decentralized customers at or near the site of consumption.
>
> (Caves and Murphy II, 1976: 574)

As a consequence 'divergent economies of scale' exist – activities associated with the promotion of a brand can best be done centrally, whereas delivery of the service/product can be done best locally (ibid).

However, New Institutionalists recognize that this alone cannot explain franchising since vertical integration can also reap the divergent economies of scale:

> There are evidently strong forces pulling for vertical integration of these activities. Apart from the problems of maintaining an intangible asset and sharing the proceeds ... the franchisor contemplates diverse local markets in which the good is produced and/or sold. Direct ownership no doubt offers a clear advantage for extracting the maximum rents from these assorted local markets ... Why does the franchisor not integrate forward into the decentralized activity?
>
> (Caves and Murphy II, 1976: 575)

According to the New Institutionalists the answer lies in the inferior transaction/agency costs attributes of company-owned and managed outlets which, either in theory or in practice, they have replaced (Brickley and Dark, 1987: 403–407).

Two inter-related transaction costs are singled out in explanation: 'shirking and excessive consumption of leisure' and weak corrective incentive structures (Rubin, 1978; Brickley and Dark, 1987: 404–405). Managers of company-owned outlets, although possibly having some form of incentive compensation, receive fixed salaries. Therefore, they do not bear the full cost of their shirking activities. Even if a manager's compensation is 100 per cent incentive *based*, it is not the same as a franchisee's whose income *is* the residual profit. The means to curb such malpractices via monitoring mechanisms are costly in sectors where decentralized production of the good (or more usually service) is required.

Once outlets/units become geographically concentrated, however, monitoring costs are likely to fall as new units are set up near to existing ones (e.g. one district manager can monitor more units in a day if the units are closer together).[1] It is for this reason that it is sometimes advantageous for franchise companies to 'buy-back' franchised units, once levels of outlet concentration rise. For example, McDonald's – the world's largest fast food franchisor – was engaged in an aggressive programme to 'buy-back' groups of its American franchisees in the late 1960s and early 1970s. The company reasoned that to operate company stores successfully, they had to be operating in a cluster. In the language of the New Institutionalists they sought to economize on uncertainty while simultaneously reducing the scope for opportunism – falling monitoring costs began to make monitoring a more attractive device for controlling agents. Since most major markets were already franchised, the only way to build a profit centre around company-operated stores was to 'buy-back' some of the largest and most successful McDonald's franchisees.

More systematic evidence, beyond the mere anecdotal, lends additional support to the notion that monitoring may eventually come back into favour as outlet concentration grows (Oxenfeldt and Kelly, 1968–69; Burr *et al*, 1975; Hunt, 1973). An examination of 'buy-back' announcements in the US over the period 1967–1983, for example, reveals that of the 60 recorded, 55 involved multiple units and 35 were confined to a specific region (Brickley, Dark and Weisbach, 1991: 34).

Furthermore, New Institutional economists argue that franchise legislation and judicial rulings in the 1970s have increased the costs of franchising relative to company-ownership in the US. By limiting the power of franchisors to terminate franchise agreements and to control inputs used by franchisees in the production process, the costs of controlling quality within a franchise system have increased, making franchising a less desirable organizational form (Brickley, Dark and Weisbach, 1989).

Nevertheless, while company-owned operations minimize transaction/agency costs in multi-store districts, the costs of monitoring the company-owned estate in smaller and more isolated single-store areas may make them uneconomic. Here, an alternative way of narrowing the scope for opportunism is to give managers the right to the residual profits of the outlet, thereby maintaining the company's presence in an otherwise loss-making area.[2] In addition, the franchisee's motivation and effort may exceed those of hired employees. For example, the franchisee often supplies much of the labour him/herself or through family workers who may be more willing to work longer hours, or as Rubin puts it 'work as hard as is efficient' (1978: 226). Negotiations with customers may be costly if entrusted to employees. For example, a commission-only car salesman will have the same incentive to sell the greatest number of cars as a franchised dealer. However, the former will be more willing to do this at the expense of higher trade-in allowances, thereby raising sales costs for car suppliers (Beale, Harris and Sharpe, 1989).

In essence, a franchisee is given the right to run the business and collect profits generated for a specified period of time; in return a franchise fee is often paid. For example, the franchise fee for a Kentucky Fried Chicken outlet is currently £10,000 whereas further down the scale a Dyno-Rod franchisee would be expected to pay £5,000. According to Rubin (1978: 227) this payment represents the present value of the expected profit stream from the outlet (adjusted downwards so as to yield normal returns on investment and risk). Indeed, the relationship between franchisee income and size of franchise fee paid has been shown to be statistically significant: generally, the higher the fee, the higher is a franchisee's income (Ozanne and Hunt, 1971: 39). In other words, franchisees work for profit, not a wage. As a result, the cost of 'shirking' by the franchisee and/or their employees will be wholly borne by the franchise holder.

In cases where the franchisee receives anything less than the entire profits of the outlet, there will be scope for residual 'shirking'. Yet, this is common practice. Many franchisors take a percentage of franchisee sales as royalties and/or mark-up the goods and services they supply to franchisees. To justify and explain the reduction in franchisee profits and the corresponding weakening of efficiency incentives, New Institutionalists turn towards the mechanisms through which the trade mark is protected (see Caves and Murphy II, 1976).

Franchisees' customers value the trade mark as providing information about the price and reassurance of a minimum level of quality of goods and services sold by establishments bearing a given trade mark. Those who buy from franchisees have this information precisely because the franchisor polices the system and maintains quality according to a predetermined set of standards. If any one franchisee allows quality to deteriorate, the establishment will still generate revenue since customers will continue to perceive it to be of an equivalent standard to those bearing the same trademark. Given opportunism, franchisees are prone to behaviour that might put the quality promised by the trade mark in jeopardy. In other words, by allowing the quality of the establishment to deteriorate, a franchisee benefits by the full amount of the savings from reduced quality maintenance, yet bears only part of the costs.[3]

New Institutionalists claim that the incentive to free ride helps to explain the pattern of company and franchise ownership within a single network. For example, consider a franchised fast food restaurant where the probability of serving repeat customers is low. The franchisee does not bear the full cost of poor quality service and thus has an incentive to free ride on the company's reputation by shirking on quality. On the other hand, company-owned units have less of an incentive to free ride because negative externalities reduce the value of the entire franchise chain. Following this reasoning, Klein and Saft (1985) argue that fast food franchisors have an incentive to locate company-owned restaurants in areas where customers have a low probability of repeat patronage, such as on motorways. However, Brickley and Dark (1987: 418) provide little empirical support for such a proposition. Even so, it is possible that the economic arguments advanced are correct, but that location on a good road network is not an appropriate proxy for the lack of repeat customers. For example, a unit's closeness to a highly developed road network can allow broader access to the unit by local residents. In this case, repeat customers may be more important for units dotted along major roads than for units in urban centres near to hotels and convention centres.

Tying the franchisor's income to the fortunes of the franchise network (either by levying a royalty on franchisee turnover, marking-up supplies or simply providing a distribution outlet for finished goods) ensures that franchisors bear some of the costs of the opportunistic behaviour of their franchisees. Franchisors therefore stand to lose out, both in terms of the falling value of the franchise chain and more immediately in falling revenue from the network, should franchisees 'skimp' on quality. The immediacy of falling revenue heightens franchisor incentives to maintain quality levels; franchisors therefore have a particular interest in closely monitoring the quality of the goods produced/services supplied. Just as the existence of management is said to stem from the lack of trust between workers and the temptation for them to shirk (Alchian and Demsetz, 1972), then *lateral* mistrust among franchisees is said to account in a similar way for the on-going role which the franchisor has via its revenue ties and quality control functions (Rubin, 1978: 229).

Criticisms of the New Institutional model of franchising

Central to the New Institutional approach to the organization of the firm is 'the archetypal Hobbesian problem of reconciling self-interested behavior on the part of individuals with collective or group interests' (Bowles, 1985: 16). Thus, it is argued that capitalist hierarchies arise because workers cannot trust one another. To substantiate the point, Alchian and Demsetz (1972) give us the following example. Although two people loading and unloading heavy cargo from trucks will find it easier and quicker to work together (as some loads may require two people), they will find it impossible to determine each individual's contribution to the total weight lifted. As a result, there is the risk that one or other, or even both, of them might shirk on their effort by lifting lighter or easier to carry loads. To prevent either of them doing so, the team's rational response is to hire a supervisor to monitor their work activities. The monitor is given the power to hire and fire, and appropriate part of the group's income in the form of a salary. In order to motivate the monitor to oversee the work of others, he/she receives any residual income or profit left after paying the wages of the cargo lifters and his/her salary. If the team decide to purchase equipment such as a fork-lift truck to increase their performance, then equity finance is required. In return, equity providers will expect to be given the right to monitor the monitor and appropriate the residual income or profit themselves, thereby assuring themselves that their investment is protected. A traditional capitalist hierarchy will be the result: shareholders, a board of directors, line management, workers and capital equipment (Perrow, 1986: 13).

The New Institutional approach to franchising is based mainly on the principles of this example. The main difference, though, is the recognition that the costs of curbing the opportunism of team members via monitoring mechanisms may outweigh the benefits of team production, especially in geographically dispersed networks. In these cases, outlet managers become franchisees: they invest their own money in setting up the outlet in accordance with franchisor instructions, run the outlet in line with their contractual obligations and take most, if not all, of the residual profits. In other words, franchised outlets become quasi-firms operating under the umbrella of the franchisor (Eccles, 1981).

In accounting for both the rise of the capitalist firm and the growth of franchising, New Institutionalists claim that the quest for greater efficiency is the driving force. It is assumed that the resulting organizational form is in the interests of all parties involved: the franchisor, the franchisees as well as all those who work for them – all parties find the avoidance of shirking desirable.

Three inter-related criticisms can be levelled at this claim. First, the use of the term 'efficiency' involves a sleight of hand as it implies neutrality – nobody can be against efficiency as it benefits all. Yet, there are two definitions of efficiency which may not always coincide: the pursuit of one is in everyone's interest, the pursuit of the other is more one-sided. The New Institutionalists use of the term 'efficiency' refers to the more one-sided version – economic efficiency. This measures performance in terms of costs and revenues from the point of view of the firm (franchisor), so that an increase in profits (i.e. revenues minus costs) signals a rise in economic efficiency and vice versa. A rise in technological efficiency, on the other hand, is usually taken to mean an increase in output produced from a given set of inputs, or the production of the same output from fewer inputs. This offers a broader societal view. Technological and economic definitions of efficiency need not coincide. For example, by securing greater effort from workers (or franchisees), employers (or franchisors) can increase output and revenues without increasing their costs. In other words, although a rise in profits might signal a rise in economic efficiency, this might be at the expense of lengthening the number of hours worked and/or the intensity of work. Thus, costs may have been minimized and profits increased, but the organization may not be technologically more efficient as both inputs (i.e. effort, intensity, length of working hours) and outputs may also have increased.

This criticism has much relevance for franchising. Comparing the performance of 22 fast food restaurants under franchise ownership with their performance as company-owned outlets, Shelton (1967) found that franchise ownership turned loss-making company-owned outlets into profit-making franchisee-owned ones (the replacement of waged managers with profit rewarded franchisees). The explanation given by company executives was that: 'franchisee-owners just watch the little things closer; *they utilize the cooks and waitresses better*; they reduce waste' (ibid: 1257, my emphasis). Indeed, the following statement by Fred Turner, the chairman of McDonald's, suggests that today's corporate leaders in the fast food industry recognize the importance that different incentives as between managers and franchisees have for the performance of franchised outlets:

> Running a McDonald's is a three-hundred-sixty-three-days-a-year business [restaurants are closed only on Thanksgiving and Christmas] and an owner-operator, with his [*sic*] personal interests and incentives can inherently do a better job than a chain manager.
>
> (Love, 1987: 292–293)

In other words, they have greater incentives to drive both themselves and their workforce harder. While unquestionably raising economic efficiency for the franchisor, this is insufficient evidence with which to argue that the development of franchising is driven by concerns of technological efficiency.

Secondly, historical evidence suggests that employers select forms and legal structures of work organization which most effectively serve their own interests (cf. Collins, 1990a). Marglin (1974) shows that early employers preferred to organize work within the factory rather than relying on putting-out, since it provided them with the means to coerce more work out of their workers. Initially, the same techniques of production were used in the factory as those used in the system of putting-out. However, when technological change did come it was developed and selected on the basis of the type of machinery that gave employers greatest control of their workforce. Similarly, Noble (1978) found that numerically-controlled machines were developed in the 1970s with the aim of 'deskilling' the labour process, thereby enhancing managerial authority (Braverman, 1974). Edwards (1979: chapter 7) suggests that machine-pacing in general was preferred for the same reason. What matters in determining the organization of production is not technological efficiency, but 'cost efficiency and predictability (enforceability) of output' (Landes, 1986: 594). Extending this argument to the growth of franchising suggests that its adoption served, above all else, the interests of the franchisor – dismissing any notion of team/partnership production.

Finally, the methodology adopted by the New Institutionalists is too narrow. The use of comparative statics places emphasis on the various states of a system and not on the processes through which one state emerges from another. Instead, organizational structures are simply isolated and compared with one another. Thus, for example, the transaction (agency) cost properties of different organizational modes (a network of company-owned and managed outlets vs a franchised network) are identified and compared, and then used to show how franchising is able to out-compete less 'efficient' modes. This is not the same as explaining how and why franchising emerged as and when it did; rather it simply provides a justification for the status quo on the grounds that only the fittest (i.e. 'efficient') organizations survive under competition.

However, organizations are shaped and moulded by employers (franchisors) to serve their own ends. A static comparative analysis of costs fails to appreciate: (a) how an increase in economic efficiency might be at someone else's expense; and (b) why one party's interests might be privileged over another's. The distinction between economic and technological efficiency, made above, advances our understanding of the former, while inequality of power explains the latter. Indeed, the competitive strategy of franchisors has been to create a distinctive image for themselves via advertising, branding and the acquisition of 'know-how' (cf. Paba, 1986). This has been used to secure greater control over their competitive environments and act as a lever over both aspiring and existing franchisees. Franchising therefore acts as a means to exercise command (or regain control) over dispersed, localized networks, thereby ensuring that franchisors' interest takes precedence over those of franchisees and/or their employees.

ALTERNATIVE MODEL

In view of the criticisms of the New Institutionalist explanation for the growth of franchising, an alternative approach is suggested. This is based on an extension of power or control models of the firm (notably Marglin, 1974; Braverman, 1974; Gordon, Edwards and Reich, 1982; Bowles, 1985). Unlike the New Institutionalists, however, power theorists have been notably slow to use their theories to understand some of the more recent real world events. This stems from their preoccupation with the exercise of power through coercive means alone. More subtle means of exercising power, such as franchising, are not considered. Nevertheless, franchisors do exercise power but in different ways: by enlisting the support of franchisees for the intensification of work rather than directly speeding-up the pace of work themselves, and then taking a part of the increased revenues generated. This section will therefore consider the power or control model of the firm and its pitfalls, and then apply an extended version of the model to the growth of franchising.

Components of the alternative model

Whereas in the New Institutional approach transaction costs drive organizational outcomes, for power theorists the distinction between work ('labour') and labour time ('labour power') and the associated conflicts over the use of labour time is given such a role. Power theorists argue that capitalists attempt to maximize profits by extracting maximum effort from workers for minimum pay. If capitalists bought labour as an input, then workers and capitalists could bargain and reach agreement over this sale, just as in any other market. However, labour input is not subject to a comprehensive transaction; the wage bargain is an inherently incomplete and ill-specified contract since capitalists do not have free and perfect information concerning worker effort and because of conflicting interests at the point of production. For a given level of technology, capitalists can only increase profits if work effort rises and/or wages fall. Therefore, capitalists and workers are caught in an inherent conflict over work effort, hours and wages.

This conflict can never be resolved under capitalism for two reasons. First, if capitalists generally do not know the precise level of effort forthcoming from workers, then some level of conflict (based on uncertainty) is inevitable. Secondly, even if knowledge concerning work effort were perfect, the system can never provide a sense of fairness since the difference between the value produced by labour and the value of labour power is the source of profit.

Given this conflict, the extraction of labour from labour power requires mechanisms of control through which capital is able to exercise dominance over labour. The original contributors to this approach – Marglin (1974) and Braverman (1974) – focused on the most visible expression of such domination: the factory system. Both writers principally sought to explain how and why the factory system rose as and when it did. For Braverman, the factory system was necessary to break worker control by separating conception from execution, thereby extending the division of labour and intensifying work. However, Marglin recognized that putting-out had already 'robbed' workers of any effective control over their output; the emergence of the factory system was seen as a further extension of this process and another way of increasing labour's input. In other words, capitalists were able to coerce more labour from workers in the factory than was previously possible when labour was undertaken in the home or cottage.

Despite their differences both writers were in agreement: factory production would become the 'norm', while production carried out outside the factory would become anachronistic relics of the past. While the New Institutionalists (e.g. Williamson, 1980) have made similar claims on the grounds of minimizing transaction costs, they have subsequently been able to apply their framework to the re-emergence of previously marginal economic forms such as franchising. The power approach has, however, been more self-limiting.

While pointing to class conflict as the key aspect of the trajectory of capitalist societies, power theorists fail to comprehend the complexities and contradictions of this struggle. They often have a naive view of employers' behaviour and a similarly undeveloped view of the character and consequences of workers' resistance (see Nolan and Edwards, 1984, for further criticisms). An attempt to formalize the power model of the firm is provided by Bowles (1985). In order to highlight the weaknesses of the approach this particular model will be considered in more detail.

Bowles begins by explicitly placing the conflict between employer and worker over the intensity of effort at the centre of his analysis. He then assumes that employers are able to compel workers to act in ways that they themselves would not choose, but that the power to do so is costly to exercise. This power is based on the ability to impose costs on the workforce for non-compliance. The principle threat is that of job loss. The extent of the threat is related to the degree to which the firm's wage level exceeds that which a worker might receive if not in the firm's employment. Increasing this threat represents a cost for the employer since to do so entails the payment of higher wages. A further cost incurred by the employer is surveillance. Implicitly, Bowles assumes that workers have an incentive to minimize their effort. The amount of effort expended is a function of the amount of supervision and the loss of income resulting from possible job loss. Assuming decreasing returns to supervision, a unique profit maximizing point is determined. Bowles demonstrates that, given a pool of unemployed labour, the profit maximizing point will always invoke some surveillance and positive opportunity costs incurred while unemployed (Marginson, 1986b).

Four major criticisms can be made of the Bowles' model. First, Bowles assumes that employer control over labour is attained by one means alone – coercion. However, several writers have stressed the importance of consent as well as coercion in achieving control over labour (for a review see P. K. Edwards, 1990). Labour enters the employment relationship in a contradictory manner. It is simultaneously flexible in the tasks to which it can be applied, and yet resistant to the intensification of effort and direction of tasks:

Unless supervision is close and uninterrupted, the conversion of labour power into productive labour must involve in part the labourer's 'voluntary' initiative, the acceptance of an obligation to perform a 'fair day's work'.

(Hyman, 1987: 40)

Total elimination of workers' discretion is impossible. Hence 'coercion must be supplemented by the organization of consent' (Burawoy, 1979: 27) to a lesser or greater extent. At one extreme, is the minimization of workers' discretion – reducing workers' responsibility by close supervision, and setting out in advance and in great detail the specific tasks each worker is to perform. This has been termed 'direct control' (Friedman, 1986). At the other extreme, is the notion of 'responsible autonomy'. Under this regime, workers are given responsibility to organize their own work tasks with only light supervision, thereby enlisting their creative potential.

Other strategies seek to convince workers that management's aims match theirs. Quality Circles, for example, are designed to foster worker identification with the quality of their own work, and so increase worker involvement with the firm (Hill, 1991). The same goes for forms of industrial democracy (Cressey and MacInnes, 1980; Ramsay, 1985), and the more recent growth of workers' financial participation in their firms through share ownership schemes and profit-related pay (Duncan, 1988; Ramsay et al., 1990). Franchising, too, aims to enlist the support of certain categories of worker for labour intensification rather than relying on the more unsubtle method of coercion.

Secondly, Bowles assumes that workers are at all times averse to work. However, ethnographic research on shopfloor workers points to the strong desire workers have to demonstrate their technical competences, thereby earning self-respect and the recognition of their peers as well as the self-satisfaction of meeting targets (Roy, 1953; Lupton, 1963). Hard work may also be recognized by management in the form of promotion. A profit-incentive and the right to hire and fire their own labour gives franchisees another incentive to drive themselves and their workforce harder.

Thirdly, Bowles concentrates on the control employers can exercise through the employment contract. As soon as the employment contract is replaced by a commercial one, the implication is that workers become petty capitalists. However, the transition is not clear-cut. Although a firm which franchises or subcontracts part of its operations no longer buys their labour time, it can still retain control over key strategic decisions and take some of what is produced as a result.

Finally, Bowles mirrors the methodology of the New Institutionalists by introducing an additional equation to the cost-minimization subject to problematic constraints. The complexity of social interaction and control cannot be captured by a single equation added to the standard neoclassical production function. To do so denies the need to harness the creativity as well as the control of labour, and the dynamics of the process.

Applying the alternative model to franchising

The criticisms of the power or control theories of the firm boil down to a general criticism of the narrowness of both how labour is conceived and controlled. Such a narrow outlook points to a single uniform trajectory for organizational change – the growth of vertically integrated companies with more and more workers on the payroll, and control exercised through coercion alone. The underlying premise of such a prediction is if you want to control something, you own it 'lock-stock-and-barrel'.

The growth of franchising, as outlined in Chapter 2, appears to be at odds with this prediction. Franchisees are legally independent of their franchisor, trading as sole proprietors, partnerships or limited liability companies. Relations with their franchisor are not governed by an employment contract but by a commercial one. Franchisees work for a profit instead of a wage, thereby raising the incentives they have to drive themselves and their workers hard without the need to resort to coercion. However, appearances can be deceptive. But it is difficult to go beyond superficial inferences without recognizing both labour's co-operative and recalcitrant nature, along with the various managerial strategies designed to heighten co-operation and/or minimize resistance. Taking on board such a recognition widens the explanatory value of the power or control theory of the firm, on which an alternative explanation of franchising can then be based.

Central to the New Institutionalist theory is the notion of mutual interest between employers and workers, franchisors and franchisees. This is summed up in Samuelson's famous axiom that it does not matter 'whether capital hires labour or the other way around' (Samuelson, 1957: 894). However, power theorists argue that the market equality between buyer and seller disappears once labour power is set to work. Employers own the machinery, raw materials, buildings and organizational 'know-how'; all that workers own is their ability to work. Concentration of the ownership of the means of production means that the many are obliged to sell their labour power to the few. Those who hire workers' ability to work organize the work process as they see fit. What workers actually produce has value and that which exceeds the value of wages, raw materials, and wear-and-tear is taken by employers as profit.

However, the appearance of franchisees investing large sums of money in the purchase of the *physical* means of production (raw materials, plant, equipment) and the hiring of their own workforce should not be taken automatically as evidence of their unambiguously capitalist credentials. To be sure, production cannot be set into motion without the purchase of the physical means of production and labour power to be put to work; but the franchisor's organizing ability, the use of a well-known trade mark, and access to a depth of experience and 'know-how' is also crucial to the success of the franchisee's business. It is through the provision of the so-called *mental* means of production that franchisors have a 'hold' on their franchisees' businesses and the grounds on which they are able to take a part of the value produced (either as a percentage of sales or a mark-up on tied sales). The fact that franchisors sign up franchisees is therefore crucial to the imbalance of power between the two parties and the contradictory position franchisees find themselves in – being the employer of others, while simultaneously being in some sense employed themselves.

The comparison of the nature of today's franchising with 'inside contracting', an arrangement prevalent in many of the staple industries (i.e. coal, cotton, and iron and steel) throughout much of the nineteenth century, provides some interesting insights. Here, too, the possession of knowledge provided a means of control. In this case, though, skilled workers rather than employers were able to use their collective knowledge of production (i.e. the tricks of the trade) to exert control. It was, for example, the skilled iron workers and cotton minders who organized, allocated tasks and determined the intensity of production, not employers (Elbaum and Wilkinson, 1979; Lazonick, 1979, 1981). These workers agreed piece-rates with their employers, and out of this price they employed their own labourers to act as underhands or assistants on time contracts. Consequently, skilled workers reaped the full benefits of driving their underhands harder, and in this respect they exercised the prerogative of employers. Since they were co-employers of their mates and unskilled helpers, Hobsbawm has coined this arrangement 'co-exploitation' (1964: 297–300).

In the case of franchising 'the tables are turned': franchisors are possessors of a brand/idea/format (i.e. 'know-how'), and although franchisees invest their own money in the business, the business is shaped according to the franchisor's accumulated experience. Without the franchisor's 'know-how' many of today's franchisees would simply not have been able to set up in business (see following section). The implication might be drawn that the franchisor's knowledge and 'know-how' is scarce, and thus a factor that a competitive market will properly reward (on the issue of knowledge and power see Marglin, 1984; Berg, 1984). Under conditions of perfect competition goods and services will command a price as long as they are scarce and possess the property of 'private' goods: that is, more for one person will mean less for another. However, the peculiar nature of the services provided by franchisors violates the latter condition. More specifically, the supply of the business format/idea/use of brand, and the knowledge and 'know-how' associated with it, to more than one franchisee does not diminish the supply available to others. As a result, each franchisor has an incentive to share his/her 'know-how' with an expanded circle of clients without reducing either the supply to existing recipients or the reward per client. Other franchisors offering competing franchise opportunities can be expected to retaliate in two ways: one is to cut the prices of their services to their existing franchisees; the other is to undercut the price of services provided by competitor franchisors, thereby invading the markets of others. The competitive outcome will be zero pricing, hence no 'reward' or role for franchisors.

In fact, many of the early business format franchisors, such as McDonald's, were often so generous in providing visitors to their stores with information about their production procedures, their equipment and their suppliers, that no one really needed a franchise to learn the McDonald's secret. However, the returns for franchisors rest heavily upon strategies that make it difficult, if not impossible, for a franchisee to operate without their assistance. By restricting the transference of relevant 'know-how' and accumulated business experience to its franchisees alone, a franchisor is able to engender a dependent relationship from which a return is then drawn. Alternatively, the pulling power of the brand may become so great that a truly independent existence outside the franchise may be too costly for incumbent franchisees to contemplate (however, this is likely to apply to only a handful of franchise systems, such as Coca-Cola; see Chapter 6).

The philosophy underlying the nineteenth century ideal of 'sanctity of contract' (a basic principle greatly relied upon by franchisors) is that both parties to the contract are approximately equal and enter into it without coercion. However, the franchisee does not bargain with the franchisor as an equal. Indeed, franchisors' unwillingness to negotiate elements of the agreement emphasizes franchisees' relative powerlessness right from the beginning of the relationship. Not only are franchisees economically inferior to franchisors, but without access to the franchisor's accumulated knowledge, experience and trade mark entry into business would, for many aspiring franchisees, remain a pipe-dream (see following section). For existing franchisees the use of a well-known national (or even international) trade mark as well as contractual ties makes business survival outside the network difficult, if not impossible (see Chapter 4). The most obvious consequence of this situation is to make the franchisee dependent on their franchisor. Pfeffer (1981) argues that this is a key source of power in an organizational setting:

> The power to control or influence the other resides in control over the things he [*sic*] values, which may range all the way from oil resources to ego support. In short, power resides implicitly in the other's dependence.
>
> (Emerson, quoted in Pfeffer, 1981: 99)

> Power is having something that somebody else wants.
>
> (Farney, quoted in Pfeffer, 1981: 100)

Given the existence of dependency, two conditions determine whether or not such dependency finds expression in the emergence of conflict. The first condition is the existence of goals which are inconsistent or at odds with one another – goal heterogeneity. The second condition is resource scarcity. The fact that each party pursues different goals will not, by itself, be sufficient to produce conflict – enough resources to satisfy everyone's goals and desires will prevent such an outbreak. However, as soon as demands exceed available resources, choices have to be made. Under conditions of resource scarcity, choices are likely to create winners and losers, generating conflict and uncertainty.

In the case of franchising, franchisors and franchisees pursue different goals. As long as franchisors receive a major part of their revenue from royalties on gross sales and/or the sale of supplies, franchisors will judge franchisees according to their sales volume. Franchisees, on the other hand, will be more concerned to increase their own profits. These inconsistent goals are evident at several points in all franchise contracts (see Chapter 4 for more detail).

A reduction in a franchisee's territory or even termination of the franchise may be held as an option by franchisors should sales fall below a certain level. Franchisors may have the option to open additional units near to existing ones if there is sufficient market potential or if the population served grows to a particular level. Even though the typical practice is to offer the opportunity to the incumbent franchise, the prospect of an additional unit being added highlights the clash of objectives – the sales maximization drive of the franchisor and the profit objective of the franchisee. A single unit with a turnover of £100,000 per annum is likely to generate more profits than two units with a combined turnover of £150,000 per annum. Higher sales, however, will raise franchisor revenue regardless of franchisee profitability.

Committing franchisees to a price ceiling on the products/services they sell is similarly revealing. Low prices will mean high physical volume, and if price elasticity of demand for the product is greater than one, this will result in high sales volume. This will benefit the franchisor since its income rises in line with franchisees' sales volume (or physical volume, where franchisor's income is derived from the sale of key supplies to franchisees). Either way, the franchisee is concerned to maximize profit not sales; as a consequence, higher prices and larger gross margins may be more desirable to the franchisee, but not for the franchisor as physical (and may be sales) volume will be reduced.

Underlying all franchise relationships is the pursuit by franchisors and franchisees of different goals. However, this alone is not sufficient for the conflict of interest to be visible to the parties involved – the self-interest of franchisor and franchisee *may* coincide. For example, both franchisee and franchisor have a common interest in intensifying the labour of those who work for the franchisee, but for different reasons. Intensifying the labour of those whom franchisees employ may reduce costs and hence raise their profits. To the extent that the benefits of labour intensification are not taken wholly in the form of reduced costs, more customers will be served or catered for, and hence sales will rise. Similarly, conflicting goals are unlikely to be evident early on in a franchisee's business career. At this stage, loss leaders and a number of loss-making years are expected as the business builds up a local reputation. Sales are therefore given priority by both franchisor and franchisee.

In the longer term, however, a conflict of interest may arise. For example, new owners of a franchise may demand a higher return from their investment than the network's previous owners (as detailed in Chapter 5). Alternatively, franchisees may no longer have the appetite for growth, they may be too small and their customers may be unwilling to deal with a fragmented network (as detailed in Chapter 6). Either way, franchising will not always be able to meet everyone's desires (i.e. a situation of resource scarcity will exist), and the inherent conflict of interest between franchisor and franchisee will become visible. The possible outcomes of this conflict are considered in Chapters 5 and 6.

REINFORCING DEPENDENCY

Franchising has few natural barriers to entry for potential franchisors. To enter franchising, huge capital outlays for manufacturing facilities are not required; a ready-made national dealer network does not have to be in place; massive national advertising campaigns are not necessary; the ownership of, or access to, unique sources of supply is not essential; and the ownership of unique patent rights is not required. Ample capital, national advertising, a well-known trade mark and patented processes are all desirable, but not necessary, for a potential franchisor to enter the industry. All it takes to enter franchising is the desire to do so, and the ability to convince at least one other person (a potential franchisee) that he/she should buy the right to operate a business under the franchisor's trade mark and to abide by certain contractual conditions (see Chapter 4).

As a result, 42 per cent of franchise systems listed in a recent directory of UK franchise opportunities are reported to have fewer than 11 franchised units, and only 8 per cent more than 100 (see Table 3.1). Therefore, most franchisors are likely to lack impressive head office facilities, have only a few existing franchise outlets to show potential franchisees, have uncertain sales levels and be relatively unknown. An examination of the channels by which franchisees made their initial approach to the franchisor bears this out. Thirty-one per cent contacted the franchisor after being encouraged or recommended to do so by friends or relations who were already franchisees in the network:

Table 3.1 Distribution of franchise systems by number of franchised units in the United Kingdom

Number of units	Number of systems[1]	%
0–10	96	42
11–25	49	22
26–50	31	14
51–100	32	14
101–150	8	4
151–200	3	1
201–250	2	1
251+	5	2
Total	226	100

Note
1. Not all of those franchise systems listed gave details of the number of franchised units in their network.
Source: Franchise World Directory 1992 (Franchise World Publications: London, 1991).

I was introduced by a friend who was already operating as a CleanCo franchisee.

A colleague from my previous job joined before me and recommended me to apply.

(written on questionnaires)

I knew the franchisor as a friend.

(field notes)

This is not unusual. Many early McDonald's franchisees in the US, for example, were personal friends of the chain's founder, Ray Kroc.

However, despite the relatively small size of franchise networks, the evidence suggests that franchisors can still be selective in whom they recruit; 14 per cent of those who enquire about taking up a franchise are interviewed, while only 4 per cent of those who enquire are actually appointed (BFA/NatWest, 1987: 36). Yet, as a franchise chain expands the direct promotional efforts of the franchisor, such as national advertising and trade shows, become more prominent in franchisee recruitment (see Table 3.2). The circle of potential franchisees widens, and with it the franchisor becomes more selective still. Thus, 'the greater the over supply of labour [would-be franchisees], the more selective employers [franchisors] can be, and the more important

Table 3.2 Channel of initial approach to franchisor by franchisee

Channel of approach	Frequency	%
Responded to an advert in a newspaper	58	29.3
Responded to an advert in a magazine devoted to franchising	24	12.1
Responded to an advert in a regular magazine	22	11.1
Attended a 'fair' where several franchisors were offering their franchises	13	6.6
Contacted the franchisor directly after being a customer of one of their establishments	9	4.5
Contacted the franchisor after talking to friend/ relations who were franchisees	62	31.3
n=198		

Source: author's postal survey of 199 franchisees.

recruitment becomes as a means of control' (Maguire, 1986: 73). As franchise systems mature, this means of control is enhanced.

Faced with lengthening waiting lists some franchisors have developed more sophisticated and thorough 'vetting' procedures. In the US, for example, McDonald's has an established programme for selecting future franchisees. The programme combines classroom, self-directed and on-the-job training. Each applicant is required to spend a substantial amount of time (usually more than 1,000 hours) in a McDonald's restaurant learning the system of operation and day-to-day management techniques. As this forms part of the training programme, franchise candidates receive no pay. The purpose of the programme is to enable the franchise candidate and McDonald's to evaluate one another in preparation for a business relationship that is intended to last 20 years. McDonald's reserves the right to terminate the programme of any potential franchisee at any time; a franchisee's participation in the training programme does not commit McDonald's to award a franchise. On occasion, the training programme can be quite lengthy as potential franchisees are asked to work part-time, keeping their full-time job in case either party to the agreement changes their mind.[4] About one in four potential franchisees who begin the training programme drop-out.

So what is the attraction of becoming a franchisee? To answer this question, we first need to consider a prior question: why do franchisees want to become self-employed? In line with a number of published surveys (Hakim, 1989: 288–290; Blackburn and Curran, 1989; *Financial Times*, 14 January 1992), the attractions of becoming self-employed can be grouped into two broad categories: 'pull'; and 'push' factors. The 'pull' factors include the benefits of being your own boss, the chance to earn more money, the notion of working for a profit instead of a wage and the prospect of a challenge. The 'push' factors refer to the lack of alternative employment opportunities and the economic reality of being made redundant. Over half of those franchisees surveyed cited independence as the primary motivator. The prospect of large financial rewards was almost negligible at 4 per cent, although being rewarded by profits instead of a wage appealed to almost one in five (see Table 3.3). The low appeal of financial benefits tallies with the finding that about two-thirds of franchisees earned about the same or less than they had prior to taking up their franchise. From this evidence, one should be highly cautious of claims that franchising is a licence to print money as is sometimes implied by less scrupulous franchisors (see Table 3.4). Nevertheless, the resale value of franchises can be quite high.

When asked about their reasons for choosing to become a franchisee instead of setting up entirely alone, almost half said they lacked a

Table 3.3 Attractions of becoming self-employed

Attractions	Frequency	%
Own boss/independent	104	52.3
Earn lots of money	8	4.0
Couldn't find employment	6	3.0
Profit for self	39	19.6
Challenge	20	10.1
Redundancy	14	7.0
Other	8	4.0
	n=199	

Source: author's postal survey of 199 franchisees.

Table 3.4 Income as a franchisee compared with income immediately prior to franchise take-up

Comparison	Frequency	%
More	70	35.9
Less	91	46.7
About the same	34	17.4
	n=195	

Source: author's postal survey of 199 franchisees.

business idea on which to base a business. This was confirmed in several face-to-face interviews:

> All the jobs I had done were in administration. I had no practical skills – no hands-on skills – I could put to use in a business of my own.

> I didn't have any ready-made business ideas I could put to good use when I came back from Saudi.

> I'd wanted to work for myself for years . . . but I'd only been in management positions, I'd no practical experience on which to set something up myself.

> (field notes)

Just over one in four admitted that they joined a franchise network for the security it was reckoned to provide:

> In theory at least, the franchisor has done all the leg work, made mistakes, providing an easier entry into business.

> I went into franchising simply because I didn't have the bottle to do it on my own.

> (field notes)

A further 16 per cent wanted to be associated with a large company in order to benefit from the national/regional identity, and the help and support it provided (see Table 3.5):

> I liked the idea of always being under the paternal protection of a large company.

(field notes)

Table 3.5 Attractions of becoming a franchisee

Attractions	Frequency	%
Lacked business idea to put into practice	91	45.7
Wanted security against failure	53	26.6
Wanted to be associated with a company	32	16.1
Wanted to make money quickly	7	3.5
Other	16	8.0
	n=199	

Source: author's postal survey of 199 franchisees.

Those who opt to become franchisees do so on the basis of a set of preceived advantages: being provided with a ready-made business idea, a tried and tested format with which to operate, and the help and support of a large company readily at hand. Wanting to use the business idea, format and brand of the franchisor puts the franchisee in a state of dependency in that they want something that somebody else has (as discussed above). Inevitably, franchisees must trade-off their desire to 'be their own boss' against the opportunity of operating a business under someone else's trade mark according to a set of contractual rules and regulations. As one franchisor put it:

> I often ask franchise prospects why they want to become self-employed. Most reply in the same vein – they say they want to be their own boss . . . I have to then explain that in franchising you can't do what you like, you must follow a proven way of doing something and abide by the contract.

(field notes)

Conversely, those with sufficient knowledge of a particular business sector, such as redundant printers or those with catering experience, are more likely to set up independently, basing the core of their operations on the skills already learnt. A survey comparing the backgrounds of 105 franchisees with 102 independent owner-operators in the US supports this hypothesis: 11 per cent of franchisees had prior experience of the industry in which they worked compared with 64 per cent of independent owner-operators (Knight, 1984: 56).

While the evidence suggests that newcomers to a particular industry or sector are more likely to be attracted to franchising as a route into business, franchisees are not self-selected but are recruited by franchisors from a pool of prospects. The likes and dislikes of franchisors are therefore crucial determinants of the socio-economic profile of those who are awarded franchises (see Stanworth, 1988; Stanworth *et al.*, 1989). For example, franchisors often express a preference for franchisees who have no prior experience in the operational area of the franchise.[5] The reasoning behind this negative preference is that novices are reckoned to be more receptive to training and direction, and bring 'no bad habits' or preconceptions with them. The long-standing policy of Wimpy, one of Britain's largest fast food franchisors, could not be clearer:

> Full training is provided and potential franchisees are not required to have catering experience. In fact, the company *prefers* to start with people *new* to the business who do not have pre-conceived ideas about running a catering operation.
>
> (*Franchise World*, July/October 1978: 14; my emphasis)

Whereas:

> those with prior restaurant experience are likely to think they know so much about the business that they try to install practices other than those specified by the franchisor.
>
> (Shelton, 1967: 1254)

Similarly, other socio-economic characteristics of franchisees are a product of who is attracted to franchising and the preferences of franchisors. Most franchisees (83 per cent of our sample) were married, and almost two-thirds had children living at home. A further two-thirds (see Table 3.6) invested some or all of their savings in the franchise – commonly in the form of providing working capital for the business in the start-up phase of development. Around four out of five franchisees raised some of the finance required to buy a franchise by moving houses, selling their homes and moving to rented accommodation (in the case of retail-based franchises in flats above the business), taking out a mortgage on their homes or using their house as collateral for a loan (see Table 3.7). Some franchisors admit that they prefer:

> to get a man [franchisee] into debt. That way we're sure that he'll be hungry for business. If he feels comfortable he might have less of a get-up-and-go mentality.
>
> (field notes)

Even if the business is fully incorporated, lenders often insist that

Table 3.6 Proportion of original set-up costs drawn from savings

Proportion of funding from savings	Frequency	%
None	65	33.0
1-20%	27	13.7
21-40%	29	14.7
41-60%	26	13.2
61-80%	4	2.0
81-100%	46	23.4
	n=197	

Source: author's postal survey of 199 franchisees.

Table 3.7 Effect of raising franchise finance on home ownership

Effect on home ownership	Frequency	%
Sell residence and buy a cheaper one	2	14.9
Sell residence and live in rented accommodation	12	9.0
Take out mortgage or second mortgage on residence	27	20.1
Use residence as collateral for a loan	59	44.0
Other	6	4.5
None	28	20.9
	n=134	

Source: author's postal survey of 199 franchisees.

directors sign personal guarantees as a condition of the loan. As a result, many franchisees' homes are at risk should their businesses turn sour.[6] Clearly, this heightens the incentives franchisees have to work themselves and their workforce (if they employ others) hard.

Almost half of the franchisee respondents claimed to work over 50 hours in a normal week with spouses (invariably wives) working an average 23.4 hours (see Table 3.8). Data derived from macro-level surveys (Curran and Burrows, 1988: 87–91; Creigh *et. al*, 1986: 191) reveal a similar picture of long working hours for small business owners in the UK: 'in this sense the idea of the "workaholic" small business owner has some foundation' (Curran and Burrows, 1988: 91). With a lot at stake – the costs of failure being high – it is not therefore surprising that working hours are lengthy.

The socio-economic profile of franchisees can also cast some light on

Table 3.8 Hours worked by franchisee

Number of hours worked	Frequency	%
11–20	7	3.6
21–30	16	8.3
31–40	26	13.5
41–50	53	27.5
51–60	46	23.8
61–70	28	14.5
71–80	11	5.7
over 80 hours	6	3.1

n=193
Arithmetic average = 49.8 hours per week

Source: author's postal survey of 199 franchisees.

the frequent claim that franchising has created both new businesses and jobs (Dutfield, 1988).[7] One cannot simply take the absolute number of franchise systems, the number of franchisees or the number of franchise-related jobs to be an accurate indicator of franchising's economic contribution. To make a more accurate assessment, a more complicated question needs to be answered: what would franchisees do in the absence of franchise opportunities? When this question was directly posed to our sample of franchisees 38 per cent believed that they would not be in business at all (see Table 3.9). However, just over two-thirds (68 per cent) of franchisees had had no prior experience of self-employment before taking up their franchise. So, although only 38 per cent believed that they would not be in business without franchising, no doubt many more would have had the will but not the wherewithal to set themselves up in business. This suggests that franchising encouraged

Table 3.9 Likely economic activity of franchisee in the absence of franchising

Likely economic activity	Frequency	%
Self-employed in the same industry (without a franchise)	41	20.9
Self-employed in a different industry (without a franchise)	80	40.8
Not self-employed	75	38.3

n=196

Source: author's postal survey of 199 franchisees.

between 38 and 68 per cent of franchisees into business who might not otherwise have considered this an option.[8] Even these figures are likely to be overestimates, since an element of substitution may be at work; franchised businesses may replace, as well as add to, the existing stock of businesses where franchisees out-compete other traders.

CONCLUSION

Despite the increased economic significance of franchising during recent years, the literature from which to draw is both patchy and poorly developed (especially in the UK). This chapter has reviewed the economic theories which might help to explain how and why a franchise structure is adopted. All theories, in very different ways, fail to meet the task, and so an alternative model has been built.

Traditionally, neoclassical economic theory has ignored the organization of the firm altogether, choosing instead a conception of production drawn purely from the engineering domain (Nolan, 1983; Green, 1988). For economists schooled in this tradition, production is represented as a set of input–output relations selected from an array of feasible technologies by a process of cost minimization with respect to market-determined prices. Production is therefore conceived of as a purely technical process. The fact that production is a social process, organized within a specific institutional and social framework, is ignored. Instead, the distinction between human and non-human factors of production is not drawn, and the organization of work is considered unproblematic. The transformation of inputs into outputs via the production function ensures the maximization of outputs from any feasible combination of inputs, thereby making the firm technologically efficient, regardless of its organizational form.

Furthermore, given the behavioural assumption of profit maximization, firms will, in the face of a set of prevailing relative prices, adopt the least cost combination of inputs. Assuming divisibility and interchangeability of inputs, the firm will, for example, respond to an increase in the relative price of labour by substituting capital for labour in the production process, and vice versa. As a result, the firm acts in ways which simultaneously make it economically *and* technologically efficient.

The traditional neoclassical theory of the firm therefore reduces to a problem of constrained optimization. Firms pursue the objective of profit maximization within the constraints set by an exogenously determined level of technology and a set of relative prices. The model offers no analysis of the internal organization of the firm, and as such is silent on the structures one might seek to explain. Implicitly, the nature of the firm – such as what will be produced (or supplied) under franchise and what will be produced (or supplied) under company ownership – is not considered an issue. Instead, the firm is reduced to little more than a production function to which a profit maximization objective is assigned – a 'black box' for short. As such, it is incapable of understanding why and how franchise structures develop.

By dropping the assumption that all inputs, including labour, can magically and unproblematically be converted into known outputs, the New Institutionalists claim to have a set of tools capable of explaining how and why franchise structures are adopted. This approach rests on two behavioural assumptions. The first is that economic actors make errors of judgement (bounded rationality), and the second is that they are prepared to cheat, lie or cut corners for their own selfish ends (opportunism). All transactions, whether the purchase of a product or labour time, incur costs on account of these behavioural traits. In other words, it may be difficult to judge the quality of the product/labour time accurately at the point of sale, and sellers or buyers may make false claims to clinch a deal. These costs will be particularly high in situations of great uncertainty and/or circumstances in which there are only a few actors with whom to trade. According to the New Institutionalists, only those organizational forms which minimize transaction costs will triumph.

To explain why franchising is prevalent in situations where a brand name is centrally promoted, yet delivery of the product/service takes place locally, the New Institutionalists point to franchising's superiority in minimizing transaction costs. A widely dispersed network will encounter high monitoring costs which may make company ownership uneconomic. Switching to a situation where franchisees work for a profit instead of a wage will ensure that opportunistic behaviour at the outlet will be wholly borne by the franchisee, thereby simultaneously minimizing the costs of bounded rationality and opportunism. Financial incentives are also placed on the franchisor to ensure that quality standards associated with the trade mark are maintained. Tying franchisors' income to the fortunes of the franchise network (either by levying a royalty on franchisee turnover, marking-up supplies or simply providing a distribution outlet for finished goods) ensures that franchisors bear some of the costs of the opportunistic behaviour of their franchisees. Franchisors therefore stand to lose out, both in terms of the falling value of the franchise chain and more immediately in falling revenue from the network, should franchisees 'skimp' on quality.

This chapter has made several criticisms of the New Institutionalist approach. These will be reviewed in brief. First, while the New Institutionalists recognize that the transformation of inputs into outputs is not unproblematic – depending, in large measure, on how hard workers work – they fail to fully follow through the consequences of their admission. For example, by securing greater effort from workers, employers can increase output and revenues without increasing the costs of labour. While costs are minimized and profits increased, the overall efficiency implications are less clear-cut as both outputs *and* inputs have increased. In other words, although franchising might be the most economically efficient means of organizing a business from the franchisor's point of view, any gains might be made wholly or partly at someone else's expense. Secondly, without a concept of power, New Institutional economics fails to appreciate why one concept of 'efficiency' takes precedence over another. Finally, comparing the various costs associated with different organizational structures provides a poor basis on which to distinguish concepts of efficiency from one another, and provides little scope to consider why one rather than the other is considered the more important organizational determinant.

With the apparent absence of any ready-made alternative explanation, many authors have tended to uncritically adopt a New Institutionalist framework (e.g. Kneppers-Heynert, 1989, 1992). However, the above criticisms suggest that an alternative explanation is desperately needed. By extending the power or control theory of the firm this chapter has offered such an alternative. While the central characteristic of the approach is the emphasis placed upon the social relations of production as the crucial determinant of work organization and business strategies, the contradictions of the capital–labour relation and hence the many and varied strategies that capital might pursue are also acknowledged. In other words, it recognizes that capital has a double-sided relationship with labour, in that it tries to reduce labour to the status of a commodity in the sphere of exchange, while also relying on workers' co-operation to set the forces of production in motion. Previously, power theorists have assumed that control can only be exercised through coercion. However, by making managers franchisees – who now work for a profit instead of a wage and who have large capital investments in the business – this co-operative component is enhanced. Franchisees have greater incentive to drive themselves and their workforces harder.

The alternative approach can draw on many of the insights provided by the New Institutionalists. For example, the greater tendency to use franchising as outlet concentration falls may be explained in terms of rising monitoring costs of branch operations for the parent coupled with rising outlet revenues associated with franchise ownership. However, the alternative approach rejects the notion that these enterprise structures must necessarily be the most efficient – greater outputs may simply be the result of more effort.[9]

The aim of getting most from the least, or driving revenues up while pushing costs down, is the guiding principle on which a business is shaped: the criteria on which businesses adopt franchise structures or not. It is on this basis that franchises are offered. The terms of association are non-negotiable, thereby ensuring that the franchisor's interests are safeguarded first. The relative powerlessness of franchisees makes this possible. Indeed, the survey of franchisees reported here provides some empirical confirmation for this. For production to take place, the physical means of production (raw materials, plant, equipment), labour power and the mental means of production ('know-how', methods of operation, etc.) are required. Many franchisees are attracted by the prospect of going into business, but rely on franchising to provide the idea or 'know-how' necessary. As such, franchising offers them a bridge into business. However, it carries a trade-off: the desire to 'be their own boss' against the opportunity of operating a business under someone else's trade mark according to a set of contractual rules and regulations. It also institutionalizes a conflict of interest between the franchisor's desire for the maximization of outlet volumes against the franchisee's desire for outlet profitability. An examination of these issues forms the bulk of the book's subsequent assessment of franchising at work.

4 Setting the legal contours of franchising

INTRODUCTION

In recent years, the role of contracting between employers and their workforces as well as between businesses has assumed great importance among politicians, commentators and academics alike (see Chapter 1). According to the UK government, for example, there has been 'a growth in the number of employers who negotiate directly with their employees on an individual basis' (Department of Employment, 1991b: 3). Yet despite anecdotal evidence there is no systematic evidence on the scale, scope and nature of these negotiations. Even collectively agreed employment contracts have rarely been subject to scrutiny (except by Leighton and Doyle, 1982).

Nevertheless, claims that employment contracts tailored to the individual and subject to periodic renegotiation are beneficial continue to be made (Hanson and Mather, 1988: 45–46). These are based on the preceived need to relate pay determination more closely to the ability of firms to pay, an attitude strongly supported by the UK government. Equally vigorous counter-claims have also been made. These are based on the argument that setting wages and conditions above market-determined levels will act to raise rather than hinder productivity growth (Freeman and Medoff, 1984; Nolan and Marginson, 1990). While this is not the place to investigate the validity of either claim, it is sufficient to note that one of the current debates in labour economics and industrial relations concerns the nature and form of *contracts* governing the employment of others.

Contracts have also begun to figure prominently in the writings of organizational and management theorists. They, too, have been prompted to consider the role of contracts in the light of what is happening or supposed to be happening to the shape of business organizations. Handy (1984: 79–82), for example, has identified a growth in the 'contractual organization', an organization with only the key functions retained in-house and the rest provided by outside suppliers on a contract basis. He cites a construction site as the most visible example of a contractual organization at work, with a small staff employed by the main contractor co-ordinating the work of bricklayers, scaffolders, plumbers, electricians, painters and so on, supplied under the terms of a commercial contract.

Others (Atkinson, 1984; Atkinson and Meager, 1986) have suggested that the workforce is increasingly being divided into 'core' and 'periphery' groups. The former comprise full-time, permanent workers, while the latter comprise part-timers, temporary workers, subcontractors, franchisees and so on. Some of these 'peripheral' workers have commercial as opposed to employment contracts. The implication that firms are able to retain control over those with whom they have a *commercial* rather than an *employment* contract is often made: 'it used to be that if you wanted to control something, you owned it. Organizations liked to have everyone working for them, *in their employment*' (Handy, 1984: 79, his emphasis). However, the empirical support for, or rejection of, such a notion remains rare. Indeed, there has been little exploration of contractual relations generally.

Like employment contracts, studies of written, legally binding contracts between incorporated/unincorporated associations (business contracts) and their use remain few and far between (Macaulay, 1963; Beale and Dugdale, 1975; Stinchcombe, 1985). By studying franchise contracts this chapter goes some way towards filling this vacuum. In addition to this, the chapter has two more focused aims. The first is to provide an analysis of the component clauses to be found in a typical franchise agreement and the bearing they have on a franchisee's independence. The second aim is an analysis of the circumstances in which they are used. In fulfilling both objectives, the chapter builds on and extends the results reported in Felstead (1991c, 1992).

The chapter therefore begins with an analysis of the composition of a franchise contract. At a general level, the agreement consists of six broad parts: the rights granted to the franchisee; the initial and on-going obligations undertaken by the franchisor; the obligations imposed on the operation of the franchise itself; trading restrictions on the franchisee; the conditions for and consequences of termination; and provisions for the assignment/death of the franchisee (cf. Mendelsohn, 1985: chapter 10). Yet beyond this, relatively little is known about what a franchise contract might contain. By examining the franchise contracts of 83 practising business format franchisors supplied to the author on request (see pp.6–7 for details), this chapter provides a clearer picture of what the franchise contract actually looks like. The analysis is organized around three key questions: where does the operational control of the business reside; what are the financial linkages between franchisor and franchisee; and who owns and controls the business assets. The degree of control formally bestowed on franchisors by contract varies significantly from franchise to franchise; an index of contractual control is devised to illustrate the degree of diversity.

The second section of the chapter moves from the formal level of *making* franchise contracts to a consideration of those circumstances in which contractual rights are actually *used*. The argument advanced is that this will depend, to a large extent, on the state of the market for franchisees and their products as well the nature of the product market they face. For example, if the demand for franchised products/ services is low and there are few would-be franchisees, franchisors are far less likely to use their contractual powers than when demand is generally good and there are plenty of franchise candidates waiting for new or existing areas. The day-to-day operations of a franchise are likely to be under far more scrutiny in situations where franchisors demand and customers expect uniformity. Similarly, where franchise agreements expire or are terminated, franchisors tend towards strict enforcement of contracts in order to restrict former franchisees from using the franchisor's 'know-how'. The chapter concludes with a summary.

MAKING CONTRACTS

The franchise agreement is the primary franchise document placing legally binding obligations and duties on both parties. As such, it plays a major role in determining the relationship between franchisor and franchisee: 'It is from this instrument and the relationship that it creates that all responsibilities and benefits flow' (Rosenfield, 1970: 67). For this reason, nine franchisors felt unable to supply a franchise contract to the author, and were prepared to say so. In four cases, words to the effect that 'due to company policy we are unable to forward a copy of our franchise agreement' (letter to author) were used. In three cases, its centrality to the franchisor–franchisee relationship was more explicitly acknowledged:

> You must appreciate that this is a legally binding business document between franchisee and franchisor and as such the 'terms' of our relationship are stated in it.
>
> (letter to the author)

Two franchisors (both of whom are large well-known operators) even went so far as to admit that only accepted franchisees are shown a contract:

> The franchise agreement . . . is a confidential document which is supplied to prospective franchisees *once they have placed a deposit* with us and shown their *commitment to proceed with a franchise.*
>
> (letter to author, my emphasis)

> The franchise contract is a confidential document which is only available to *accepted* franchisees.
>
> (letter to author, my emphasis)

In other words, a franchisee has to be acceptable to the franchisor, show a willingness to go through with the purchase and/or pay a non-returnable deposit to even see the franchise agreement. In this situation, a franchisee is indeed 'buying a pig in a poke'.[1] The suspicion must be that some of those who did not supply a franchise contract for analysis (and there were three times as many of those who did as those who did not) guarded the terms of their contract, not only from research scrutiny but from franchise candidates as well.

Franchisees are offered a standard-form contract drawn up in advance by the franchisor. It is very rare indeed for there to be any departure from the printed form; often the only point subject to variation is the site location or geographical area of the franchise and even here there is little or no room for negotiation.[2] In all other respects, the contract is non-negotiable and is offered on a take-it-or-leave-it basis. Franchisees have little bargaining power on account of two factors. First, in seeking to use the accumulated experience, 'know-how' and trade mark of a franchisor (even if limited), franchisees are in the position of wanting to use something the franchisor has. The prospective franchisee is given no choice over the terms and conditions of association: he/she is simply told to take them or leave them. This imbalance of power is more pronounced where there are few 'open points' in network that need to be filled; it is at its least pronounced where small companies are using franchising to widen their geographical coverage (Hough, 1986: chapter 8; Felstead, 1991b).[3]

Secondly, not only is the franchisee economically inferior to the franchisor, but he/she suffers from unequal access to all the relevant information. The franchisor understands the implications of the agreement it has devised, and provides the bulk of information about the franchise. For example, if the area was previously worked by a franchisee, but is now dormant, only the franchisor will know the exact circumstances of the previous franchisee's departure. There is no legal obligation on the franchisor to disclose this information, and no way of corroborating any explanations given (short of tracking down the former franchisee). Taking up a franchise can therefore be risky or, at worst, a trap for the trusting. To restore some balance, a former franchisee advises prospective franchisees thus:

> [they] shouldn't take what their bank managers or accountants say as gospel, they can only see figures on a page, they have no idea of whether they are appropriate to that particular business. Instead talk to as many franchisees and people in the business, so that you can assess the franchisor's claims with greater knowledge.

> (field notes)

The imbalance of power between franchisor and franchisee extends to the franchise agreement itself. Even a cursory examination of a few franchise agreements suggests that the basic franchise document imposes far more obligations on the franchisee than on the franchisor. A detailed examination of a large number of franchise agreements, as carried out here, reinforces this impression.

Not only are the clauses that impose requirements on the franchisee many and on the franchisor few, but differences in detail, level of specification and degree of flexibility are also worthy of note. The provisions applying to the franchisee tend to say that 'the franchisee will do such and such at a given place, in a specific amount of time, and in a particular manner'. On the other hand, franchisor provisions are inclined to be more vague and are hedged in limiting phrases, such as 'the franchisor at its sole discretion', 'at a time and place chosen by the franchisor' and 'the franchisor reserves the right to vary its policy with regard to X, Y and Z from time to time in the light of experience'.

Nevertheless for tax, social security and labour law purposes franchisees are deemed to be legally independent. Indeed, most franchise contracts go out of their way to underline the arm's length nature of the relationship:

> The parties hereto agree that the franchisee is an independent contractor. Nothing herein contained shall constitute the franchisee as an agent, legal representative, partner, subsidiary, joint venturer or employee of the franchisor. The franchisee shall have no right or power to and shall not bind or obligate the franchisor in any way, manner or thing whatsoever, nor represent, that he [*sic*] has any right to do so.

> (contract no. 4)

Clauses of this type deny that the franchisee is an agent, employee or legal representative of the franchisor, and that he/she has any legal authority to bind the franchisor to contracts with third parties. In other words, the legal boundaries of the franchisor–franchisee relationship are set; franchisors' legal responsibilities do not extend either to franchisees as employees, to those whom franchisees employ or to the ultimate purchasers of the franchise system's products and services. Yet franchisees are bound to operate their businesses according to the terms of franchise agreements which place many more obligations and duties on them than they do on franchisors.

Several studies have begun to raise doubts about how real legal independence actually is. Notable studies on homeworking (Allen and Wolkowitz, 1986, 1987; Rubery and Wilkinson, 1981) and subcontracting (Rainbird, 1991; Evans and Lewis, 1989) have raised question marks over the implied differences between a *firm–client* relationship and one based on the worker–employer model. Indeed, Chapter 1 discussed how tolerant UK law has now become: 'a man [*sic*] does not cease to run a business on his [*sic*] own account because he [*sic*] agrees to . . . accept another's superintendence'.[4] Yet 'independent' businesses can often find themselves in a subordinate market position by virtue of their being dependent on a small number of 'clients' – in many cases just one (Rubery, 1988: 267–268). Consequently, hours of work are determined by completion dates, the pace of work by piece-rates and the quality of work by 'client' specification (see Figure 4.1). Trading under the label of a legally independent business can therefore conjure up an image of work autonomy which can be quite misleading.

The same can be said of the franchise relationship. In spite of the sizeable financial investment often required to buy a franchise and the fact that franchisees trade as legally independent businesses serving numerous clients, they do so by using the accumulated 'know-how', experience and trade mark of a franchisor located upstream in the productive process (see Figure 4.1). Even though the contract governing the relationship between franchisor and franchisee is commercially grounded, franchisees find themselves dependent on the franchisor for the business idea/format/trade mark in much the same way as a worker is dependent on an employer for a job. Although a firm which franchises part of its operations no longer buys franchisees' labour time, it can still retain control over key strategic decisions and take some of what is produced as a result. This is revealed in the franchise contract in three ways: the controls and regulations placed on the operation of the business; the payments made by the franchisee to the franchisor; and the retention of key elements of the business apparatus by the franchisor.

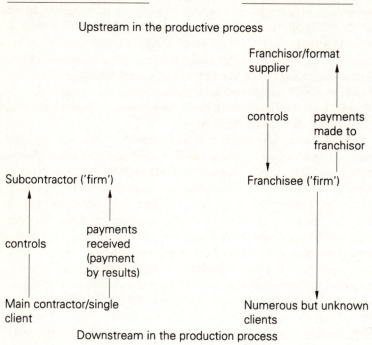

Figure 4.1 Subcontracting and franchising mechanisms

The remainder of this section will consider each dimension in turn, before constructing an index of contractual control.

Operational controls

Although franchisees are considered to be formally autonomous from their franchisor, there are a number of contractual clauses designed to keep franchisees operationally bound in the way they do business. These fall into two categories. The first are those designed to regulate the day-to-day operation of the franchised business so as to convey a common, uniform image to the purchasing public; and the second are those intended to shape the longer-term development of the franchisee's business (see Table 4.1 for a summary).

Putting franchisees into business inevitably involves specifying and regulating how the business should be run on a daily basis. Indeed, one of the attractions of taking up a franchise instead of setting up

Table 4.1 Components of a franchise contract: day-to-day operation and business trajectory of a franchisee's business

Contractual clauses	Percentage presence
Day-to-day operation	
Franchisor has right to unilaterally change the Operations Manual	88.0%
Opening/working hours of business specified	47.0%
Franchisee cannot to be involved in any other business during the life of the franchise without franchisor's consent	83.1%
Prior approval for holidays required	6.0%
Franchisees committed to a minimum level of local advertising expenditure	26.5%
Franchisor influence on prices	45.8%
Franchisor right to monitor quality of product/service	59.0%
Business trajectory	
Minimum sales and/targets	33.7%
Expansion triggers	8.4%
Granted exclusive trading rights within a specified trading area	49.4%
Option to renew	90.4%

Source: author's survey of 83 franchise contracts.

independently is the rights it gives franchisees to operate on a pre-determined basis. In the case of product franchises these regulations apply to the quality of the product and no further, whereas in business format franchising they extend beyond to the operation of the business itself (see Chapter 2 for distinction). Without exception, all the contracts examined here provide the franchisee with a business format on which to run their business. As such franchisees are contractually bound to:

> operate ... in accordance with the standards, specifications and procedures as set out in the Manuals.
>
> (contract no. 80)

> act strictly in accordance with and undertake ... that all his [*sic*] staff are obliged to act ... strictly in accordance with the Policy and Procedure Manual and the Logo Book.
>
> (contract no. 11)

operate the system properly and strictly in accordance with the provisions of the operational manual.

(contract no. 2)

The operations manual is likely to lay down a set of minimum standards to which franchisees must adhere. These standards may relate to the actual premises, their size, layout and decor, to the organization and staff levels, to technical training, service facilities and equipment, to receiving and handling customers, to accounting and stocking systems, and to advertising and sales promotion.

The apparent preference of many franchisors for franchisees unfamiliar with the operational area of the franchise (see pp.84–85) raises the likelihood that they will follow the franchisor's methods and procedures to the letter. Indeed, much of the franchisee's operational activities are not directly controlled by the franchisor, but are instead controlled at one remove. As one franchisor candidly put it:

> We brain-wash them [franchisees] into our way of thinking, so that in actual fact we don't need to stand over them telling them what to do, they will do what we want them to without that.

(field notes)

However, by retaining the right to make on-going operational changes, most franchisors are able to modify the way their franchisees do business throughout the trading life of the franchise. Eighty-eight per cent of the contracts examined allow the franchisor unilaterally to change the way the business is run by making amendments, alterations and improvements to the operations manual. This is often couched in terms such as 'the franchisee will conform with the amendments/ updates/revisions made to the operations manual from time to time'. Sometimes much stronger language is used to underline the unconditional right of the franchisor to change how franchisees operate and provide an assurance that franchisees comply:

> The franchisee agrees . . . to *obey the franchisor's orders and instructions* . . . and act in such a manner as . . . to be most beneficial to the franchisor.

(contract no. 74, my emphasis)

Franchisees are contractually required to follow franchisor-inspired changes without question. Consultation with franchisees on any proposed change often takes place, but is rarely specified contractually (such a clause was found in only two of the contracts examined). In effect, this commits the franchisee to an open-ended agreement:

Since the provisions of the operating manual can be changed at the prerogative of the franchisor, the franchisees find themselves in the tenuous position of being bound to a contract that can be modified *unilaterally* by the franchisor.

(Hunt, 1972: 36–37, his emphasis)

Operationally, franchisees are therefore bound to follow detailed methods and procedures, which may, in turn, be subject to franchisor-inspired change or modification. However, changes can only be made if they do not contradict other clauses in the contract. For example, the introduction of a national discounting scheme *wholly financed* by the franchisee will only be permissible if the contract does not contain a clause requiring the franchisor to make a *contribution* (albeit un-specified) to the financing of any such schemes (Horne, 1992).

Almost half of the franchise systems examined specify the *minimum* trading hours of the business in the contract itself; the likelihood is that the remainder lay them down in the operations manual. Some of the clauses simply give the franchisor the right to determine at their sole discretion the days and hours in which franchisees must be open for business. In other cases, they are more specific:

The operator's [franchisee's] hours of business are from 7.30 am to 6.00 pm Monday to Friday and 7.30 am to 1.00 pm Saturdays. The operator [franchisee] must maintain a telephone and the telephone must be manned [*sic*] between the hours of 9.00 am and close of business Mondays to Saturdays. No answer phone shall be used during business hours.

(contract no. 38)

In the case of franchise systems which provide an emergency service, such as drain cleaners for example, franchisees are required to provide a 24 hour 365 days a year service:

In order to ensure that the service is available twenty-four (24) hours a day for every day of the year, the franchisee may consult with other franchisees to organize a rota and in any case the franchisee shall keep the franchisor's Central Message Handling Service fully in-formed of the rota arrangements prior to implementation and also of any unavailability for work for any reason. Notice of such unavail-ability must be given in advance and as early as possible.

(contract no. 22)

For the one-person franchise, setting trading hours determines the minimum number of hours the franchisee works (or is on call). Even for those franchisees who might employ others, clauses requiring the franchisee to devote their time and attention to the business during the hours of operation determines the minimum number of hours they work. To ensure a franchisee's commitment to the business, 83 per cent of franchisors claim the right to give or withhold consent from franchisees who wish to become involved in other business ventures while also operating a franchise. Five (6 per cent) of the contracts examined go one stage further and specify the number of working days the franchisee is permitted to take as holiday:

> [the franchisee] shall be entitled to take a holiday at such times as he [*sic*] may chose but not exceeding 25 working days per annum provided that he [*sic*] shall give the franchisor sufficient notice of such holidays and provided that sufficient arrangements can be made in advance to ensure that the service can be properly provided.
>
> (contract no. 21)

Slightly more than one in four franchisors require that their franchisees do a minimum amount of local advertising, while all reserve the right to approve any advertising material used. This is either expressed as a commitment to a percentage-based level of local advertising or as a commitment to bear the financial cost of local advertising and promotion campaigns as specified in the operations manual. In more than three-quarters of these cases, this is in addition to a commitment by the franchisor to fund national advertising campaigns out of revenues raised by levies on the network. While this is likely to raise franchisee sales, its effect on franchisee profits is more uncertain (i.e. expensive giveaways such as 'buy two get one free' reduce profit margins and may do the same to franchisee profits).

The stresses and strains within the franchise relationship are also evident when it comes to determining what prices franchisees charge for their services/products. As long as franchisors receive a major portion of their revenue from royalties on gross sales and/or the sale of supplies (see below), there will be a conflict of interest between franchisors and franchisees over what prices to charge. Low prices will mean high physical volume and (if demand is price elastic) high sales, which will unquestionably benefit the franchisor since its income rises and falls according to physical volume and/or sales.[5] It should therefore come as no surprise that almost 50 per cent of franchisors influence their franchisees' pricing policy in some way or another. However, this influence ranges from one extreme to the other. For example, 26 per cent of these franchisors merely suggest prices to their franchisees, whereas 18 per cent issue a set pricing structure for franchisees to follow. In between these extremes, franchisors specify maximum prices (37 per cent), minimum prices (13 per cent) and upper and lower pricing bands which franchisees must not breach (5 per cent). Imposing a ceiling on the prices charged by franchisees prevents them from simply raising their prices, and hence profit margins, at the cost of volume. Such a course of action would limit the franchisor's ability to recoup profits from franchisees. On the other hand, imposing a price floor restricts the degree to which the franchise can provide a cut-price, low quality service to the detriment of the entire network. The franchisor can indirectly influence the pricing policies of franchisees as well. By including price information in national advertising campaigns, the prices charged by franchisees are influenced by their customers' price expectations (Caves and Murphy II, 1976: 579).

In order to ensure adherence to the provisions of the franchise agreement and the methods and practices as set out in the operations manual, almost 60 per cent of contracts contain a clause which gives the franchisor the right to inspect the franchisee's business, and in four-fifths of these cases this can take place without notice being given. In mobile operations, for example, this is extended to communicating or interviewing the franchisee's customers in order to assess the quality of the service provided to the ultimate user.

The lines of contractual control do not simply relate to the day-to-day operations of the franchisee's business, but extend far beyond to shape the longer-term development and performance of these 'independent' businesses. By measuring franchisee performance in terms of outlet turnover, franchisors exercise wide-ranging control over their franchisees' businesses. Franchisors make this the key yardstick against which to measure the success or failure of their franchisees, since their income rises and falls according to outlet turnover (by taking a percentage of outlet turnover and/or supplying a key ingredient). However, this highlights an area of potential conflict between franchisor and franchisee. The aim of the franchisor – maximization of outlet turnover – and that of the franchisee – profit maximization at the outlet – may not always coincide. An increase in a franchisee's turnover is *neither a necessary nor a sufficient* condition for an increase in franchisee profits. For example, the costs of generating an increase in sales may outweigh the benefits, i.e. slimmer profit margins per sale may not be compensated for by increased sales. However, the aim of the franchisor takes priority with the franchisee agreeing 'to procure the greatest volume of turnover for the business' (contract no. 82) or 'to use [their] best endeavours to establish, maintain and increase the turnover of the said business at the said premises' (contract no. 20). Although worded somewhat differently from contract to contract, all of those examined contain clauses intended to have a similar effect.

In terms of promoting the volume of the business, some franchise agreements go much further than simply obliging franchisees to seek the greatest turnover for their business – not an altogether obvious goal given a franchisee's greater interest in profitability. Some franchise contracts set minimum turnover targets and provisions to trigger a franchisee's expansion once certain turnover levels are reached, regardless of a franchisee's profitability.[6] One in three of the franchise contracts analysed have a minimum sales or performance requirement. These targets can take the form of a specified level of turnover, a minimum number of vehicles or teams per outlet, a percentage of outlet turnover forecasts, or a level of turnover deemed to be 'reasonable' or 'substantial' by the franchisor:

> In the event that a turnover of £50,000 arising from the business is not achieved within two years of the date of this agreement or for a continuous period of twelve months at any time thereafter . . . the franchisor will have the right (but not the duty) [to do X, Y and Z].
>
> (contract no. 28)

> The franchisee undertakes to maintain available for rental a minimum yearly average of cars, vans and trucks as below.
>
> (contract no. 9)

> The franchisor may terminate this agreement in the event of the franchisee failing to achieve a minimum annual sales turnover . . . amounting to 75 per cent of the turnover calculated in the finalised cash flow and trading forecast, as supplied to the franchisee.
>
> (contract no. 25)

> The franchisor may at its sole discretion terminate this agreement in the event that substantial turnover arising from the business . . . is not achieved within eighteen (18) months of the date of the agreement or for a continuous period of six (6) months at any time thereafter.
>
> (contract no. 40)

In each case, the targets are set unilaterally by the franchisor. Should franchisees fail to meet these performance targets, three remedies are open to franchisors.[7] First, one-third claim the right to appoint a manager, at the franchisor's expense, to assist in the development of the business. Second, 36 per cent have the right to reduce the size of the territory in which franchisees work, offering limited compensation. And finally, there is the ultimate sanction of revoking the agreement, a remedy open to 71 per cent of those who have performance targets.

In addition to avoiding the sanctions which can be imposed on those franchisees who fail to meet the franchisor-set turnover targets, those who do well may be forced to expand. Nearly one in ten contracts were found to contain provisions relating to the point at which the franchisee is contractually required to expand his/her business:

> Where annual turnover of the business exceeds £40,000 in any calendar year the franchisee shall make arrangements for the acquisition of a second vehicle if the franchisor reasonably requires him [*sic*] to do so for the purpose of business development. Further vehicles shall be acquired by the franchisee for every extra £40,000 in annual turnover thereafter.
>
> (contract no. 21)

> In the event that the franchisor decides that the territory is sufficiently large geographically and has sufficiently large population to justify one or more further outlets . . . in the territory . . . the franchisee shall have the right to open such further outlet . . . In the event that the franchisee fails . . . to open such further outlet, the franchisor shall have the right to reduce the territory to enable it to provide an exclusive area in which a new franchisee may trade.
>
> (contract no. 77)

Since it is the franchisee who provides most of the money capital for expansion, fixed costs for the franchised business may rise by proportionately more than turnover, and hence overall profits for the franchise may fall. Over the longer term, profits for the franchisee may improve, but there is, of course, no guarantee. However, the franchisor's gain will be much more immediate as its income is directly tied to franchisee turnover, a business indicator likely to rise long before expansion begins to show a profit for the franchisee. Although relatively rare, clauses designed to trigger business expansion are intended to prevent franchisees from reaching a 'comfort zone', thereby stifling the growth of their franchisor.

Franchise territories, too, are often defined in such a way as to privilege franchisor interests over those of franchisees. The extent to which exclusivity is granted has important consequences for both franchisee and franchisor. For franchisees, it determines the extent to which they are insulated from competition from others within the chain, i.e. dilution of any monopoly power they might have. For franchisors, it determines the leeway with which they can expand in order to increase market share without being solely reliant on the business plans of their franchisees.

The results of the contract survey suggests that just under one-half of franchisors offer their franchisees exclusive territories within which to operate.[8] More often than not these are defined by using postal codes or the catchment areas are covered by advertising mediums such as the *Yellow Pages*. A slight majority of franchisors, however, offer either qualified exclusivity or no exclusivity at all, thereby giving themselves another lever over the development of their franchisees' businesses. One in six give their franchisees limited exclusivity. This might entail dividing the territories into primary and secondary areas, giving the franchisee the right of first refusal if another outlet is opened nearby, making exclusivity contingent on attaining franchisor-set performance targets, or simply giving franchisees prime responsibility for an area provided they can reasonably meet customer demands. The remaining one-third of franchise contracts grant no exclusive territorial rights, often going out of their way explicitly to deny that such rights are granted or implied. In other words, the franchise relates to that location alone and no further. Consequently, single store franchisees have no automatic right to expand their business, nor are they sheltered from competition from other franchisees in the same chain should the franchisor appoint additional franchisees nearby. The addition of a new franchise close to existing outlets may reduce the sales of existing operators and hence reduce their profitability, but raise the total revenue generated across both outlets and with it the franchisor's revenue stream. The ability to open up more franchised outlets, even alongside existing ones, allows franchisors to recoup more of franchisee profits for themselves.

On the other hand, granting unqualified exclusivity to franchisees prevents the franchisor from expanding total sales and limits the repatriation of franchisee profits. Instead, the franchisor may be forced to see sales opportunities go begging. If minimum sales targets are reached and there are no expansion triggers in the contract, the franchisor will be left with few levers on which to pull. The franchisee may be happy with his/her lot, and therefore unwilling to 'bust a gut' in search of extra sales. The franchisor's efforts will be confined to persuasion and suggestion alone. For example, the franchisor may suggest that the franchisee 'put another team on the road'. The franchisee may, however, reject the idea on the basis that 'he/she can do without the added headaches of employing more people and equipment' and would rather 'enjoy what little spare time I have'.

Franchise contracts are overwhelmingly of a finite duration – on average lasting around seven years, with almost 50 per cent lasting for five years and 20 per cent for ten. Only two of the franchise contracts examined could, theoretically at least, last forever provided either party does not wish to terminate. Nine out of ten contracts give incumbent franchisees the option to renew their franchise for a further specified period, but only if they have 'performed satisfactorily' during the currency of the agreement. Once again, franchisors can exert influence on the operation the franchisee's business by withholding (or threatening to withhold) renewal from an operator considered slovenly or whose performance has been poor. Furthermore, most franchisees who wish to exercise this option have to post adequate notice, modernize, renovate or repair equipment if so directed, take refresher courses and abide by the terms of the then current franchise agreement. While most franchisors waive the franchise fee on renewal, about 7 per cent were found to charge a renewal fee, either based on a proportion of turnover or the then current franchise fee.

Both in terms of the day-to-day operation of the franchised business and in terms of its longer-term development, franchisors are armed with a whole battery of control mechanisms designed to induce franchisees into their service. The contract gives franchisors powers to curb individual flair for the sake of uniformity, and to ensure that their economic interests are given primacy in the running of the outlet, despite a substantial sum of investment by the franchisee.

Financial linkages

Relying on the use of franchisees' money capital to expand their network substantially lessens the risks to which the franchisor is exposed should an outlet fail. Franchisors are even insulated from the losses often incurred during the early years of setting up satellite branches as their income is related to turnover (and/or volume), not profits. Instead, the franchisee bears the greater financial risk should the business make a loss (or become bankrupt), yet shares the profits of the business with the franchisor when trading becomes profitable. A franchisor executive has even been reported as joking: 'we're just like the Mafia: we skim it right off the top' (quoted in *Time*, 17 September 1973: 89–90).

The mechanism through which this is achieved is the royalty levy. In three out of four cases this is expressed as a percentage of franchisee turnover, averaging 9.3 per cent (according to Table 2.1). Only a very small minority of franchise systems *apparently* do not commit franchisees to make any direct payments (see Table 4.2 for a summary). However, in these cases the levy is simply less obvious by virtue of the fact that franchisors generate their revenue from the mark-up on the goods they supply. This is more commonly used by product franchisors (see Chapter 2). The most notable franchisors here are the soft drink companies, such as Coca-Cola, who sell concentrate to their franchised bottlers (see Chapter 6), petrol and new car suppliers, such as Shell, Esso, Ford and Rover, who sell petrol and cars to their networks, and breweries who supply their 'tied estates' (cf. Monopolies and Mergers Commission, 1989). Even so, almost 45 per cent of business format franchisors require that specific consumables be ordered and paid for via them. This implies that a significant minority of franchisors actually have two sources of income – turnover related payments and revenues generated by marked-up supplies. Furthermore, about one franchisor in every eight guarantees that they receive a certain annual payment from each franchisee in the network, irrespective of their turnover. This takes the form of either a flat rate fee linked to the Retail Price Index as well as a percentage of turnover, or a percentage but with a guaranteed minimum payment adjusted for price inflation.

Table 4.2 Components of a franchise contract: financial linkages

Contractual clauses	Percentage presence
Royalty { Management services fee	94.0%
Advertising levy	67.5%
Order consumables through franchisor	44.6%

Source: author's survey of 83 franchise contracts.

Royalties often include levies which are channelled into an advertising fund. Just over two-thirds of franchisors collect separate funds for advertising purposes, of which 90 per cent make their collections based on a percentage of franchisee turnover. Where expressed as a percentage, the advertising levy averages 2.7 per cent (cf. Table 2.1). These funds are set aside to promote the trade name of the franchise on a national basis, although doubts are sometimes expressed that they are also used to advertise for additional franchisees. Taken together, the management services fee and the advertising levy are referred to as royalties, averaging about 9.3 per cent.

The large, sometimes considerable, investment required of franchisees and the tying of their income directly to the profits generated by the outlet are often uncritically taken to denote their capitalist credentials. If the defining feature of wage labour is the payment of a wage, then franchisees do indeed fall outside the category of wage labour, taking on the hallmarks of the capitalist class. If, however, wage labour is defined as the contribution labour makes to the process of capital accumulation, then franchisees may, in part, constitute a form of wage labour. Payments are made to the parent company (usually in proportion to turnover as indicated above), thereby contributing to a process of capital accumulation *outside* their own limited sphere of autonomy (cf. Birkbeck, 1978; Gerry and Birkbeck, 1981; Gerry, 1985).

Constructing the financial linkage between franchisor and franchisee in this way has considerable advantages for the franchisor. By granting franchisees property rights in the business (i.e. the right to profit from their own, and others', labour), franchisors may benefit from increased effort on the part of franchisees, reflected in higher levels of turnover, and consequently larger payments being made to the franchisor via royalty payments and/or the mark-up on any goods and services they supply. Franchisees, for example, work long hours (see pp.86–87) and often draw on a pool of family labour. Indeed, many franchisors are keen to recruit only those with the complete backing of their family in the hope that family labour can be tapped upon whenever needed (Edens *et al.*, 1976; BFA/NatWest, 1989: 33). The outcome is to raise labour's input (that of both the franchisee and their staff) without any direct physical supervision being required of the franchisor.

Although franchisees can make additional profits by working harder themselves (and/or intensifying the work of others), they do so only after they have made turnover-related payments to their franchisor. Trading losses, too, are compounded by turnover-related payments, sometimes set at nominal levels below which they cannot fall. In this sense, the legal 'independence' of franchisees belies the economic fact that, despite bearing most of the risk of setting up a branch, they are not able to reap the full rewards of their own efforts.

Ownership and control of business assets

In addition to posing questions such as who controls the business, who bears the financial risk, and who is likely to profit (or lose) from the venture, the question of who owns, or has control over, the assets necessary for the performance of the task must be answered. At a superficial level, the often significant investment required of franchisees (cf. Table 2.1) would suggest that the ownership and control of the business assets resides with them. A more detailed investigation, however, reveals that franchisees do not have outright ownership of the business assets with which they work. Not only do franchisors retain ownership of the intangible business assets (intellectual property rights,

Table 4.3 Components of a franchise contract: ownership and control of business assets

Contractual clauses	Percentage presence
Intangibles	
Restrictions on setting up a competing business on departure	84.3%
Restrictions on soliciting customers and employees on departure	64.9%
Tangibles	
Franchisor 'stake' in telephone lines/sites/equipment	66.3%
Franchisee's right to assign only to approved buyer	94.0%
Commission/fees paid to franchisor when a franchisee sells their business	63.9%
Franchisor's right to assign	49.4%
Franchisor approval for changes in the voting capital of the franchisee and/or specifications on its composition	60.2%

Source: author's survey of 83 franchise contracts.

'know-how' and the like), but they also exercise a 'hold' on many tangible assets too. Both elements are considered below (see Table 4.3 for a summary).

In order for production to take place tangible business assets (raw materials, plant, equipment), labour power and intangible business assets ('know-how' and methods of operation) are required. Before production can be set in motion, money capital must be advanced for the purchase of the tangible assets for each outlet established, while the intangible assets must also be acquired. In the more conventional small business start-up, the skills, knowledge and 'know-how' acquired from a prior period as an employee often form the basis for the business idea or concept. However, most of those who become franchisees do so because they want to become self-employed, but lack the specific business idea with which to achieve this end. Therefore, the franchisor is able to secure an on-going source of revenue on the basis of supplying franchisees with a business format and/or trade mark under which to work.

To sustain such a financial flow, however, access to the business format must be limited, otherwise it would be available to all at no cost.

In fact, many of the early business format franchisors failed to appreciate this point. McDonald's, the hamburger chain, for example, was often so generous in providing visitors to their stores with information about their production procedures, their equipment and their suppliers that no one really needed a franchise to learn the 'secret' of McDonald's. This quickly became apparent as imitators set up in competition. However, modern-day franchisors are acutely aware that their returns rest heavily upon strategies which make it difficult, if not impossible, for a franchisee to operate without their assistance. By restricting the transfer of relevant 'know-how' and accumulated business experience to its franchisees alone, a franchisor is able to engender a dependent relationship from which a return can then be drawn.

Control of the intangible business assets of a franchise is retained by the franchisor through the non-competition and non-solicitation clauses prevalent in franchise agreements. The former clause was found in 84 per cent of franchise contracts examined, the latter in 65 per cent of them. Briefly, the non-competition clause prevents former franchisees from setting up in direct competition to the franchisor or its franchisees. Its duration is often short – from just three months to three years – and its geographical coverage equally modest – from the territory previously worked to 50 miles from the former franchisee's premises and those of other franchisees. However, it is interesting to note that several contracts prohibit competition over a much wider area than the territories within which franchisees operate (cf. Ozanne and Hunt, 1971: 278–279). Even so, restrictive convenants of this type must not be too onerous; to be enforceable in court they must be of a relatively short duration and be of limited geographical scope (cf. *Financial Times*, 27 March 1991; Aikin, 1991). Mindful of this, one of the contracts examined maintains the right to enforce more limited, yet more 'reasonable' restrictive covenants, in the event of the initial clause being considered by a court of law to be too broad in duration or geographical scope to be enforceable. The non-solicitation clause is designed with a similar intent in mind: to prevent former franchisees from using the business contacts and acquaintances they may have made while a franchisee for the purpose of setting up a competing business.

Franchisors have sometimes gone a stage further by taking a 'stake' in the tangible business assets as well. In retail-based franchise systems, this commonly takes the form of franchisors taking the head-lease and offering franchisees an under-lease. In the United States, franchisors often hold outright ownership of the property and land on which outlets are built. McDonald's provides a classic example of this sort of strengthened tie. The enhanced control which this gives the company over its franchisees was not lost on the chain's founder, Ray Kroc:

> I have finally found the way that will put every single McDonald's we open under our complete control . . . It [the franchisee's sub-lease] says that if at any time McDonald's System Inc. notifies Franchise Realty Corporation that the operation does not conform in every way to the McDonald's standards of quality and service, this lease will be cancelled on thirty-day notice. Now we have a club over them, and by God, there will be no more pampering or fiddling with them. We will do the ordering instead of going around and begging them to co-operate.
>
> (quoted in Love, 1987: 156–157)

With similar intent in mind, other examples can be drawn from the United States. Dunkin' Donuts, for example, controls the real estate from which two-thirds of its franchisees operate, either through outright ownership, or holding the head lease for property and/or the land on which its outlets are built (Kaufmann, 1988).

In the UK, only 17 per cent of the contracts examined give franchisors a 'stake' in the properties from which franchisees trade, either by offering franchisees an under-lease, or else requiring them to surrender their lease on termination or expiry of the agreement (cf. Fox, 1988). However, one would expect the contractual analysis to be an underestimate of the true 'stake' franchisors have in their franchisees' trading locations owing to two factors. The first is that many franchise systems are not premises-based, and the second is that leasing arrangements for premises are more often than not concluded by separate agreement.

Almost 10 per cent of contracts confer on franchisors a similar 'stake' in all or part of the franchisee's operating equipment, either by requiring franchisees to lease equipment through the franchisor or by giving franchisors the right to purchase equipment on termination/ expiry of the agreement. This, too, is likely to be an underestimate, since leasing arrangements which specify that the franchisor has some sort of 'stake' in the franchisee's operating equipment can be made outside the franchise agreement itself.

In many mobile franchise operations, control of well-publicized telephone numbers is likely to give franchisors much greater leverage. The contract survey therefore found that two-thirds of agreements contain clauses which give franchisors some 'hold' on telephone lines. This 'hold' commonly takes the form of either outright ownership as the official subscriber (46 per cent) or a requirement that franchisees do all such acts as are necessary on expiry or termination to ensure the transfer of the telephone number to whomsoever the franchisor directs (41 per cent). By 'lending' franchisees a telephone line, the franchisor is able to retain the goodwill associated with that number should the franchisee cease to remain with the franchisor for whatever reason.

Some franchisors have taken this further by channelling all telephone calls (either through a freephone number or by diverting locally dialled calls, often a 'cosmetic', i.e. easy-to-remember number) to a centralized booking office operated by the franchisor. Work schedules are then drawn up and transmitted by mobile telephone to franchisees. This triangular relationship – customer–franchisor–franchisee – further enhances the franchisor's grip over the franchisee. It enables the franchisor to monitor (and set) the franchisee's movements and pace of work and to track, with greater surety, whether a franchisee is under-reporting their turnover and hence lowering the royalties paid.

The best way to answer the question of who owns and controls the business assets with which franchisees work is to consider what happens when a franchisee decides to sell 'their' business. Unlike the conventional business, a franchised concern has certain elements (particularly intangibles such as the trade mark) in which the franchisor has a 'stake' (see above). In order to protect and maintain their value, 94 per cent of franchisors require franchisees to seek the approval of anyone who wants to buy the business. A quarter reserve the option to purchase the business on the same terms as offered by the proposed buyer. A further 10 per cent claim the right of first refusal should the franchisee wish to sell. And one contract restricts the franchisee's right to sell to a number of years before the end of the agreement.

Associated with the sale of any business are the costs of making such a transfer. In the case of franchising, there is the additional cost of franchisors vetting suggested purchasers. To cover these costs, 64 per cent of those who allow franchisees to sell their businesses levy a commission on the sale price. This commonly takes one of two forms. First, a dual levy structure, where a certain percentage of the sale price is payable if the franchisee introduces the purchaser, with an additional percentage if the purchaser is found by the franchisor. The second is a percentage figure of the purchase price irrespective of whoever introduces the purchaser.

In contrast, franchisors in nearly half of the contracts examined explicitly reserve the right to assign franchise agreements to others without seeking the consent of any franchisee. Consequently, franchise contracts can change hands by assignment as well as by the more conventional route of takeover – as in the case of Grand Metropolitan's recent takeover of the Wimpy chain and the subsequent resale of its table service restaurants back to a group of former Wimpy managers (*Financial Times*, 9 August 1989; *Financial Times*, 17 April 1990).

Similar conditions are also placed on the trading structure of the franchisee during the term of the agreement. Sixty per cent of contracts restrict the changes that can occur in the franchisee's trading structure. These range from approval for any change in the beneficial ownership or de facto control of the franchise, to allowing the limited transfer of a certain proportion of voting shares. In this way the franchisor retains control of who actually runs the business at the outlet level.

In terms of the ownership and control of the business assets, the franchisee's position is therefore ambiguous. Despite investing large sums of money, often their life savings and/or funds raised by taking out a second mortgage on their homes, franchisees have virtually no ownership rights in the intangible business assets and only restricted rights in the more tangible ones.

Devising an index of contractual control

As a summary of the discussion above, an index of contractual control has been devised in order to identify the different levels of independence, and therefore the level of franchisor control, franchisees might experience (this is shown as Table 4.4). To do this, six key elements in a franchise contract have been selected, which are considered to have a major bearing on how independent franchisees are. Each element is allotted a score – 0 if absent, 1 if present and, where appropriate, 2 if it is present in a stronger form. Although the scoring framework does not 'weight' each of the components, it does enable identification of 'hard' franchise systems (where the lines of contractual control are tight) from 'softer' forms (where franchisees enjoy greater levels of autonomy). About two-thirds of the franchise systems examined fall somewhere in between the two extremes. However, the overall distribution of the 'scores' is skewed towards the 'hard' end of the spectrum.

Although the survey was self-selective, the pattern of response matched the distribution of franchisors across trade categories. So, for example, retailing accounted for 23 per cent of franchisors listed and 18 per cent of the franchise contracts provided. Similarly, 14 per cent of franchise systems were classified as providing building services compared with 16 per cent of our sample contracts. The third largest category of franchise system – commercial, domestic and personal services – also figured in the contract survey in a magnitude (14 per cent) representative of its presence in the total population (13 per cent).

Table 4.4 Index of contractual control[1]

Component elements	Score	%
(a) Non-exclusivity:		
Exclusivity guaranteed in territory	0	49.4
Qualified exclusivity	1	16.9
Non-exclusive franchise	2	33.7
(b) Performance targets:		
None	0	62.7
Turnover targets/expansion triggers	1	37.3
(c) 'Stake' in tangible business assets:		
No 'stake' evident in contract	0	33.7
'Stake' in telephone lines/sites/ equipment	1	66.3
(d) Operations Manual:		
No rights to unilateral change	0	12.0
Rights to unilateral change by franchisor	1	88.0
(e) Post-termination restrictions:		
None	0	13.3
Non-compete or non-solicitation	1	25.3
Both non-compete and non-solicitation	2	61.4
(f) Monitoring of output quality:		
No rights to police system	0	41.0
Rights to inspect/communicate with clients on *reasonable* notice	1	10.8
Rights to inspect/communicate with clients *without* notice	2	48.2
Index of contractual control		
'Soft' franchising (0–3)		13.3
'Medium' franchising (4–6)		65.1
'Hard' franchising (7–9)		21.7

Note:
1. Contracts are individually assessed on six key components with a score of 0 indicating the component's absence, 1 its presence and, where appropriate, 2 indicating its presence in a stronger form. The scores for each contract are then added together producing an index of contractual control ranging from 0–9. Those falling in the 'soft' (0–3), 'medium' (4–6) and 'hard' (7–9) categories are then expressed as a percentage of the total.
Source: survey by author of 83 franchise contracts, first developed in Felstead (1992).

However, it is not possible to be so sure of the representativeness of the nature and content of the contracts. Indeed, the survey probably underestimates the number of 'hard' franchise contracts on account of franchisors being more unwilling to share the terms of their 'harder' franchise relationships without also having the opportunity to explain through interviews why each clause is considered necessary.

At the formal level at least, it would appear that franchisees occupy an ambiguous position of being neither fully in control of 'their' business nor fully controlled. This section has identified three factors which make the point (Felstead, 1991c and 1992). First, despite operating without close and direct supervision, franchisees are required to operate within procedures laid down and often subject to unilateral change. Moreover, franchisees are sometimes committed to adhere to franchisor-set performance targets, and, in any case, to give the aim of the franchisor (turnover maximization) primacy in the running of the business. Secondly, while they appropriate the profits (and losses) of the business, they do so only after they have made turnover-related payments to their franchisor. Thirdly, although franchisees buy or lease much of the physical business apparatus, some parts remain in the hands of the franchisor, and some have franchisor-imposed restrictions on their use both during and after the currency of the agreement. Furthermore, franchisees have no ownership rights in the intangible business assets – they simply 'borrow' the business idea, trading name and/or format.

USING CONTRACTS

Franchisees are often reliant on a franchisor for their business existence. Small wonder then that the relationship is highly formalized in lengthy written contracts, that it gives franchisors more power to influence the actions of their franchisees and that it commits them to make fewer, less detailed obligations than are placed on franchisees. Franchise contracts are often made with little or no negotiation taking place, and as such are more like insurance policies which are sold and not negotiated (Hunt, 1972: 37). That said, one needs to consider the extent to which the contents of these contracts actually shape business practice. In other words, one needs to pinpoint those circumstances in which franchisees may be rigidly held to the terms of their contracts as well as situations in which franchisors may choose to turn a blind eye.

Franchise contracts may be 'used' in two ways (cf. Macaulay, 1963; Beale and Dugdale, 1975). First, they may be used to regulate the ongoing relationship with certain clauses taken up by the franchisor and enforced. Second, contractual remedies may be used in the event of something going wrong: for instance, the franchisee may wish to sell the business before the end of the contract, but will only be able to do so provided certain conditions are met; certain restrictive covenants may also be enforced. Like the contract itself, the use of contractual powers varies from franchise to franchise. While a systematic analysis of what a franchise contract actually looks like has been possible, the collection of evidence on the use of contracts has been more difficult. Without exception, all of the contracts examined carry the disclaimer that:

> no failure of the franchisor to exercise any power given to it hereunder or to insist upon strict compliance by the franchisee with any obligation hereunder . . . shall constitute any waiver of any of the franchisor's rights under this agreement.
>
> (contract no. 50)

The use of contractual powers is at the franchisor's sole discretion and is therefore difficult to detect.[9] Often contracts are used against a single current or former franchisee, and are rarely challenged. Evidence for this section is drawn from a variety of sources: secondary literature, industry-level interviews, case study material, and the press (both trade and non-trade).

The two ways in which franchise contracts may be used are not mutually exclusive, indeed they often merge. For example, in using franchise contracts to regulate the franchisee's business, the franchisee will be aware, or made aware, of the remedies available should he/she not comply. However, franchisors and franchisees do not quote legalistic contract clauses at one another on a daily basis, rather it is used as a last resort. Thus, it is not surprising that only 20 per cent of franchisees surveyed in a previous study claimed that their franchisor referred to the contract in everyday relations (Stanworth *et al.*, 1986; Stanworth and Smith, 1991: 66–76).

Broadly speaking, there are three situations in which franchise contracts may be used. First, in situations where franchisees are not following the operations manual, are discovered to be doing so and where even one maverick operation could do great harm to the entire chain. Secondly, where franchisees are in breach of other aspects of the agreement (such as turnover targets) or where the franchise does not carry an exclusive territory, yet demand for franchised products/services is buoyant and there are plenty of suitable franchise candidates waiting for a franchise. Thirdly, where a former franchise continues to use franchisor's 'know-how' (and possibly trade mark) as well as the tangible assets in which it has a 'stake' at the end/termination of the agreement. Each of these circumstances is considered in turn.

Nature of product market

The most obvious way in which the franchise contract allows the franchisor to determine the daily operation of the franchisee's business is through the incorporation of the operations manual in the agreement. The extent to which this clause gives franchisors control over the operational activities rests on four inter-related factors. The first is the completeness and detail of the operations manual itself: the greater its breadth and depth the more operational control the franchisor has and the increased potential for uniformity. McDonald's franchisees in the United States are currently supplied with an operating manual which runs to 600 pages. It covers cooking methods and procedures, standard food portions, daily cleaning requirements, quality control, as well as specifying the organization of production and the division of labour. McDonald's, along with other fast food companies, has changed the nature of not only the food service industry but that of the food processing industry too. The number of suppliers has been reduced from around 200 supplying 1,500 stores in 1970 to around ten supplying the chain's network of around 7,000 American stores today. Store deliveries have been reduced, from 25 to three a week. More significantly for our purposes has been the tendency to shift more and more product preparation back to the processing plant. Specifications such as the size of french fries, the thickness of cheese slices, and how to make a milk shake are no longer relevant for store-level operators, but are instead prepared by manufacturers according to McDonald's stipulations *before* they reach the store (Levitt, 1972; Love, 1987: chapter 14). Most franchisors have the right to make these operational changes at will; some regularly issue bulletins announcing new regulations thereby strengthening their operational control (Luxenberg, 1985: 78–79).

A second factor which will influence the extent to which franchisors have operational control over franchisees, concerns the specificity of the product or service supplied by franchisees to customers at the level of the outlet. In sectors such as fast food, the product supplied to customers is highly specified – much of the guess-work is removed and replaced by pre-packaged supplies, cooked at specified temperatures over a stipulated time period. For example, Dunkin' Donuts offers detailed cooking instructions for each kind of donut – honey-dip donuts should be fried at 375 degrees Fahrenheit. In other sectors, such as mobile vehicle tuning, however, the service is difficult, if not impossible, to instil into a single operations manual that covers every eventuality. Instead, the quality of the service is often determined by the level of expertise attained by the franchisee (*Financial Times*, 20 April

1990). Even in sectors like high street print, where product variation is more narrow, the operations manual can only provide a guide to bespoke production (Felstead, 1988).

A third factor is the need for uniformity. Despite the importance placed upon uniformity in the franchise literature (Rubin, 1978), its significance varies widely between sectors. The stress on the importance of uniformity is often couched in terms of an externality problem. If any one franchisee allows quality to deteriorate, he/she will generate revenue because customers perceive him/her as being of the same quality as other outlets bearing the same trade mark. Thus, if one franchisee allows the quality of the establishment to deteriorate, he/she benefits by the full amount of the savings from reduced quality maintenance, but he/she bears only part of the costs since this is shared between other franchisees. All franchisees would lose something as a result of this deterioration, and consumers would therefore have less faith in the quality promised by the trade mark. The externality problem is a varying one. It is greatest in sectors serving a significant number of repeat customers to the chain, yet not for a given unit, e.g. hotels, motels, fast food restaurants and car rental agencies. In other words, it is in travel-related businesses that the scope for comparison across the chain is at its most potent. The externality problem, and hence the need for uniformity, is lowest in sectors serving a local population, e.g. automotive services, homecare and personal services, business services, printing.

Finally, the importance placed on uniformity has a determining influence on the degree of store/outlet monitoring required. Three in every five contracts examined contain a clause giving franchisors the right to inspect the franchisee's business, on reasonable notice or without warning (cf. Table 4.1). Where applicable, this is extended to communicating or interviewing the franchisee's customers in order to assess the quality of the service provided to the customer.

A review of particular franchise systems reveals how the sophistication of monitoring procedures varies considerably in practice. The example of fast food provides the clearest case of a situation where policing is at its most developed. McDonald's in the United States gives each store a grade on its quality, service and cleanliness (QSC) as well as an overall grade on a scale ranging from A to F. Currently, the company employs nearly 300 field service consultants, each of whom visits and evaluates about 18 stores four times a year. On each visit, they assess a store on more than 500 items using a standardized inspection form which spans 27 pages. The inspection takes two to three days to complete and covers everything from the cleanliness of the toilets to the quality of the hamburgers and french fries. The consultant returns in 30–90 days for an unannounced follow-up visit before assigning the restaurant its grades. These are complemented by 'customer visits' and spot checks (Love, 1987: 143–146).

If the operator is not meeting McDonald's QSC standards, the field consultant will set up a programme to work with the operator to correct any deficiencies. If the field consultant is unsuccessful in assisting the operator in curing these deficiencies, then the regional manager is called upon. If after this process the regional director determines that the operator is unable or unwilling to meet McDonald's minimum standards, then McDonald's will suggest that the operator sell to an approved buyer. If the franchisee refuses to sell, then McDonald's will begin default proceedings. For example, McDonald's successfully defended the legality of the termination of a franchisee who operated 12 outlets in Paris from 1970 to 1978 on these grounds.[10] The company's strict specifications on food products had been blatantly ignored. Hamburgers were prepared without the standard ingredients. Food was held so long and served so cold that McDonald's inspectors visiting the stores found it difficult to eat. Standard equipment was either missing or poorly maintained, and the grills were improperly calibrated. Food supplies were even found next to cleaning compounds. The court ruling upheld McDonald's action:

> The credibility, viability and enforceability of the McDonald's System is at stake and if Dayan [the franchisee], a grade 'F' operator in Paris, can thumb his nose at the System and its standards then so too can operators everywhere.
>
> (quoted from Mr Judge Curry's Opinion, *Dayan v. McDonald's Corporation* [1982], unpublished: 83)

Kentucky Fried Chicken makes similar detailed inspections, both behind and in front of the counter. Inspectors examine the dates on the products to ensure that chickens are less than six days old, the gravy mix is less than six months old, and that the chicken has been properly prepared. Inspectors move around the store with a thermometer and a stop-watch. In addition, Kentucky Fried Chicken relies on 'mystery shoppers', incognito inspectors posing as customers who make purchases and then report to central headquarters. Franchisees who fail inspections may eventually lose their franchises, as has happened to a number of franchisees in the UK (*Popular Food Service*, March 1987; *Guardian*, 31 March 1992). Similar steps have also been taken by Body Shop, a natural cosmetics retailer, to regain control of six franchised branches in the UK which it alleged had fallen into a 'deplorable condition' (*Financial Times*, 17 August 1992; *Daily Mail*, 13 June 1992).

Other franchise systems reliant on travel-related trade also have sophisticated monitoring procedures. Inspectors for Holiday Inns spend about three hours thoroughly reviewing a unit from top to bottom. Randomly selecting about 10 per cent of the rooms, they look at the ceiling for marks. Light bulbs must be of the correct wattage, walls must be clean, skirting boards dust free, carpets must not be frayed or discoloured, proper door locks must be fitted and smoke alarms must be in working order. Motels rated fair or poor are inspected again in sixty days. If they fail the second time round, the franchisee may be declared in default and so lose the franchise. However, while revoking the franchise is the ultimate sanction, the company inspectors commonly take the lesser step of requiring the franchisee to replace worn-out facilities (Luxenberg, 1985: 89).

In sectors where uniformity is less important, monitoring is less stringent. The classic examples are services supplied to customers in their own homes by franchisees operating in well defined territories. The scope for the consumer to make comparisons across the chain is limited, as are the opportunities for franchisors to make inspections while work is in progress. In these situations, standards vary, with franchisors often content to place minimum quality standards on their outlets. These are then maintained by keeping track of the number of complaints received by head office or by conducting a periodic postal survey of customers.[11] In these businesses initial training, instead of monitoring, becomes the most important standardization device.

In spite of the inclusion of a contractual clause relating to the operations manual in all business format franchise agreements, the level of control it gives franchisors over franchisees varies. Our discussion has identified four inter-related factors on which this leverage turns: the depth and breadth of the manual itself; the specificity of the product/service supplied by franchisees to customers; the need for uniformity; and the enforcement practices of franchisors. The potency of these factors is determined by the franchisor through the tightness or otherwise of the franchise contract, and the nature of the product market which franchisees are 'fitted out' to face.

Demand for franchises and their products

The demand for franchises and the products/services they supply to end-sers can also have a major bearing on whether franchisors decide to use their contractual powers or not. In times where the demand for the products/services of franchisees is buoyant and there are many more suitable franchisees ready to take up a franchise, one would expect the franchisor to use clauses designed to prevent additional sales from going begging. For example, those with a 'street address only' franchise may well see additional franchisees appointed nearby, they may even be offered the chance to buy the franchise themselves.[12] Either way, the combined turnover of the stores will rise more quickly than their combined profitability – favouring the franchisor rather than the franchisee since its income rises with franchisees' turnover and/or physical volume.

Such circumstances are not merely theoretical. Benetton, the knitwear and clothing chain, has recently used the absence of exclusivity obligations to its store owners to achieve just such an end (*Financial Times*, 3 November 1989). Based on a strategic decision that Benetton's future growth will come from opening stores close to the 5,900 already in operation, clusters of outlets have been opened in locations where the group is already well established. Consequently, several dissatisfied franchisees have voiced their concerns as the profitability of their outlets has fallen when competing Benetton stores have opened nearby (*International Business Week*, 14 March 1988; *Financial Times*, 7/8 July 1990).

Similar moves have also been detected in mobile franchises, where the franchisee serves a well defined geographical area from a van, often using their home as a base. These franchisors realize that:

> the 'comfort' level of our franchisees is never the level of actual business available in that market area. That's why we need a non-exclusive clause in our contracts to protect ourselves against a plateau of income beyond which we cannot expand.

> (field notes)

This is achieved by dividing territories into primary and secondary areas, thereby allowing the franchisor to appoint another franchisee in the secondary area at a specified date or if the franchisee underperforms. A major drain cleaning franchisor admits using this sanction 'as retaliation' against those franchisees who claim the right to pick and choose what work to do and where.

On the other side of the coin, a franchisee's suitability to run another franchised outlet will depend on his/her past performance and, *inter alia*, the 'realization of maximum sales' from their existing outlet (McDonald's Rewrite Policy).[13] Even for those franchises offering unqualified exclusivity, conditions may be placed on existing franchisees wishing to purchase other areas to ensure that the existing territory has been fully worked. For example, as a rule of thumb, a major network of car valeters in the UK requires expanding franchisees to have at least two vans on the road serving the existing territory before they are considered 'expandable'.

In times of economic downturn – with demand for franchised products/services falling and fewer would-be franchisees willing to risk setting up a business in less than fortuitous circumstances – franchisors are likely use the franchise contract more leniently (*Observer*, 28 April 1991). Targets may be disregarded, royalties may be deferred and credit may be extended. However, this provides franchisees with only temporary respite. In the end, the franchisor may terminate the franchisee rather than underwrite a franchisee's mounting royalty debts. The Tie Rack, the retail group specializing in ties, scarves and accessories, recently terminated contracts with eight franchisees who ran 19 shops between them. The terminations were issued on the grounds that franchisees 'breached their contracts with us in relation to standards of operation and payment of debt' (*Financial Times*, 8 April 1991; *Franchise World*, May–June 1991; *The Franchise Magazine*, Summer 1991). Other franchisors have repossessed and/or closed down franchisees who have failed to clear their debts with them, but without much publicity. For example, a sizeable (though not the largest) group of natural cosmetics shops closed 12 franchised shops and repossessed 17 during a four-year period from 1987. The franchisor bought back heavily indebted franchisees at a fraction of their initial set-up costs, leaving franchisees with bank debts often secured on the basis of personal guarantees backed by the collateral of their homes. Using the power to terminate appears widespread: over one-half of the franchisees who responded to our postal survey reported that they believed their franchisor had used the contract to terminate franchisees, mostly on the grounds of non-payment of royalties.

Although relatively rare, there are cases where franchisors may hold franchisees rigidly to the terms of their contracts even in times of recession. For example, during the recession in the 1930s and again in the 1950s, US car dealers were 'pushed . . . relentlessly for more sales, sales which were extremely difficult to make' (Macaulay, 1973: 24). Short of forfeiting the franchise, dealers could only sell more cars by reducing their profit margins to unprofitable levels. Many dealers were forced out of business as a result. This is likely to be the exception rather than the rule, however. Franchisors will want to maintain their networks with as few casualties as possible so as to safeguard their own revenue stream. Assisting franchisees with support teams, extending credit arrangements and restructuring payments can only provide franchisees with temporary breathing space. Franchisees may choose of their own accord to cease trading or, if royalty debts continue to mount, franchisors may have no alternative but to bring their agreements to an end.

Restricting the use of franchisor's intangible and tangible assets

The contractual powers designed to limit former franchisees' use of the franchisor's 'know-how' and the tangible assets in which it has a 'stake' are more uniformly deployed. Indeed, a franchisor's revenue stream rests heavily upon strategies that make it difficult, if not impossible, for a franchisee to operate without their assistance. By restricting the transfer of relevant 'know-how' and accumulated business experience to its franchisees alone, a franchisor is able to engender a dependent relationship from which a return is then drawn. This is an integral part of the franchise contract. Clauses relating to the disclosure and resale of 'know-how' and restrictions on ex-franchisees from operating similar types of businesses are aimed at tying a franchisee to a franchisor, thereby legitimating and sustaining the income of the latter. Issues of this kind were recently raised in a High Court action by Prontaprint, a chain of high street print shops, against one of its former franchisees (*Prontaprint Plc v. Landon Litho Limited* [1987] FSR 315). Given the importance of this case to franchising generally, it is worth a more detailed examination.[14]

The case concerned a Prontaprint franchisee who declined to renew his contract, but continued to trade at the same premises in the same type of business yet under a new name. The terms of the original agreement entered into, however, contained specific clauses restraining ex-franchisees from engaging in similar types of businesses, either directly or indirectly. The restrictions were to operate for a period of three years following termination/expiry, with the geographical extent of the limitation confined to within half a mile of the original premises and three miles from existing Prontaprint outlets (most franchise contracts contain similar restrictions, see Table 4.3).

Prontaprint claimed that by entering into an agreement of this kind, the franchisee was supported in the setting up and successful operation of a business about which they knew very little until Prontaprint's 'know-how' was made available to them. They also benefited from the goodwill attached to the Prontaprint name. Counsel for the ex-franchisee did not dispute that Prontaprint was a name which in fact acquired considerable goodwill. Rather, the franchisee's position was that the restrictions on ex-franchisees was unreasonable. Prontaprint had already received an initial payment – the franchise fee – for the use of the trade mark, 'know-how' and for the help and support given in setting up the business. In so far as additional assistance and 'know-how' was given thereafter, a percentage charge on turnover was levied. The ex-franchisee submitted that the business was one mainly built by the franchisee with Prontaprint having been paid for such contribution as they made during the life of the agreement. On expiry, Prontaprint no longer had an interest in the business, and as such it would be unreasonable for the franchisor to restrict the activities of an independent business.

The judgment found in favour of the franchisor upholding the duration of the restraint and its geographical coverage. Two main grounds for doing so were offered. The first was that if the former franchisee were entitled to operate from the same premises, albeit with a different name (Laserprint), they would still draw advantage from the Prontaprint name. In all local directories, including the *Yellow Pages*, anybody seeking printing services would, for some time, find under the name of Prontaprint the address and telephone number of Laserprint.[15] Furthermore, existing customers returning to where they would naturally expect to find a Prontaprint service, would find a competing service yet with the same faces greeting them. They might well assume that it was, in substance and effectively, the same business and they would not bother to go elsewhere. Indeed by displaying a notice on the window bearing the words 'Same Team, New Name' shortly after the franchise agreement came to an end, the ex-franchisee actively encouraged old and new customers to make just such an assumption.

The second reason for ruling in favour of the franchisor, lay in Prontaprint's 'know-how'. Without making this available to the franchisee it was argued that the business would not have been set up, let alone become a success:

> It is apparent that he [the franchisee] knew little about printing, buying paper, stationery and other things, and indeed about retail selling ... the defendants [the franchisee] were supported in the setting up of a business about which they really knew nothing until the plaintiffs [Prontaprint] told them what they should do to set up and successfully run a business of this kind.
>
> (Whitford J in *Prontaprint Plc v. Landon Litho Limited* [1987] FSR 315 at 317, 322)

On these grounds the court upheld the restrictions placed upon former franchisees. In giving his judgment, Mr. Justice Whitford, recognized the importance of the case to franchising more generally:

Quite plainly, if a covenant of this kind [restrictions on the activities of ex-franchisees] is unenforceable, as soon as they [franchisees] have managed to get going on the expertise, advice and assistance given to them by the plaintiffs [Prontaprint as well as franchisors more generally], other franchisees are going to either withdraw or not renew their agreements and franchising will, effectively, become inoperable. They [the franchisor] say that this is a perfectly reasonable restriction to protect the interest which they legitimately have in running a franchising business because, without a restraint of this kind, effectively running a franchising business is going to become impossible. (Whitford J in *Prontaprint Plc v. Landon Litho Limited* [1987] FSR 315 at 322)

In upholding the terms of the franchise agreement the court therefore maintained the franchisor's 'hold' over the franchisee by declaring it lawful for restrictions to be placed on the activities of the latter on termination or expiry of the agreement. As a result the franchise relationship and the contract in particular makes it difficult, if not impossible, for the franchisee to do without the franchisor. 'Know-how', like capital itself, becomes a social relation of production, and as such a source of power from which income can be drawn. The outcome of the specific case itself was that the former Prontaprint franchisee rejoined the chain, and as a result royalties continue to be paid.[16]

However, much uncertainty surrounds the enforceability of restraints of trade – clauses preventing competition against existing franchisees from persons who built up their knowledge and interest as former franchisees must not be too onerous.[17] Even so, the clause is often used to threaten those contemplating leaving their franchise networks in order to set up independently acting largely as 'a "club" to keep franchisees in line' (Ozanne and Hunt, 1971: 280). For example, a car valeting franchisee remarked:

Even if you simply terminate, the contract says you must give at least six months' notice and for a further six months you can't valet [in the territory]. With three more car parks likely to be offered to me [providing valeting on-site in supermarket car parks], I can't take this risk, so I'm tied to X almost indefinitely.

(field notes)

This clause, though, is weak in situations where the 'know-how' is commonplace and where the equipment supplied as part of the franchise package can readily be found elsewhere. Of this, many franchisees may simply not be aware.

Franchisors have a more secure 'hold' over franchisees in terms of the 'stakes' they often have in the tangible assets of the franchisee's business. For example, taking the head lease or owning outright the properties from which franchisees trade, offers franchisors a larger say in the operation of the business – both now and in the future. Franchise arrangements are not static: franchisees retire or die, occasionally they do not live up to their franchise obligations and must be replaced, and even if no such contingency occurs the agreements normally come to an end at a particular date. If franchisees own their own stores or hold the lease, any of these events could disrupt the franchisor's business and have an adverse effect on the system's goodwill. For example, buildings whose architecture identifies them as former McDonald's stores may sit idle or be used for other purposes. Replacement franchisees would have to acquire new and perhaps less desirable sites, a much more difficult process after the surrounding business area has matured. By owning its own stores (in the US; they are more likely to be leased in the UK), McDonald's assures its continued presence on the site, maintains the store's patronage even during management changes and avoids the negative publicity of having former McDonald's stores used for other purposes.[18]

Franchisors who hold the head lease or outright ownership of the properties from which franchisees operate therefore claim the right, as part of the sublease, to evict terminated franchisees or those who leave of their own accord. Franchisees terminated for non-payment of royalties, for example, can be replaced by company managers relatively easily. Indeed, the recent termination of eight Tie Rack franchisees and those of a natural cosmetics retailer have been made all the smoother by the franchisor–franchisee/head lease–sublease arrangement (*Franchise World*, May–June 1991). Similarly, those who leave their franchise networks voluntarily have been prevented from continuing to trade from properties in which their former franchisor has a say. For example, a Kall-Kwik franchisee gave due notice of their intention to leave their franchisor's network of high street print shops. However, after the period of notice had expired, they carried on the operation of an independent print shop from the same premises, refusing to assign with vacant possession the premises to the franchisor despite an agreement to do so (i.e. deed of option). The High Court upheld Kall-Kwik's right to exercise its contractual powers to take over the premises once the franchise contract came to an end (*Kall-Kwik Printing (UK) Ltd. v. Baypress and others* [1988] Journal of International Franchising and Distribution Law 152).

In mobile operations, the goodwill attached to the telephone number is often vigorously defended as it is invariably the only means by which customers can get in contact with the franchisee for the offer of work, requests for estimates and so on. This became particularly evident, for example, following the resignations (21) and terminations (5) which halved the number of franchisees in a major damp-proofing and timber treatment network in 1988. The franchisor's response was to use the contract to ensure that *inter alia* former franchisees would not be able to reap the advantages of a telephone number associated with the franchisor (especially as it would remain listed for some time in local directories such as the *Yellow Pages*). All former franchisees were therefore required to relinquish these telephone numbers, transferring them instead to the franchisor as per the franchise agreement. These telephone numbers were then reallocated to incoming franchisees to the vacated territories.[19]

While the making of franchise relationships is highly contractual – often encapsulated in lengthy and detailed documents – their usage is more difficult to gauge. This section has, however, provided some pointers as to circumstances in which franchisees are likely to be held to the terms of their contracts and those where franchisors are more likely to turn a blind eye. But as a rule 'when push comes to shove' franchisees are bound by a contract, the terms of which have been subject to little or no negotiation, but designed instead to safeguard and privilege the interests of franchisors ahead of theirs.

CONCLUSION

The chapter began by setting the growing interest in contractual relationships alongside the relative dearth of empirical evidence on their creation and use. Studies of written, legally binding contracts between businesses remain few and far between. Those which do exist have tended to focus on specific business contracts such as car dealerships (Kessler, 1957; Macaulay, 1973; Beale, Harris and Sharpe, 1989), construction contracts (Lewis, 1982) and petrol stations (Rehbinder, 1973).

This chapter was written in the same vein; it has focused on the contractual underpinnings of the franchisor–franchisee relationship. By analysing the contents of 83 franchise contracts it has answered three key questions: where does the operational control of the business reside; what are the financial linkages between franchisor and franchisee; and who owns and controls the business assets. None of the answers to these questions has been unambiguous or clear-cut. First, despite operating without close and direct supervision, franchisees are required to operate within procedures laid down and often subject to unilateral change. Moreover, franchisees are sometimes committed to adhere to franchisor-set performance targets, and, in any case, to give the aim of the franchisor (turnover maximization) primacy in the running of the business. Secondly, while they appropriate the profits (and losses) of the business, they do so only after they have made turnover-related payments to their franchisor. Thirdly, although franchisees buy or lease much of the physical business apparatus, some parts remain in the hands of the franchisor, and some have franchisor-imposed restrictions on their use both during and after the currency of the agreement. Furthermore, franchisees have no ownership rights in the intangible business assets – they simply 'borrow' the business idea, trading name and/or format.

Franchises also differ from one another quite markedly in terms of what is included and what is left out of a contract – there is no typical franchise contract. The index of contractual control makes this point – some contracts are 'harder' and some 'softer' than others. Whether contractual powers are used, however, is another matter. This will depend to a large extent on the nature of the market franchisees are 'fitted out' to face – a franchisor's desire for and customer expectation of uniformity will make the franchisor less tolerant of franchisees who do not follow the operations manual than a situation where uniformity is of lesser import. Franchisors are also unlikely to turn a blind eye to other contract violations (such as falling short of turnover targets, non-payment of royalties) and more likely to refuse to renew contacts, where the demand for franchised products/services is buoyant and there are plenty of suitable franchise candidates waiting for a franchise. Also, contractual powers to limit the use by a former franchisee of a franchisor's 'know-how' and any tangible assets in which it has a 'stake' are likely to be vigorously deployed.

The franchise contract sets the parameters of the franchisor–franchisee relationship, it is referred to if things go wrong, used to bring wayward franchisees back into line and protect the franchisor's goodwill. It is not surprising then that it shapes the franchise relationship, and that attempts to change its contents often prove contentious. The following two chapters consider the reasons behind and consequences of contractual change in two very different franchise networks – one successfully carried out, the other far less successful.

5 Changing franchisor ownership and its consequences

INTRODUCTION

The commercial environment in which franchising takes place is prone to change – franchisees may no longer have the appetite for growth, they may be too small to deliver low cost products and their customers may be unwilling to deal with a fragmented network (see Chapter 6). Alternatively, the franchisor may decide to sell the business. Quite apart from the uncertainty this will generate, the new owner may wish to make changes which significantly alter the nature of the franchise relationship. Changing franchisor ownership and its possible consequences is therefore the focus of this chapter.

In recent times, several franchisors – some with large networks – have been acquired by new owners. For example, in late 1988 Grand Metropolitan, the UK drinks and food group, acquired from Pillsbury the Burger King chain which comprised 5,900 restaurants worldwide with 86 per cent of them owned by franchisees (*Financial Times*, 21 November 1988). The acquisition of United Biscuits Restaurants a year later boosted Burger King's UK presence; it acquired a franchised estate of 381 Wimpy restaurants and 130 Perfect Pizza outlets, and 131 company-run Pizzalands (*Financial Times*, 9 August 1989). Since then it has converted 160 Wimpy restaurants to the Burger King format (adding to the 30 already operating in the UK) and sold the remaining table service restaurants to a group of former Wimpy managers (*Financial Times*, 17 April 1990). Pronuptia-Youngs, the complementary bridalwear and menswear hire chain, has also gone through several bouts of ownership change – rescued from receivership in the mid-1980s, sold in 1988, sold again in 1990 but not as a whole (Youngs stayed with its previous owner), and then reunited when the new owner of Pronuptia bought Youngs in the early part of 1992 (*Financial Times*, 29/30 December 1990; *Franchise World*, January–February 1992).

Other franchisors have also changed hands: in 1988 Prontaprint, the high street print chain, was bought by Continuous Stationery; while later on in the same year Kwik-Fit, the replacement exhaust and tyre chain, bought out Midas, one its competitors; at about the same time Curtainz, a retailer of ready-made curtains, was sold to Lonhro Textiles; and more recently Interlink, the express courier service, has been purchased by an Australian investor.

The recession which marked the beginning of the 1990s served to heighten the comings and goings of franchisors still further. Several franchisors have gone into receivership and have subsequently been sold to new owners. For example, a rival retailer of ready-made curtains bought the rights to acquire the shop leases and franchise contracts of 54 franchisees whose franchisor – Curtain Dream – had suddenly collapsed (*Independent*, 2 November 1989; *Franchise World*, January–February 1990). Similarly, Autosheen, a network of mobile car valeters, has been acquired by a group of investors from the receiver. New owners of the Body and Face Place, a retail chain of natural beauty products, and the hairdressing chains of Alan Paul, Raymond and Andre Bernard have been put in place in a similar way (*Franchise World*, January–February 1992).

Whatever the route – whether 'voluntary' or 'forced' – a change in who owns the franchise can have a dramatic effect on the nature of the franchisor–franchisee relationship. This chapter traces the consequences of one such ownership change at close quarters (Felstead, 1991a). It is based on a case study of a well-known and long established UK business format franchise of mobile car engine tuners taken over by another company in 1987. The new franchisor was a much larger company with interests in the import and sale of foreign cars in the UK, and ambitious plans to expand both its size and profits within ten years (*Motor Trader*, 16 July 1988). With little, if any, negotiation the new owners presented new contractual terms to franchisees designed to help them meet this corporate goal. Unwilling to go along with the proposed changes, 76 of the 113 CarCo[1] franchisees left to form AutoCo, a rival franchise network, 4 retired or else went independent, 32 signed the new agreement and one remained with CarCo but under the terms of the old agreement. Legal battles then ensued as Vehicle Dealers Limited (VDL) – the new owners of CarCo – tried to enforce a number of restrictive clauses on the activities of the break-away group. These actions were largely unsuccessful on the grounds that the clauses were too widely drawn to be enforceable. In the main, this was as far as the reports in the trade press went (e.g. *Franchise World*, May–July 1988; *Franchise Magazine*, Autumn 1988).

Even from these reports, it was apparent that research into the origins of the AutoCo break-away would provide a fitting case study for a project that sought to focus on the dynamics of the franchise relationship. After all, two-thirds of the fleet were clearly dissatisfied with the new terms and conditions they were offered. They voted with their feet and decided to *collectively* break-away, risking the uncertain and costly consequences of litigation.

In the light of previous chapters, the case study raises two sets of questions. The first concern the reasons why franchisees were unhappy with the new terms and conditions under which they were expected to operate. How did the franchise operate before the take-over? What difference would the proposed changes make? The second set of questions concerns the enforceability of franchise contracts. What terms of the old contract were used by the new owners to limit/stall the break-away? Why were they largely unsuccessful? This chapter attempts to provide answers to both sets of questions. The chapter is based on evidence collected via a survey of those franchisees who broke away, drawing upon completed questionnaires, follow-up interviews, and access to business and court documents. In addition, franchisor personnel, industry officials, consultants and solicitors were questioned about their role in the break-away (see pp.8–9 for further details).

The chapter begins by analysing the way in which franchisees operated prior to the take-over. Following the argument made in Chapter 4, three questions are considered with respect to the way franchisees conducted their mobile engine tuning businesses: where did the operational control of these businesses reside; what were the financial linkages between franchisor and franchisee; and who held the ownership title to, and control of, the business assets with which franchisees worked. The chapter then goes on to look at what difference the new contract would make to the way in which franchisees ran 'their' businesses. By adopting the 'hard–medium–soft' continuum the chapter argues that the proposed changes were intended to tighten the reins of control the franchisor held over the franchise network, shifting the franchise from the 'soft' towards the 'harder' end of the spectrum. An account is then given of the reasons why the franchisor was unable to make restrictive clauses in the old contract stick and therefore unable to prevent the break-away group from setting up in competition. This further underlines the 'softness' of the original franchise relationship. The chapter ends with a summary.

ORIGINAL FRANCHISE STRUCTURE

CarCo was established as one of the earliest business format franchisors in the UK in 1968. The franchisor was a family-owned and family-run business which actively sought to cultivate a paternalistic relationship between franchisor and franchisee (cf. Goffee and Scase, 1982). Its public pronouncements were that a franchisee was 'a customer, a partner and a friend, developing in that order' (franchise prospectus, 1985). Its actions appeared to support this philosophy. For example, in 1975 the franchisor set up and contributed to a Charitable Fund which deserving franchisees and their families could call upon in times of need. CarCo also helped to set up a franchisee association (known as the Franchise Advisory Board or FAB) whose six members stood for election annually with one-third standing down every three years. Its purpose was to remove the 'them and us situation' (quoted from letter setting up the FAB, March 1982) and replace it with stronger bonds of 'togetherness'.

The franchise itself is based on a system of tuning cars and a novel way of delivering the service to the customer. The system operates on site – either at the customer's home or their place of work – avoiding the inconvenience of taking the car to the garage and having to arrange alternative transportation. The franchisee takes a fully kitted vehicle – equipped with an electronic analyser and a stock of replacement parts – to the customer's car and carries out a 74-point check and adjustment programme which electronically diagnoses engine performance and identifies problems.[2] The complete process takes between one and two hours, leaving the car engine running more smoothly, starting better and using less fuel than previously.

The amount of investment required to become a CarCo franchisee was modest; franchisees operated from home, and the set-up costs could be further reduced if franchisees took up the option to lease both their van and equipment. Prior to the takeover it took £8,500 to become a CarCo franchisee. The franchise network grew to a peak of 240 vans on the road operated by 120 franchisees in 1981. But by 1987 the number of vans on the road had shrunk to 180 operated by virtually the same number of franchisees (113). To assess the nature of the franchisor–franchisee relationship three dimensions need to be considered: the conditions under which engine tuning was carried out; the on-going payments made to the franchisor; and who owned, and controlled, the vans, equipment and telephone lines with which franchisees worked. Each is considered in turn in the remainder of this section as they applied under the original regime; the following section considers the same dimensions under the new regime with comparisons being drawn.

Operational controls

Definitions of business format franchising (such as the one given in Chapter 2) often refer to the supports provided by the franchisor to ensure that the franchisee is able to duplicate or clone the success of the franchisor. Indeed, the British Franchise Association requires that its members have successfully piloted their operation before being admitted to membership.[3] However, CarCo never piloted its operation, nor was any territory ever run by the company to keep track of developments in the market.

Furthermore, many of the supports that should theoretically have been provided by the franchisor were never provided, or else were reported to be of a poor quality. Over 50 per cent of the break-away respondents, for example, reported training to be poor to the extent that one franchisee remarked that it 'was marginally better than pathetic' (field notes). Instead franchisees often made private arrangements to obtain training in order to keep themselves abreast with the rapid changes in engine technology. The operations manual – theoretically thought to lay down guidelines covering all aspects of the business – was similarly less than extensive and was reported to cover just four pages. Only after pressure from the fleet through the Franchise Advisory Board was a technical manual covering mobile vehicle tuning produced. Even then it was written by some of the franchisees, and simply edited and circulated by CarCo. Field support was virtually non-existent with almost three-quarters of respondents reporting that it was either poor or simply not provided by the franchisor. Forty per cent believed CarCo employed no one to visit franchisees in the field, while over 50 per cent reported that they had either never received a visit or that these had taken place at yearly or longer intervals (most visits coming in the year before their departure, and then only to encourage or cajole them to sign the new agreement).

In this respect CarCo was far from unique. Franchisors are often vague when it comes to detailing the services they provide franchisees (cf. p. 96). Commitments to provide an operations manual, on-going support, training and technical advice can be minimally fulfilled. Franchisors need only prepare a flimsy manual, provide training only at the time of entry, and respond reactively, rather than proactively, to franchisees' technical and business enquiries. Rarely, if ever, are the obligations on franchisors made specific. This makes for the possibility of a serious mismatch of expectations between franchisees and franchisors as to what support services the franchisor will provide in practice, and has consequently been the most common source of disputes in the past (and one suspects in the future too). This is compounded further by the fact that any oral commitments given by the franchisor detailing the more specific support services to be provided are not enforceable in law.[4]

The lack of a detailed operations manual, the lack of regular visits and the nature of the work itself gave CarCo franchisees significant scope to tune cars in whatever way they saw fit. Rather than providing a tried and tested formula or system of operation, CarCo franchisees were often 'told to get out tuning' (field notes) and many simply learnt on-the-job. The looseness of this arrangement is best explained by the nature of the product market franchisees served – customers would rarely be in a position to compare the standards of service offered between franchisees, and in any case this would be dependent on the diagnostic skills of each franchisee and not on the close adherence to a manual.

Indeed, the changing nature of engine tuning itself further emphasized the importance of the 'know-how' acquired by franchisees on-the-job. The increased use of electronics in many new cars has broadened the skills required of engine tuners. As yet affordable tuning equipment capable of removing much of the discretion and skills associated with the increasingly varied diagnostic process is not within sight. Area testing rather than detailed testing is the best the equipment can do, leaving the exact pinpointing of faults to the skills acquired by the tuner. As one franchisee put it:

> engine tuning is not like cooking a burger, or a fried chicken, or even selling cars. I've been tuning since 1974 and I'll never stop learning. Most franchise operations can be learnt in a very short time, this one can't.
>
> > (written on questionnaire)

The comparison with other sectors where franchising has taken root is particularly interesting since, in most, the labour process has become increasingly de-skilled. This is most striking in fast food and many of the retail-type franchises where stores are 'fitted out' with automated equipment (such as electronic point of sale tills and automated cookers), and where many of the products supplied are prepared by manufacturers *before* they reach the store (cf. Bluestone and Huff Stevenson, 1981; Levitt, 1972; Dunne, 1988). Even the small amount of discretion that remains is closely monitored through an analysis of franchisees' inventory and sales reports, which can in turn be used to determine whether the store is getting the appropriate yields and meeting minimum standards. For example, McDonald's can check a franchisee's order for supplies against their actual sales to indicate whether the store is putting the correct amount of ketchup on the hamburger, the appropriate amount of french fries in a bag or achieving wastage rates not significantly different from the average (burgers should stand for a maximum of ten minutes and then be thrown away). In short, the separation of conception and execution of tasks is most sharply delineated in these types of franchise, whereas in engine tuning the division appears, if anything, to be increasingly blurred, offering little scope or incentive for uniformity.

In addition, CarCo's policy of granting franchisees an exclusive territory within which to work gave franchisees autonomy to shape the development of their businesses as they saw fit. In order to expand their businesses without buying neighbouring territories, franchisees were allowed to increase the number of vans they had on the road by taking on sub-operators. Under this arrangement the franchise holder could pyramid his/her (almost invariably his) territory to a second tier of operators who would be supplied with vans, equipment and work directly for the franchisee. The sub-operator would typically retain 45 per cent of the labour cost of the tune, the franchisee would receive 45 per cent and CarCo the remaining 10 per cent (as it would have done if the tune had been performed by the franchisee). The recruitment of sub-operators was the franchisee's responsibility subject to CarCo's approval, while their training was the responsibility of the franchisee.

The three-way relationship between franchisor, franchisee and sub-operator has clear parallels with territorial or master franchising. Under the latter arrangement a franchisor sells an exclusive area, either a country or state, to a master/territorial franchisee (Justis and Judd, 1986). While the franchisor might be obliged to provide some very basic assistance in setting up the first operation and some fundamental training concerning the system of operation, most of the initial fees collected from the master/territorial franchisee drop to the franchising company's bottom line. Master/territorial franchisees then sell parts of their territory to a second tier of operators, collecting up-front fees from each one. Although the sub-operator structure operated by CarCo did not entail the sale of territories, its systemwide effects were similar to that generated by the sale of master/territorial franchises.[5] This had a number of consequences.

First, this structure made it extremely difficult to exert central control over the development of the network. Territorial franchisees could either increase the number of vans operating in their area or else remain a one-person van operation. The franchisor had little control over this, despite the fact that its income rose and fell according to the numbers of tunes completed. In well developed territories 'so-called baron operators emerged wielding a great deal of power, influence and large amounts of turnover within the fleet' (field notes). Or as one franchisee put it, the sub-operator structure made for 'an uncontrollable feudal-type franchise' (field notes). With almost all parts of the UK having a CarCo franchisee, CarCo had little ability to raise its market share and generate enough profit for the new owners under this set-up. Secondly, by training sub-operators themselves, franchisees could inculcate them with their own particular methods and practices and hence add a further tier over which the franchisor had little or no operational control.

Given the situation outlined above, it is perhaps rather unsurprising that when asked to rate the level of independence they enjoyed under the original regime, over 80 per cent gave scores of 1 or 2 on a scale ranging from 1 (total independence) to 5 (manager in all but name). Similarly, almost 70 per cent of our respondents reported that they exercised 'a great deal of freedom in running their business', while the remainder reported that they exercised 'a reasonable amount within guidelines'.

Respondents were further asked to give a score between 1 and 6 to indicate where the burden of responsibility lay on seven key strategic business decisions – hours of operation, book-keeping systems, product range, local advertising, price setting, the number of sub-operators and the terms under which they were required to operate. A score of 1 indicated that CarCo had complete responsibility, a score of 6 that the franchisee had complete responsibility, and there were gradations in between these two extremes. Over all but two of the seven decisions – price setting and the terms and conditions on which sub-operators worked – franchisees claimed to have more responsibility than their franchisor. This prompted one respondent to write:

> I suspect we were given too much freedom for CarCo to exist as a true franchise.
>
> (written on questionnaire)

Indeed it may not be too wide off the mark to suggest that CarCo franchisees 'behaved more like "licensees" than franchisees' in that they received little or no ongoing operational support (quote taken from a circular letter from VDL to all members of the CarCo fleet shortly after the take-over).

Financial linkages

Despite the absence of many operational controls found in 'harder' franchise systems, CarCo franchisees still remained part of a wider process of capital accumulation. Although franchisees retained most of their own profits, they still contributed to the profits of their franchisor. CarCo levied a 10 per cent royalty on the labour content of each tune, and marked-up or else retained the commission it received on the products and services it supplied to its franchisees (such as spares, insurance, equipment and out-of-guarantee repairs). It was recognized by the fleet that while 'the 10 per cent was theoretically for a lot of things, in reality it simply gave eight letters down the side of the van and technical back-up if required' (field notes). In other words, the franchise amounted to little more a rent-a-name scheme. Once the name had been promoted by the franchisee in his/her territory, though, the 10 per cent royalty plus mark-ups represented retainers on the use of a trade name they had themselves helped to promote. This was less so for 'baron' operators since their sub-operators paid the 10 per cent royalty charge to CarCo.

Interestingly enough, the original contract made no levy for advertising (compared with two-thirds of those franchise contracts examined in Chapter 4). However, a 4 per cent advertising levy was introduced, albeit briefly, in 1982. For existing franchisees, it was introduced under a clause in the agreement which bound franchisees to matters not included in the agreement but approved by at least 75 per cent of franchisees. One-half of each franchisee's payments could be recovered for approved local advertising and marketing expenses (such as *Yellow Pages* advertising), the remainder was used for national campaigns which the franchisor 'shall in its discretion think fit'. After two years the marketing levy was removed in the same way as it had been introduced – 75 per cent of franchisees voted against it. But once again the original franchise regime gave franchisees greater latitude than is common in many franchise agreements. This was used to reject what is a central pillar of many franchise agreements, further underlining its 'softness'.

Ownership and control of business assets

The link between franchisor and franchisee is commonly buttressed by the franchisor taking propriety rights over some aspects of the business in addition to the trade name. Typically this amounts to a contractual clause which attempts to maintain the franchisor's proprietary rights over the 'know-how' or intellectual property associated with the business. As a consequence, former franchisees are prohibited from competing directly with the franchisor or the company's franchisees for a specified period of time within a clearly defined geographical area (known as the 'non-compete' clause). Courts demand a very precise definition of what the former franchisee is barred from doing, for whom, and for how long, as well as where. Furthermore, without a secret process or the use of secret equipment this clause is weak. In the case of CarCo, the use of a piece of car tuning equipment that could be readily found in other mobile car tuning organizations as well as in garages and tuning centres hardly constituted a trade secret, making its enforce-ability doubtful. The non-solicitation clause – preventing former fran-chisees from touting customers, whom they had served while a fran-chisee, for business – needs to be similarly drafted, so that it protects the franchisor's legitimate client base while not being unduly restrictive on the activities of former franchisees (see pp. 152–155).

Franchisors often seek to strengthen their control over the franchisee through the ownership of some of the physical as opposed to mental means of production. As illustrated in Chapter 4, this commonly takes the form of franchisors taking the head-lease and offering franchisees an under-lease in premises-based franchises. This policy has been declared publicly by major franchisors:

> If your business needs sites, you should find them and keep them under your control. The occupation of a site by a franchisee should depend on the continuation of the franchise relationship . . . With the control of the sites you have real control of your business . . . Once you have them they should not be handed over to the control of franchisees.
>
> (*Franchise World*, May–July 1988: 18)

CarCo's policies to control franchisees through the ownership of some of the physical means of production remained weak. Only those franchisees with limited capital resources were 'tied' to CarCo through the restrictive clauses written in to leasing agreements on vans and equipment which lowered the capital threshold on entry and/or expan-sion. The leases were provided through CarCo's leasing arm and as such contained clauses which gave CarCo the right to remove or repossess any equipment under lease in the event that the franchise agreement was terminated for any reason. More important, however, telephone numbers were the property of the franchisee. Since these represent the 'front door' for mobile tuners (and many home-based franchises for that matter), CarCo's lack of control over such a 'life-line' (field notes) severely diluted its control over franchisees. As soon as a franchisee ceased to remain with CarCo for whatever reason, the goodwill associated with the original telephone number was retained by the franchisee but lost by the franchisor.

Under the original franchise structure, operational controls, revenue links with the franchisor, and the ownership and control of the business assets with which franchisees worked all pointed towards a 'soft' franchise relationship. Shortly after the take-over, it became clear that the original franchise structure would be unable to meet everyone's desires. The new owners had ambitious expansion plans which could not be accommodated within the existing structure; a show-down therefore seemed inevitable as they sought to 'harden' the franchise relationship.

TIGHTENING THE REINS

The new owners (VDL) took over CarCo with two inter-related aims in mind. First, by acquiring relatively small businesses with growth potential, VDL aimed to double its size within ten years and thereby help it to meet its publicly declared profit target of £8 million by 1995. Second, it sought to acquire complementary businesses to its core motor trade activities and those additional interests it acquired. As a result, it acquired the master franchise to set up a chain of quick lubrication centres in the UK in 1986 (by that time there were already over 500 franchisees operating the system in the US). The plan was for the quick lubrication centres to act as a base and a regional booking office for about ten CarCo vans. However, both aims could not be achieved without change, or in the words of an internal management report, without 'a tightening of the reins'.

The acquisition itself was made through a rather unusual route. The original franchise agreement contained no clause permitting the franchisor to assign franchise agreements to another company. Since VDL was only interested in buying the CarCo franchise and not other parts of CarCo's business (e.g. CarCo's leasing arm), franchisees were asked to sign a 'letter of novation' transferring their contracts from CarCo Ltd to CarCo (UK) Ltd. It also extended the terms of franchisees' original agreements to 31 March 1988 if they were due to expire before that date (this applied to about one-half of franchisees). At this stage, franchisees were unaware that the franchise system was under new ownership. However, when the change in ownership was announced, it was accompanied by the news that a new agreement would be prepared and presented to the fleet, but only after consultation with the FAB.

Despite the uncertainty generated by the takeover and the suddenness with which it took place, over half of those who eventually broke-away to form AutoCo thought the take-over was a good thing. Yet for months little, if any, consultation took place on the changes VDL intended to make. The feeling of being left out was further compounded when an internal management report on the CarCo franchise was leaked to the FAB. Rumours and uncertainty were rife. When the franchise agreement was finally presented to the fleet it was unanimously rejected. Minor modifications were made, but the spirit of the new agreement remained intact. Fearing the consequences for the operation of their businesses, 76 franchisees 'voted with their feet' by leaving the network to set up a rival franchise. This section considers in what ways the new agreement sought to 'tighten the reins' (see Table 5.1 for chronology).

Table 5.1 Presentation of new contract: a chronology

Date	Event
12 February 1987	Letter of novation – assigning contracts from CarCo Ltd to CarCo (UK) Ltd, extending contracts which expire within the next year to 31 March 1988, reinstating those whose contracts have already expired up to 31 March 1988 (extension and reinstatement affecting about 55 franchisees) and leaving the expiry date of those with more than a year to run unaffected.
5 March 1987	Franchise founder announces that CarCo has been sold to Vehicle Dealers Limited.
14–15 March 1987	Annual CarCo Conference – VDL present themselves and an outline of their plans to the fleet. Announcement that a new franchise agreement will be prepared. All franchisees will be asked to sign, but only after full consultation with the FAB.
14 April 1987	FAB meet VDL for a tour of office and warehouse facilities.
May 1987	Regional meetings with franchisees to discuss their views and fears on points of contention within a new franchise agreement (meetings of about 10 franchisees). Internal document is produced for VDL management. It warns of 'exodus' if 'strong' agreement is sought. The document is leaked to the FAB.
29 July 1987	Meeting between the FAB and VDL at VDL's headquarters. Frustration that the FAB is not being consulted on matters of concern to franchisees – no clear idea of what VDL intends. VDL unwilling to present draft new agreement to the FAB until it has been given to the entire fleet.
2 September 1987	Presentation of new contract to Franchisee Conference. Brought forward from original date in November. All 113 franchisees attend. The draft new agreement is rejected unanimously by a show of hands.
20 September 1987	FAB meet to discuss response. Ten-point list of objections drawn up. Entire fleet is contacted by telephone to test response to the new terms: 80 per cent of the fleet are not prepared to sign the new contract.

Table 5.1 contd

Date	Event
21 September 1987	FAB asks VDL to reconsider the contract in the light of the fleet's response.
7 October 1987	FAB meets VDL, but only cosmetic changes to the draft agreement are made – replacing royalties of 14 per cent of turnover with 17.5 per cent of labour content.
8 October 1987	VDL writes to the fleet making it clear that 'no further changes to the agreement are possible' and that 'it is now up to each individual to decide what is best for himself and his family'.
October 1987	VDL management begin to meet franchisees on an individual basis.
18 October 1987	Franchisees meet to discuss their collective response. Eighty-one out of a possible 113 attend. Seventy-nine franchisees sign petition declaring their intention to refuse to sign the new agreement, 77 declare their willingness to join a cooperative. £1,220 is raised in 'whip-round' for fighting fund.
18 November 1987	New prices for leasing vans and equipment from VDL's finance arm, only 'available to those who have signed the new agreement'.
18 December 1987	Waiver agreements on telephones – (1) allows franchisees wishing to keep their telephone numbers to do so, provided they join regional booking offices if set-up and provided they undertake to give up their telephone number on termination; and (2) allows franchisees to keep their booking centres provided they meet certain specified standards and provided they agree to assign their telephone numbers when their franchise terminates. Franchisees are also advised that 'the Board would approve no further changes to the agreement'.
24 January 1988	FAB organizes a meeting of the CarCo fleet to consider response. Seventy-six franchisees agree to resign or not seek renewal after the 31 March 1988.
9 March 1988	British Franchise Association tries to mediate in the dispute, but is unsuccessful. Thirty-eight franchisees have already served notice of their intention to leave the network on 30 April 1988.
31 March 1988	Thirty-eight franchisees leave the CarCo network and join AutoCo instead.
30 April 1988	After serving three months' notice, a further 38 CarCo franchisees leave to join AutoCo.

Source: sworn affidavits, correspondence and interview material.

Operational controls

> In all honesty, we *will* be more demanding, we *will* demand that operators commit themselves to success; commit themselves to professional standards; commit themselves to growth.
>
> (letter circulated to all CarCo franchisees from VDL, sender's emphasis)

A simple comparison of the obligations placed upon franchisees under the old contract with those placed upon them under the new contract bears this out. Franchisee obligations grew from four to eleven pages and the clauses themselves became much more extensive. Three examples can be cited to illustrate the point. First, a set of new clauses allowed the franchisor to insist that all supplies of equipment and consumables must be purchased from them. This imposed a severe restriction on the franchisee while adding to the franchisor's income. Furthermore, in the absence of a pricing provision the franchisee could not be certain that the franchisor's prices would be competitive. Secondly, under the new contract franchisees were obliged to provide the franchisor with any information it deemed fit, thereby providing CarCo with a carte blanche. Thirdly, the new contract obliged franchisees to use their best endeavours to meet targets set down by the franchisor. There was no provision for the franchisor to act reasonably, seek independent advice or consult with the franchisee. While it is doubtful whether any court would allow this to be used to engineer grounds for termination, it could certainly be used to harass a franchisee.

Granting franchisees an exclusive territory within which to work – as CarCo had previously done – was a 'double-edged sword'. On the one hand, it prevented competing franchisees from free-riding on the activities of others, thereby strengthening the incentives to develop the market. But, on the other hand, franchisees may have reached 'comfort levels' from which they were unwilling to expand and develop their territories any further. The evidence suggests (or at least there was the belief) that many in the CarCo network had reached this point:

> [Franchisees] feel resentful that [VDL] ... now expects them to contribute further sweat and funds at a time when many were growing accustomed to a level of comfort.
>
> (letter circulated to all CarCo franchisees from VDL)

Under the original regime, the only control CarCo had over the development of a territory was the setting of a minimum number of tunes to be completed one year after setting up. This was set at 40 tunes per month; a level widely recognized within AutoCo to be low, to the point of it being difficult to keep the business afloat at such a level. CarCo's right to terminate the franchise contract should the number of tunes fall below this level was therefore something of an empty threat as bankruptcy/the cessation of trading probably loomed much larger.

The new contract, on the other hand, contained much stronger powers to penalize those who fail to develop their territories sufficiently. Three separate sets of clauses gave the franchisor these powers. First, in the event of a franchisee failing to achieve 'substantial' turnover within one year of the agreement or any other 12 month period, the franchisor had the option to terminate the agreement, appoint others to help the franchisee (at the franchisee's cost) and/or reduce the primary area of the franchise. This clause would have been particularly hazardous for franchisees whose business was slow to develop or those who suffered from a slack trading period. It also gave the franchisor wide scope in its interpretation of 'substantial'. It may well be that a court would impose a very strict obligation of implied reasonableness upon the franchisor, but not many franchisees would have been able to afford to litigate the point or would have wished to do so if the franchisor decided to take up its options.

Secondly, franchisees' existing territories were split into primary and secondary areas with the franchisor having rights to expand or contract the boundaries of either. The new contract made retention of the former contingent on hitting franchisor-determined performance targets (as outlined above). It also allowed the franchisor to 'at any time . . . vary the extent of the Secondary Area either by increasing or reducing the same or by substituting one area for another'. This gave the franchisor greater control over the development of the business, a point readily acknowledged by CarCo's new management:

> We reserve the right to place a vehicle in the franchisee's secondary area if he does not wish to, or if he is not ready to expand through poor performance. There would be an element of negotiation before we place a new franchisee in a secondary area, but it would not be legal negotiation.
>
> (internal management report: 3)

Clauses on the placement of additional vans were drafted in a similar spirit. The new contract gave the franchisor the right to require that more vans be placed on the road in any primary area if *it* decided that the area is 'sufficiently large geographically or has a sufficiently large population or sufficient customer demand to justify one or more further vans'. Should the incumbent franchisee refuse to put another van on the road, the franchisor had the option to reduce the size of the franchisee's primary area. Franchisees would be given financial compensation if their areas were reduced in size. However, this was set at £10 for every tune carried out in the reclaimed area for the previous 12 months, with no account for inflation or the cost of the tuning service being made.

Measuring the performance of franchisees according to franchisor-determined targets, making territories dependent on 'good' performance and requiring additional vans to be placed on the road when the franchisor thinks fit, would have altered the way in which franchisees operated their businesses in two ways. First, the quality of the service to the customer would have suffered. The incentive to take as read many of the checks necessary for a thorough engine tune would be increased. First, and even second, order faults found on verification would go unnoticed as franchisees sought to meet monthly tuning targets. Secondly, a franchisee's security of territorial tenure would be severely undermined, it would be 'a case of heads they win, tails you lose' (field notes). The contract gave the franchisor the powers to constantly reset targets that were met at higher and higher levels, while those who failed to reach these targets would face the prospect of having their ' "undeveloped" territories [and even their primary area] confiscated' (written on questionnaire) and then sold for a further one-off franchise fee to a new recruit.

Financial linkages

In addition to raising franchisor income by increasing the number of tunes completed, the new contract was designed to achieve the same objective through a more direct route. Under the old agreement the management services fee was set at 10 per cent of the labour content of tuning work (i.e. excluding parts). Initially, it was proposed to broaden the method of calculation to franchisees' *turnover*, thereby raising the payments made to the franchisor. An additional payment of 4 per cent of turnover was also proposed as a marketing fee. This was eventually changed to 12.5 per cent and 5 per cent of the *labour content* respectively – making it one of the most visible changes to the franchise relationship. To ensure that the increased fees were actually paid in full the new contract permitted franchisor access to franchisees' VAT returns, thereby preventing franchisees under-declaring their income for the purposes of royalty calculation.

Apart from increasing payments to the franchisor, franchisees had at least two further reservations about the change. In the first place, the franchisor must or should have been using at least part of the original 10 per cent management services fee on advertising, so the marketing services fee had the effect of replacing some of the pre-existing advertising budget, thereby generating greater profit for the franchisor. Secondly, the way in which the franchisor was permitted to use the marketing fund could be broadly interpreted. It committed the franchisor to use the funds 'to promote, market, extend and develop the Service and the Trade Name in such manner as the Franchisor in its absolute discretion thinks fit'. This could enable the funds to be applied to the general development of CarCo's business, including the extension of the franchise network, in a manner that would not necessarily be to the benefit of franchisees. However, although these were the most visible and immediate changes to the franchise relationship 'it soon became the least of our worries as our independence was threatened far more in other ways' (field notes).

Ownership and control of business assets

One of these changes concerned the proposed ownership arrangements for the business telephone line, vans and equipment. Under the new contract, CarCo would be the sole subscriber for all telephone lines used by its franchisees for business purposes. Franchisees were fearful that 'by taking our phone lines – our life-line – the franchisor would be able to pull the plug at any time, if they so desired' (field notes). The importance of who owns the telephone line should not be under-estimated. During one month a franchisee who signed the new agreement but has since left recorded the diversion of 113 customer calls from a telephone line in his house to CarCo's headquarters. However, the concern was compounded by a clause committing franchisees to participate in the setting up of a regionalized or centralized booking office should the franchisor deem it appropriate.

If implemented, regionalized or centralized booking offices were thought to have two consequences. First, they would break the link between the customer and the tuner since all customer calls would go through a third party. As a result the personal touch would be diluted, and the number of call-backs increased as queries could no longer be dealt with directly over the telephone by the tuner. Secondly, for many franchisees who broke away the prospect of centralized booking offices meant that CarCo had the 'makings of becoming another AA-type service, with head office taking the calls, farming it out to patrol men who would then do the work' (field notes). Franchisees would be left with little control over the planning of their working day, what cars they were prepared to tune, what areas they were prepared to work, and for how long. Even holidays would have to be booked in advance. In short:

We wouldn't really control our own businesses, but would instead be controlled by an anonymous person. We had become franchisees to control our own destiny, and so we didn't want to be told what, when and where to do our next tune.

(field notes)

VDL foresaw the reaction of franchisees to the proposed changes to telephone ownership, but did too little too late to successfully counteract it. The ownership of telephone lines was:

one of those areas that hardly raises eyebrows at the start of a franchise, but can cause endless trouble if changed . . . their [franchisees'] reaction to losing (as they see it) their phones is likely to be very strong.

(internal management report: 6)

Only belatedly was the clause waived and replaced with two slightly weaker options (see Table 5.1). One allowed franchisees to retain ownership of their telephone numbers for the time being provided they agreed to join regional booking offices if, and when, they were set up and provided they undertook to give up their telephone number on termination. The other option allowed franchisees to operate their own booking centres provided they met certain specified standards and provided they agreed to assign their telephone numbers when their franchise came to an end. Yet either option simply delayed rather than annulled the switch from the franchisee owning and controlling the telephone line (i.e. the source of work) to the franchisor. Given the five-year term of the agreement, this could only postpone the inevitable for at most five years.

The new owners of CarCo were also keen that franchisees either lease their vans and testing equipment (i.e. digital engine analyser) through its financing arm or else rent them directly from CarCo. Both would ensure that franchisees did not hold outright ownership of the operating equipment, thereby further enhancing their dependence on CarCo. However, this preference could only be pursued with new recruits to the fleet 'who will accept what we say' (internal management report: 4) or existing operators who qualified for expansion.

As indicated in Chapter 4, the making of contacts can differ from their actual usage. This point was repeatedly made by CarCo's new owners:

There has been disquiet at the determination we have shown, and the fact that we have only been willing to consult, not negotiate [on the new contract]. There is a real concern that once they [franchisees] sign the new agreement, independence will disappear, and that we will 'hound' them with its detailed requirements . . . let me assure you that whilst *we certainly expect all its provisions to be performed*, we are not so stupid as to have it at the forefront of every franchisee conversation.

(letter circulated to all CarCo franchisees from VDL, my emphasis)

Many of those who left to form AutoCo were in little doubt that the contract was there to be used to further VDL's aggressive growth plans. VDL expected the proposed contract to provoke 'one almighty punch-up' and that some franchisees 'would vote with their feet' (internal management report: 8–9). Presumably, however, VDL judged that this short-term cost – measured in terms of lost royalties from those who left – was worth the long-term benefit of a contract 'drawn up to control and drive the franchise forward' (internal management report: 1).

The new contract was designed to tighten the reins: targets were set and could be varied from area to area; the decision to place so many vans in any area was switched from franchisee to franchisor; areas were no longer treated as exclusive; royalties were raised; and ownership of the business telephone lines, vans and equipment was placed more firmly in the hands of the franchisor. This strengthened CarCo's contractual powers, shifting it towards the 'harder' end of the 'hard–soft' continuum. Recognition of the shift was the root cause of the franchisee break-away:

> The contract was very draconian, they'd thought of every way they could to pin you down, everything was designed to keep us under control. They were talking about partnership, but the contract meant that we'd lose control over our businesses.
>
> (field notes)

The new powers given to the franchisor were considered too broad and intrusive to be acceptable to two-thirds of the fleet. Almost nine out of ten franchisees who broke away held the view that the new contract would convert them from entrepreneurs into employees. It would represent:

> no more working for yourself than working for British Leyland [*sic*], yet with none of the benefits of employee status and all of the disadvantages of self-employment.
>
> (field notes)

It was on this basis that 76 out of 113 CarCo franchisees voted with their feet, by leaving the network to set up a rival chain.

VOTING WITH THEIR FEET

To counterbalance the power of franchisors, franchisees have sometimes grouped together to form associations.[6] Some franchisors have actively encouraged the setting up of franchisee associations in the hope that they will encourage two-way communication between franchisor and franchisee on ways and means to improve the system. However, franchisee associations have often found it difficult to be effective. The distances separating franchisees may make regular meetings difficult, franchisees put in such long hours that they may not have time to attend meetings and, regarding themselves as 'independent entrepreneurs', they are more likely to shun, rather than embrace, activities associated with collectivism (Bechhofer and Elliot, 1978). A common threat, though, is likely to coalesce the interests of franchisees and activate their association, if they have one (or prompt the setting up of one if they do not).

The presentation of a new contract, the perception that VDL intended to 'tighten the reins' over the franchise network and expiry of about half of the fleet's contracts on the same day all served to lay the foundations for a collective response. The Franchise Advisory Board became the nucleus around which this response was formed. Whereas the threat of litigation against individual franchisees might have been enough to ensure that the new owners of CarCo got their way, the presence of a collective grouping allowed a pooling of resources and gave franchisees an ability to resist CarCo's demands.

The FAB decided to make plans to break away if the contract was not radically revised. VDL's reply was two-pronged. First, it continued to approach franchisees on an individual basis in an attempt to allay their fears and persuade them to sign the new contract – 85 franchisees were reportedly approached in this way (*Motor Trader*, 21 May 1988). Second, it 'tried every trick in the book to make things difficult for the break-away group' (field notes, interview with CarCo management). This included attempts to prevent preparatory arrangements being made for a break-away, protection of the goodwill attached to telephone numbers advertised in CarCo's name, and enforcement of a clause limiting by whom and how former customers can be approached for business once the break-away has taken place. The outcome of these court room battles is important for two reasons. First, for the practical reason that they allowed the break-away group to set up virtually unhindered by legal restrictions. Second, since the legal arguments used serve to further underscore the 'softness' of the original franchise relationship. With these points in mind, the main areas of the legal battle are considered below. A chronology of the legal battle is given in Table 5.2.

Table 5.2 A chronology of the legal battle

Date	Event	Outcome
23 December 1987	VDL claims four franchisees are in breach of contract: (1) engaging in another 'business activity' without consent – attempting to recruit shareholders/franchisees, preparing stationery and trade marks and sorting out finance while still CarCo franchisees; and (2) 'passing off' by using a similar sounding name to CarCo.	Denial that franchisees are in breach of contract since the company is inactive and the company's name has in any case been changed.
28 January 1988	Writ served on four CarCo franchisees and a summons seeking an injunction restraining their involvement in any non-CarCo business activity without the consent of the franchisor.	Undertaking that until their contracts expire, they will not be involved in any other business activity. They will not seek to encourage or solicit the resignation of CarCo franchisees/ employees or custom for any other business than their CarCo franchise. Also they will not seek to promote or advertise any other business.
3 May 1988	CarCo instructs British Telecom to transfer Auto-Co's telephone numbers to its head office and allocate new numbers in their place. AutoCo seeks injunction preventing transfer.	Injunction granted – provided callers are made aware that they are no longer associated with CarCo but trade under the name of AutoCo, all advertising linking the telephone number with CarCo ceases, all reference to CarCo ends and instructions to remove CarCo entries in telephone directories are dispatched forthwith.
24 June 1988	Committal proceedings brought against two franchisees for allegedly breaching undertaking given above – referring to CarCo in an advert in local weekly newspaper.	Inadvertent nature of breach accepted by the court.
19 July 1988	Evidence of circular being widely distributed to former CarCo customers – offering discount on work and referring to former association with CarCo. Flagrant breach of undertaking given above and post-termination clause of non-solicitation.	Non-solicitation too wide to be enforced – type of business/area not specified and time frame too broad. Undertaking not to use 'CarCo' in any customer communication, and agreement to drop claims to enforce the non-solicitation and non-compete clauses, and action relating to circulars sent out before 19 July 1988.

Sources: sworn affidavits, correspondence and interviews.

Maintaining franchisees' fidelity

Some time before resignations were formally given, the FAB had begun to consider the possibility of breaking away; it had sought legal advice, set up an incorporated company, engaged the services of a management consultant, prepared stationery and trade marks, and was attempting to recruit shareholders/franchisees. Yet their franchise contracts placed quite severe limitations on the extent to which they could 'feather their own nests' before leaving the network (cf. *Wessex Dairies Ltd v. Smith* [1935] 2 KB 80 CA; *Sanders v. Parry* [1967] 1 WLR 753 CA). Franchisees were bound by a fidelity clause preventing them from engaging 'in any business activity other than that of [CarCo] without the prior written consent of the Company'.

Leading members of the FAB were in breach of this clause in two respects. First, they were not devoting their full-time attention to the single-minded development of their CarCo business. Instead, they were placing themselves in a position whereby there was a conflict of interest between themselves and the franchisor, which was being resolved in their own favour. Secondly, while not actually 'trading', they were involved in a much wider set of 'business activities' than operating their CarCo franchise. While franchisees would be permitted to take some minimum steps to prepare for a new job or new business on termination of the franchise, this would only include job applications, obtaining an off-the-shelf company, commencing discussions for finance but nothing of any more substance or detail. CarCo brought an action seeking to enforce this clause on four members of the FAB (see Table 5.2). An undertaking of compliance was given to the court, but it was more of a case of 'bolting the stable door after the horse has bolted'; many of the break-away preparations had already been made (cf. Table 5.1).

Protecting goodwill

Once the break-away group began trading on 1 May 1988, CarCo instructed British Telecom to reallocate new telephone numbers to the break-away group and to divert all calls to the original telephone numbers to CarCo's headquarters. This request was made in spite of the fact that franchisees were the sole subscribers to their telephone lines, and in the absence of any suggestion that leaving the CarCo network would result in their ownership of telephone numbers being challenged. The court ordered against CarCo's interference with AutoCo's telephone lines. However, it also gave limited protection to the goodwill these telephone numbers carried on account of their previous association with CarCo. Callers had to be made aware that the franchisee was no longer associated with CarCo, but was trading as under the name AutoCo, all advertising linking the telephone number with CarCo had to be stopped, and references (such as 'former-CarCo franchisee') in advertising materials had to cease.

The break-away would have been more difficult to effect had CarCo retained a 'stake' in other parts of franchisees' physical business assets. Interestingly enough, the original owners did – equipment and vans could be leased through CarCo's leasing arm provided they agreed to their removal once the franchise was terminated. However, the transfer of contracts from CarCo Ltd to CarCo (UK) Ltd closed off this option. The leasing agreements 'tied' franchisees to CarCo Ltd *not* CarCo (UK) Ltd, and, as such, clauses relating to the removal and repossession of leased assets were no longer enforceable. This meant forfeiting the 'tie' on 46 per cent of the vans and 35 per cent of the tuning equipment which franchisees took with them to form AutoCo.

Enforcing restrictive clauses

Clauses which place restrictions on the activities of franchisees once outside the network are more far-reaching in their intended effect, and they are also more difficult to enforce. Both the non-compete and non-solicitation clauses to which AutoCo operators were bound were loosely worded to the point of being unenforceable. The courts demand very precise definitions of what former franchisees are barred from doing, for whom, for how long and where (*Financial Times*, 12 January 1990, 27 March 1991; Aikin, 1991). Imprecision is likely to be costly, and so it proved for CarCo.

The original contract to which AutoCo operators were bound prohibited former CarCo franchisees from entering into 'direct competition with the Company or any of its Franchisees in the field of mobile engine tuning for a period of two years from the date of termination'. This clause was so loosely worded that no attempt was made to enforce it. Its weakness stemmed from three factors. First, franchisees were barred from setting up in competition within too wide an area. If enforceable it would have had effect of barring former franchisees from contact with customers with whom they had never had any previous dealings simply because they were customers of an existing CarCo franchisee or of the franchisor.[7] In general, one would expect to be able to enforce such a restraint provided it was limited to the franchisee's operational area (as in the Prontaprint case, see pp.124–126). However, it is more difficult to argue that the franchisee acquires any special advantage outside that area or that the franchisor has a legitimate interest to protection outside that area. Furthermore, there is a potential 'springing contingency'. For example, if a former franchisee sets up in business well away from existing CarCo operations, he/she may be considered in breach of this restraint if the CarCo network then expands into this new area. Former franchisees may not know whether their customers are or have previously been customers of CarCo, or whether they are competing with the CarCo network. They will therefore be unaware of whether or not they are in breach of contract.

Secondly, the time restraint might be considered too long. It is set on the basis of allowing a reasonable period of time to appoint and train a replacement franchisee for each territory. While by no means fatal to this argument, the new contract reduces the period of restraint from two years to one year. This provides some evidence that the franchisor now considers one year to be the duration reasonably required to protect the area while a new franchisee is introduced.

Thirdly, the absence of information constituting 'trade secrets', which was shared with franchisees as part of the franchise relationship, weakens the case for the enforcement of restrictive clauses. A 'trade secret' is a body of information: (1) which is not in the public domain; and (2) the disclosure of which would be to the detriment of the owner. In the light of the customs and practices in the car tuning business, it is unlikely that CarCo could claim that becoming one its franchisees allowed franchisees access to 'trade secrets' so defined. The car tuning equipment used by CarCo franchisees can commonly be found in other mobile tuning organizations, in garages and service centres. CarCo simply communicated to franchisees how the equipment is used as part of a method or system that also incorporates sales techniques, the use of the name and other advertising and promotional techniques. The use of less commonly known and operated machines would strengthen the grounds for restraint (cf. *Faccenda Chicken Ltd v. Fowler and others* [1986] 1 All ER 617 CA).

CarCo was in a better (though not a winnable) position to enforce the non-solicitation clause. By operating through a franchise network, the franchisor has limited contact with existing and potential customers. Franchisees, on the other hand, have very close contact with regular customers who have their cars tuned at intervals of between six and nine months. It is therefore an obvious and substantial advantage to have available a list of customers who are not only prepared to pay to have their cars tuned but with whom one already has established a trading relationship.[8] The non-solicitation clause is designed to prevent franchisees using this information received in the course of working in a franchise network for their own personal profit once they leave the network. By distributing a circular to former customers shortly after the break-away, AutoCo sought to challenge the validity of this restraint (see Table 5.2). In the court order which followed, CarCo dropped its claims to enforce both the non-competition and non-solicitation clauses as its chances of success appeared remote.

Like the non-compete clause, the non-solicitation clause was imprecise. It required that former franchisees would 'not tout or solicit for business any person who was at any time during the period of two years prior to such termination a customer of or in the habit of dealing with the Franchisee's business'. First, it restricted ex-franchisees from approaching former customers in respect of *any* business. However, courts have been willing to construe restraining clauses with more limited meaning. For example, restrictions on a former milkman selling 'milk or dairy produce' were construed to be limited to the activity of a milk roundsman mentioned elsewhere in the agreement, and not to his employment in, say, a grocer's shop where butter or cheese happened to be sold. Similarly, a clause preventing a former salesman from canvassing anyone who was a customer of his former employer while he was in their employ, was construed to apply only to those goods sold by the employer (*G W Plowman and Son Ltd v. Ash* [1964] WLR 568 CA).[9] It is therefore possible that the court would have interpreted CarCo's non-solicitation clause in more limiting terms: restraining former franchisees from approaching CarCo's customers as potential customers for a new but similar mobile car tuning service. The substitution of literal interpretation for one of purposive construction is made on the grounds that the courts should try to give such clauses the effect intended by both parties. This policy usually benefits the party seeking to enforce the restraint – in this case CarCo. However, the clause had a second, more damning flaw – no time limit was placed on the restriction. If enforced, no-one who was a customer of an ex-CarCo franchisee two years before the former franchisee's departure could be approached by that franchisee for business *at any time in the future.*

Consideration of some of the legal arguments on which action was brought against AutoCo serves to further underline the 'softness' of the original franchise relationship as well as highlighting the 'hardness' of its replacement. Crucially, the original CarCo contract gave the franchisor little control over the franchisees' business assets and therefore provided it with limited powers to keep the network intact. Franchisees were able to 'vote with their feet' taking with them their telephone numbers, vans, equipment, customer lists and were able to set up a competing network. Had they been subject to the terms of the new

CarCo agreement (or many of the ones analysed in Chapter 4), things would have been very different, making the prospect of a break-away on such a large scale remote.

CONCLUSION

'Change is the only constant' is a commonly used business adage. It is often used by management to justify and smooth the introduction of changes which may have far-reaching consequences for employment levels, pay, methods of working, conditions of employment, work intensity and so on. Yet while franchising is neither immune nor insulated from change, little is known about sources of change and its consequences in a franchise context. Clearly, one of the most dramatic changes that could possibly confront franchisees is a change in franchisor ownership. Whether initiated voluntarily or as a response to compulsory pressure (i.e. liquidation), franchisees may have to face a new owner. They may be unaware of their intentions, suspicious of their motives, have little knowledge of their background and will certainly not have any (formal) say in their appropriateness. Yet they will be expected, or formally obliged by contract, to follow their strategic lead. This chapter has provided an insight into what *can* happen when a franchise changes hands. Its generalizability is limited by its focus on a single case study, but even so it provides several important lessons for the study of the franchise relationship.

First, assessments of franchisees' independence within a particular franchise system are historically specific, i.e. they can change. An examination of how the CarCo franchise operated before the takeover strongly indicates that the relationship stood towards the 'softer' end of the 'hard–medium–soft' spectrum. Operational controls were weak, franchisees relied more on the skills they had learnt on-the-job than adherence to an operations manual, and they worked their exclusive territories with as many vans on the road and worked as intensively as they saw fit. Even the introduction of an advertising levy was short-lived as franchisees were able to vote against its retention. Similarly, the franchisor had only a weak 'hold' on the tangible (and, as the court battles subsequently proved, intangible) assets with which franchisees operated.

However, franchisees may find that the rules and regulations (either explicit or implicit ones) governing the franchise relationship change dramatically when their franchise system is acquired by new owners. In the case of CarCo, this amounted to a 'tightening of the reins'. Formal targets were introduced with the possibility of penalties being used against franchisees who fell short; the decision to place so many vans in any one area was switched from franchisee to franchisor; territorial boundaries were no longer treated as sacrosanct; royalties were raised; and ownership of the business telephone lines, vans and equipment was placed more firmly in the hands of the franchisor. This represented a shift in the nature of the franchise relationship from the 'softer' towards the 'harder' end of the independence–dependence spectrum. Furthermore, the new owners had ambitious growth plans for the network both in terms of further penetration of the market and profit generation. This made the use of the new contractual powers they were seeking all the more likely.

Secondly, the presence or otherwise of restraining clauses is one thing, their enforcement by the courts is quite another. The enforcement of non-solicitation and non-competition clauses faces a stern test once the legal process is called upon to uphold their validity. Despite initiating legal action against the break-away group, the loosely worded and imprecise nature of the restraining clauses forced CarCo to make 'out of court' settlements before judgments were made. This would seem to underline the point that:

> a good deal of legal 'know-how' is required for the successful drafting of a restrictive covenant.
> (Pearson LJ in *Commercial Plastics Ltd v. Vincent* [1964] 3 All ER 546 at 555)

Much turns on the court's interpretation of the wording used. CarCo was therefore left with little ability to prevent or stall the break-away from taking place – had the contract been more tightly drafted its powers would have been greatly enhanced. Instead, CarCo started off from a weak position with a duff contract in several important respects. This made the 'hardening' of the franchise relationship risky at best and, as it turned out, insufficient to carry even a majority of existing franchisees.

In addition to a change in the ownership of a franchise, changes in the commercial environment that franchisees face can also prompt a radical reshaping of the franchise relationship. The is the focus of the following chapter.

6 Managing a franchise in a changing commercial environment

INTRODUCTION

Franchisors have limited access to the market their franchisees actually serve on a day-to-day basis. Nevertheless, franchisor income rises and falls according to how much franchisees sell. Yet what may have maximized franchisee sales in the past may not necessarily do the same in the future. Since the network was first established the commercial environment may have changed significantly, calling into question some of the fundamentals of the franchisees' business set-up. For example, outlets may be located in the wrong places, the network may cater for a declining market segment, outlets may have a limited appeal and they may provide few facilities considered necessary to fully maximize franchisee sales. The franchisor may therefore seek to reshape the franchise to meet the changing commercial environment which the network faces.

Several franchisors have, in recent times, sought to mould their franchise networks to meet the changing commercial environments they now face. For example, the imposition of Value Added Tax (VAT) on hot take-away food in 1984 and the declining sales turnover which followed, prompted Kentucky Fried Chicken to reappraise its approach to the UK fast food market.[1] The provision of in-store seating became a top priority. The franchisor publicly declared its firm intention to convert Kentucky Fried Chicken's image from a chain of side street take-aways into a chain of fast service high street restaurants. Those franchisees unwilling or unable to convert their outlets to the new style format were refused a new contract once their franchise came up for renewal. Instead, they were asked to close down existing, profitable outlets (even though hefty investments had sometimes been made in 'repositioning' the outlet) and relocate to high cost, new style outlets (*Popular Food Service*, March 1987).[2]

Similarly, Prontaprint sought to change its corporate image and improve the layout of its stores in the late 1980s. The new layout did away with the counter and replaced it with a layout which allowed the customer to move towards the services or products which were found in a series of sales points around the perimeter walls. Along with the new layout Prontaprint also changed its logo and company colours, and introduced soft lighting, 'help-yourself' coffee and cleared all 'clutter' from its window (*Inplant and Instant Printer*, March 1987). The changes were designed to convey a broader business centre image. However, the refits were often made as a condition of renewal, since what the franchisee might gain in increased turnover was more than accounted for in increased costs (a refit costs £10,000–£15,000).

A more competitive commercial environment, a shrinking market and a change in franchisor ownership have prompted an overhaul at Holiday Inn, the middle-range hotel chain. Bass, the UK hotel, brewer and leisure group, acquired Holiday Inn in the US in 1989. This move added almost 1,400 Holiday Inns, many of which are run by franchisees, to those it already owned outside the US. On taking over the US chain, Bass publicly said that '80 per cent were in very reasonable condition', leaving the implication that several hundred left something to be desired. A fairly tough tug-of-war seems to have ensued to persuade franchisees to upgrade their properties. More than 90 properties have dropped out of the Holiday Inn system since March 1990, although new franchises, notably for a replacement downmarket chain under the Holiday Express banner, have taken their place. With about 40 per cent of franchisee contracts expiring during the next five years, the new owners are well placed to insist that operators spend more on their units to meet an increasingly competitive environment or risk losing their franchise (*Financial Times*, 12 May 1992; cf. Luxenberg, 1985: 268–269).

Missed market opportunities have prompted some franchisors to take a more active involvement in their franchisees' businesses, either through take-overs or a tightening of the franchise relationship or both. For example, during the past 30 years or so the oil companies have presided over an increase in the number of petrol stations they own – rising from 14 per cent of the total number of petrol stations in 1964 to about 33 per cent today. At the same time, the proportion of petrol stations directly run has almost doubled – from 5 per cent in 1977 to around 9 per cent in 1988 – and franchise arrangements have replaced tenancies as the most popular form of 'arm's length' management. Whereas tenants may seek to lower their costs by operating for shorter hours and having less people working at the site, franchisees must keep to the opening hours they are set. In addition, slim retail margins further heighten the incentive for volume growth because petrol is supplied to retailers at wholesale prices minus rebates subject to a maximum retail price and the rigours of competitive pressure (Monopolies and Mergers Commission, 1990: 38, 368–369; cf. Rehbinder, 1973).

Changes in the commercial environment franchisees are 'fitted out' to face also serve to highlight some of the contradictions inherent in the franchise relationship. For example, although refitting existing locations may be enough to reverse declining outlet turnover, relocating to new style higher-cost outlets may boost outlet turnover more dramatically. Replacing low turnover outlets with high turnover ones will raise franchisor revenue regardless of franchisee profitability. While the franchisor is more likely to prefer outlets which generate high turnover, franchisees are more likely to have their eyes on outlet profitability (for them the business adage 'turnover is vanity, profitability is sanity' applies). Yet with franchisors in strategic control their interests are put first; franchisees who are unwilling or unable to go along with the change are replaced by those who are.

This chapter analyses the reshaping of a franchise relationship at close quarters. It examines the reasons why the Coca-Cola Company's original franchised bottler structure in Germany[3] had by the 1980s outlived its usefulness, and why a reshaped franchise structure was put in its place. The chapter argues that the changes stemmed from two contradictory tendencies within the franchise relationship itself, yet were prompted by the changing commercial environment. First, franchisees and franchisors have different incentives; franchisees may seek to maximize or simply sustain *their own* profits, thereby selling a smaller output, at a higher price and with less promotional support than would maximize the profits of the franchisor whose income is derived from the sale of the beverage base to the franchisee. In other words, the interests of the franchisor and those of franchisees may be in tandem for *some* but not *all* of the time – franchisees may reach a level of sales which maximizes their profits well before the franchisor reaches theirs (cf. Felstead, 1991c, 1992). Second, the image of a national/global product may come into conflict with the decentralized nature of franchising; those with whom franchisees do business may find it difficult, or even refuse, to recognize the sovereignty that *each* franchisee has over pricing and supply conditions within *their own* territorial boundaries. They may choose instead to seek national agreements.

Both contradictions were exposed by the changing commercial environment the Company and its franchisees faced – the addition of new products and packages, the increase in the minimum efficient scale of bottling and the concentration of retailing (cf. Hyman, 1987). The Coca-Cola Company's response was to tighten its grip on, and reshape, the franchise structure to ensure that future sales growth would not be jeopardized. Discussions with bottlers took place on how this might be achieved. Territories were enlarged, the number of franchisees was reduced, production was concentrated in fewer plants, franchisees were required to hit minimum sales or investment targets, and franchisees' pricing autonomy was narrowed. These changes were designed to safeguard and promote sales growth above all else, and to instil a similar commitment among franchisees.

This chapter traces the whys and wherefores of the Coca-Cola Company's changed franchise structure in Germany (and elsewhere). The chapter therefore begins by analysing the historical origins of the Coca-Cola Company's franchise relationship in Germany. It then discusses the changing commercial environment which came to a head in the 1980s, and the contradictions which this began to expose. The resulting means of reshaping and tightening up the franchise relationship are then given consideration. Finally, the chapter ends with a summary.

ORIGINAL FRANCHISE STRUCTURE

Almost all producers of carbonated soft drinks manufacture their product not from fruit or other primary inputs but from a syrup or concentrate produced by a specialist firm. At the risk of over-simplifying, the soft drinks industry can be categorized into two distinct kinds of operation. First, there are those producers who purchase syrups or concentrates from specialist firms. The drinks are then bottled and sold under their own labels; such firms are often small to medium-sized firms operating in a local or regional market. Secondly, there are firms which specialize in the manufacture of syrups or concentrates. These firms typically award franchises to local bottlers to produce and market their range of soft drinks over a specific area. Here, the brand belongs to the upstream producer of the concentrate, although advertising and marketing of the brand may be carried out jointly with franchisees. The Coca-Cola Company is the archetypal user of this second type of operation. It pioneered this type of operation in its domestic market, and then used it to penetrate other markets worldwide. Its method of entry into the German market was no different.

Under the franchise arrangement, the Coca-Cola Company manufactures and sells syrup (a mixture of ingredients in liquid form which, when properly mixed with carbonated water, becomes the finished product) and concentrates (a mixture of the same basic ingredients minus sugar[4]) to a bottler who has the exclusive right to bottle according to the Company's quality standards and specifications, and distribute the beverage in a clearly defined geographical territory for a finite period (except in the US, where contracts run for perpetuity, see pp.182–183). The Coca-Cola Company participates, conceptually and financially, in many of the advertising and promotion programmes made in connection with their trade-marked products, provides advice and technical assistance on production, quality control, management and sales problems, and engages in development and test marketing of new products and packages. In the original franchise structure the bottlers, for their part, decided on the plant and equipment to be used, total production by size and type of container, their product mix, the price to be charged, and the manner in which to penetrate the market and secure the widest possible distribution of the product throughout their territory (as required by contract).

As in the US, the Coca-Cola Company adopted a two-tier franchise structure shortly after its entry to the German market.[5] On 8 April 1929 the first bottle of Coca-Cola was filled in Germany. A year later, the local franchisee who had filled the first bottle was given the right to sub-franchise distribution and bottling rights to others across Germany (a system known as 'parent bottling'). The parent bottler recruited two types of franchisee, both of whom were very small companies or even individuals: distribution-only franchisees; and those who bottled and distributed the finished product. For the former, the parent bottler acted as a wholesaler of Coca-Cola, while, for the latter, it collected payments for concentrate delivered to bottlers by the Company (where the difference between the monies collected and the amount charged represented the parent bottler's commission or royalty). The Company bought out the parent bottler in 1937 and a wholly-owned subsidiary was subsequently put in its place (Giebelhaus, 1988).

Initially, predominantly distribution-only franchisees were recruited. Often they were small family-run businesses which had already acquired valuable experience in beverage distribution either as wholesalers, breweries or mineral water producers.[6] This is in marked contrast to the recruitment of inexperienced franchisees by many of today's business format franchisors (cf. pp.84–85). Distribution-only franchisees were supplied with the finished product from a nearby Coca-Cola plant, and were required by contract to secure the widest possible distribution of the product. In return, franchisees were granted exclusive territories within which to operate. This limited the franchisee's right to sell Coca-

Cola only for ultimate resale within the franchisee's exclusive territory, thereby eliminating *intra*brand competition.

The main effect of exclusive territories was to reduce the risk to which franchised distributors of the relatively unknown soft drink exposed themselves. It ensured that at least they, rather than some 'free rider', would realize the full gains of their merchandising, servicing and advertising efforts, as well as offering some protection for the specific assets in which they had invested.[7] For example, distributors often opened and serviced accounts which were unprofitable to them in the short term. The hope was that frequent delivery of even the smallest quantities, the supply of coolers (either free or for a nominal charge), the cleaning and filling of coolers, the issuing of point-of-sale advertising material and the negotiation of shelf space for the product would raise sales and eventually make the account profitable. In the absence of exclusivity, it is unlikely that distributors would have made such efforts, since rivals carrying the same brand would simply undercut the 'opener's' prices once sales began to rise, making the account theirs. As a result, the incentive to make Coca-Cola available 'around the corner from anywhere' (1927 advertising slogan) would have been weaker, bottle sales would have been lower, and concentrate sales would not have been as high.

A similar argument applies to advertising and investment in specific assets such as buying a stock of supplies and parts, trucks for distribution, sending staff on training courses, and so on. Without territorial exclusivity, any local advertising expenditure and specific investments which may have increased sales of the bottled beverage (and hence concentrate sales) would not have gone ahead for fear that competing distributors would 'free ride' on these efforts (Katz, 1978; Larner, 1977). Once again this would have dented franchisees' incentive to make Coca-Cola 'within easy reach of . . . thirst' (1940 advertising slogan) and would have shifted much more of the cost of doing so back on to the Company itself.

Territorial exclusivity also made monitoring the performance of franchisees easier and less costly. Before the outbreak of the Second World War, monthly sales quotas were issued to each franchisee. Those falling below these targets were asked to explain why, and were required to remedy the situation. The ultimate sanction was termination of the franchise agreement for failure to increase market coverage, or a refusal to renew the contract at the end of its term. However, this sanction was rarely used.[8]

A more potent means of increasing sales was the use of peer pressure. Coca-Cola GmbH (the wholly-owned German subsidiary of the Company) encouraged franchisees to compare and compete with others in the network in terms of their sales achievements. Annually, the best sales performers (as measured in terms of sales per capita) were chosen to form a 'Ring of Honour'. They were praised at the annual convention of franchisees, given ceremonial awards and taken on a partly-paid trip. This was the main mechanism used to inspire commitment to the organizational goal of opening up more and more markets for Coca-Cola (indeed these 'first hour' franchisees are often referred to as 'Coca-Cola missionaries').

Within five years of entry into the German market, 124 distribution-only franchisees had been added to the network, and by 1939 there were 616. During Coca-Cola's first decade in Germany sales had risen from 5,840 cases in 1929 to 4,451,355 cases in 1939.[9] With few districts left without a Coca-Cola franchisee, the Company had begun to franchise bottling rights as well. It was becoming increasingly uneconomic to supply a dispersed network of distribution franchisees with the product from a few Company-owned plants. Franchisees prepared to invest in bottling lines were therefore given filling rights; by 1939 thirty-four plants were operating as franchised bottlers.[10]

However, the development of Coca-Cola in Germany was interrupted by the Second World War. Concentrate ceased to be shipped, sugar was rationed and by the end of the war almost two-thirds of the distribution network had been wiped out.[11] Of those who remained many were seeking to renew their contracts. Coca-Cola, however, was only prepared to renew the contracts of those who were willing and able to build their own bottling facilities and become franchised bottlers. Territorial boundaries were redrawn and bottling contracts awarded only to those who could prove that they had an investment capability of at least DM1.00 per inhabitant.[12] By 1954 there were 96 bottlers, and by the early 1960s the process of conversion was at an end with 123 bottlers all told (see Table 6.1).

EXPOSING THE CONTRADICTIONS

The franchise structure created a patchwork of 'little kingdoms' throughout Germany. Vertically imposed territorial exclusivity eliminated direct competition between Coca-Cola bottlers, and as a result bottlers enjoyed monopoly power in the filling and distribution of Coca-Cola within their own territorial boundaries. While this proved advantageous to the Coca-Cola Company and its bottlers initially in that it encouraged widespread distribution, over the longer term it was to become the system's 'Achilles' heel' (contrary to Katz, 1978: 88). This

Table 6.1 Evolution of Coca-Cola's franchise structure in Germany, 1929–1962

Year	Bottling franchises (company-owned bottlers)	Year	Distribution franchises
1929	1 (1)	1929	first issued
1930 (beginning)	1 (1)	1930	7
		1930 (end)	31
1931	1 (5)		
		1934	124
1938	27 (14)		
1939	34 (15)		616
		1944	234 (at least 382 lost) – drive to consolidate into larger units begins
1954	96		
1962	123		

Source: Archives, Coca-Cola GmbH, Essen.

was vividly exposed by three major developments which came to a head in the 1980s: (1) the addition of new products and packages; (2) the increase in the minimum efficient scale of bottling; and (3) the concentration of retailing. In this section, we consider each of these dimensions of the changed commercial environment in turn.

New products and packages

Originally, Coca-Cola was a one product/one package company – the 6.5 fluid ounce (192 ml) glass returnable Coca-Cola bottle.[13] This had at least two advantages. First, the hobble-skirted bottle made Coca-Cola easily identifiable over its competitors who were using the more conventional straight-sided bottle. Second, a single package protected the investment bottlers had made in returnable bottles and bottling lines. However, competitive pressure and the opportunity of increasing sales by selling larger packages prompted the Coca-Cola Company to abandon its single package/one product philosophy in 1955. Modern self-service supermarkets were becoming more widespread and with them purchases for home consumption (which were typically larger than those for immediate consumption) were beginning to rise. Without a larger package, the Company faced the prospect of losing out to its competitors who already sold soft drinks in larger packages.[14]

Today, Coca-Cola in Germany is sold in many different package types (returnable glass, returnable plastic, one-way plastic, cans), sizes (0.2 litre to 2.0 litre) and configurations (6-packs, 18-packs, 24-packs). In addition, vending units which automatically mix syrup with chilled carbonated water at the point of sale and dispense the beverage into a cup or glass (post-mix) are in place. Extensions to existing brands have been launched, most notably low-calorie versions of existing brands such as Coca-Cola Light (known as Diet Coke in the UK and US). New products, too, have been added to Coca-Cola's range – Fanta Orange, Sprite, Bonaqa, Aquarius and so on (known as allied products) – as well as extensions to these new brands. The introduction of each of these package/product variations raised bottle sales and with it concentrate sales as well (see Figure 6.1).

However, no bottler was able to produce the entire Coca-Cola range of products, and many did not package all the sizes for which they were authorized. Instead, the Company gave bottlers supplementary agreements to their original contract allowing them to sell the complete

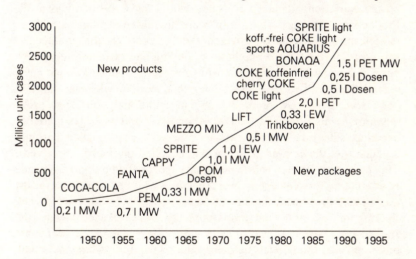

Figure 6.1 Growth of case sales and new product/package introductions in Germany, 1950–1990

Key
MW = glass returnable
PET MW = plastic returnable
EW = one-way
Dosen = cans
Trinkboxen = boxes
PEM = pre-mix containers
POM = post-mix containers
Source: Archives, Coca-Cola GmbH, Essen.

range, as long as each product and package was furnished by authorized suppliers (either the Company's own bottling plants, franchised plants with a toll filling agreement or canning co-operatives). Franchisees, for example, were authorized to distribute cans in their territories following the introduction of cans onto the German market in 1963. However, the right to fill cans for sale within an exclusive territory was never relinquished. Given the high investment costs required to build canning lines and the small size of their territories, few, if any, franchisees would have been able to make the necessary investment. Even if they had, investments expanding the market for Coca-Cola products, such as advertising and marketing campaigns, might have been jeopardized as a result. However, several franchised bottlers combined to form separate canning co-operatives filling cans for Coca-Cola on the basis of a toll filling agreement (cf. Beale and Dugdale, 1975).[15]

Although the addition of each new product and package raised beverage sales (and hence concentrate sales), economic *theory* suggests that had franchisees been able to produce, package and distribute *more* of the variations themselves, sales would have been higher still. Products and packages 'bought in' were purchased at wholesale prices (which must at least have covered average costs for the producer to survive). The cost to the purchaser of buying one extra unit must have been higher than the marginal cost of production (since average costs spread fixed and variable costs over total output, whereas marginal costs record the cost of producing one additional unit). The profit maximizing distributor of 'bought in' products and packages therefore expanded sales up to the point at which marginal cost equalled marginal revenue (i.e. the cost of the extra sale equalled the income received). This point was reached before marginal cost equalled marginal revenue in production (or at an even lower level of sales if the distributor sought goals other than profit-maximization; see below). In other words, the 'buying in' of more and more products and packages meant that franchisees reached a level of sales which maximized their profits (or other considerations) well before producers, and the Company which supplied the concentrate, reached theirs.

Economies of scale and technological advance

Bottler territories were originally drawn up on the basis of producing and packaging a 6.5 fluid ounce (192 ml) returnable Coca-Cola bottle using 1950s technology, and distributing it within a serviceable territory (i.e. vehicle-round-trip-in-one-day measurement). Today, the growth of packages and products (see above), technological advances in soft drink bottling and improvements in Germany's transportation system have all helped to raise the minimum efficient scale of operation. Bottling lines have got faster (today a 100 spout bottling filler can fill a fifth as many bottles again as it could in 1970) and hence production costs have been reduced. Transportation costs have similarly fallen, although traffic congestion following is beginning to jeopardize these gains.

However, three factors confined bottlers to production units with higher costs than those attainable in an efficiently-sized plant. First, the most efficient bottling lines required large investments: for example, a new plastic bottling line with an annual capacity of 66 million litres currently costs about DM12 million (Monopolies and Mergers Commission, 1991: 58; Coca-Cola GmbH sources). Second, territorial restrictions prevented bottlers from growing to the minimum efficient scale by expanding the geographical boundaries of the market in which they sold Coca-Cola products. Growth could come only from population increases or higher per capita consumption of brands within the franchise territory. Third, although investment costs could be shared and territorial boundaries enlarged if neighbouring franchisees merged, many resisted doing so voluntarily (see below). Most bottlers were family-owned and run businesses, and many had family members such as wives, grandparents and children working there in some capacity. Although a merger would have increased the financial strength of their businesses, many family-owned bottlers feared that it would also dilute their control – reducing their ability to make family appointments, preventing them giving themselves pay rises, and weakening their economic influence and status within the community. Furthermore, many were content with the level of profits their business was able to generate without the upheaval of organizational change (that is, they had reached their 'comfort level').

These factors held sway until bottling contracts came up for renewal in the late 1980s. Bottling continued to be carried out in plants whose level of production fell below the minimum efficient scale. As a result, higher costs pushed up prices and/or reduced bottler profit margins compared with those of an efficiently-sized plant. Higher prices reduced sales in the short term, while slimmer profit margins narrowed the scope bottlers had to make investments in the market (e.g. vending machines), thereby depressing sales over the longer term. In both of these ways, maintaining the status quo reduced volume sales (and hence concentrate sales) from what they might have been. In other words, a franchise network of 100 or so bottlers was increasingly becoming an obstacle rather than a tool for the maximization of

concentrate sales: the Coca-Cola Company had a network of bottlers
whose volume sales goals were incompatible with theirs.

Retailer concentration

It is conventional in the soft drinks industry to distinguish between two
channels through which products are distributed to the trade: the at-
home-market; and the away-from-home market. The labels given
indicate the essential difference between the two: drinks purchased for
consumption at home as opposed to those drunk at the point of sale.
Most of the retail outlets supplied through the at-home channel are
shops of one type or another ranging from supermarkets to corner
stores. The outlets comprising the away-from-home market are more
varied. These include bars, fast food outlets, clubs, restaurants as well
as leisure parks, sports centres and works canteens.

Concentration has taken place in both channels of distribution. The
share of the grocery business won by the German supermarket chains
such as Tengelmann, Spar, Metro, Aldi, Karstadt and so on has
increased substantially over time. Their growth has largely been at the
expense of the independent corner store. Over the period 1970–1989
more than 100,000 retail stores have closed throughout Germany, while
the sales of those remaining has leapt by 234 per cent (see Figure 6.2).
Even the smaller retailers have joined buying groups in order to buy
larger volumes from manufacturers, and have gradually expanded their
operations (cf. Pleijster, 1992). The growth of fast food and other
restaurant chains such as McDonald's, Burger King, Nordsee, Möven-
pick and so on has concentrated the away-from-home market in a
similar, albeit less dramatic, fashion.

Furthermore, many of the largest retailers launched their own-label
range of soft drinks designed to give the consumer a cheap alternative to
the brand leaders. During the 1960s and 1970s they provided just that –
a cheap, but lower quality alternative. However, throughout the 1980s
retailers improved the quality of their own-label soft drinks considerably as part of a wider process of 'retail branding' their stores.[16]

The development of own-label soft drinks offered three advantages to
the retailer. First, stocking own-label soft drinks gave them the opportunity to increase their margins by avoiding the advertising and marketing costs of supporting a brand. Secondly, it gave them a more detailed
knowledge of the costs of production and hence a better basis on which
to negotiate with soft drink bottlers. Thirdly, it heightened competition
for shelf space (or a single source of supply), and provided retailers with
another lever over those who bottled soft drinks. The threat to devote

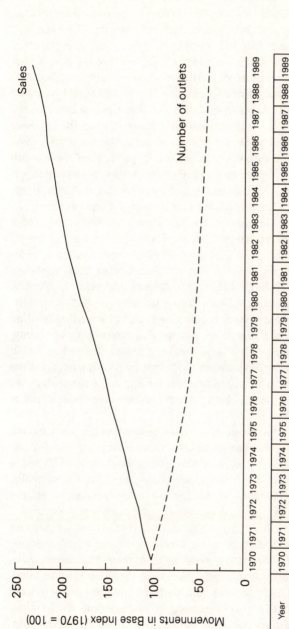

Year	1970	1971	1972	1973	1974	1975	1976	1977	1978	1979	1980	1981	1982	1983	1984	1985	1986	1987	1988	1989
Sales	100	109	114	123	129	137	146	152	161	169	180	187	195	200	206	210	217	219	225	234
No of outlets	100	93	86	80	75	69	64	60	57	55	53	51	50	48	46	45	43	42	41	40

Figure 6.2 Number of grocery stores and sales in Germany 1970–1989

Note:
This figure takes as its base the number of grocery stores and sales for 1970. In that year, there were 172,576 stores and sales were running at DM57,573 million per year.

Source: Nielson Universum, 1990 (Nielson Marketing Division: Berlin), p.16.

more shelf space to own-label soft drinks, or a major rival such as Pepsi-Cola, if terms were not improved, was a credible one.

Originally, each franchisee was able to negotiate their own terms and conditions of supply with retailers in their territory: most were single outlet operations, and few had outlets in more than one franchise territory. These negotiations included: prices, volume rebates, participation in special promotions, delivery arrangements and the allocation of shelf space. However, while concentration in the retail trade gradually pushed purchasing decisions from the local to the regional and then the national level, the right to sell remained decentralized in the hands of more than one hundred bottlers. At the same time, the buying power of these retail chains increased. For example, 45 per cent of the sales of Coca-Cola brands in Germany currently goes to just ten customers.[17] Moreover, the progressive dismantling of trade barriers between European Community (EC) states meant that transportation costs were the only factor protecting German bottlers from low-cost bottlers elsewhere in Europe supplying Germany's large retail chains.

The initial response of the German Coca-Cola organization to these changes was the establishment of Key Account Committees consisting of bottler and Coca-Cola GmbH representatives, and central billing of major customer accounts. These Committees negotiated with purchasing managers of each major account on behalf of the entire bottling network. However, the Committees had no real authority to set pricing and supply conditions with whom they negotiated. Instead, a single bottler could hold the entire network to ransom by refusing to accept the outcome of the negotiations, holding out instead for a better deal. At best this could delay the deal being struck, at worst the entire national account could be lost.

Some accounts were considered by the Company as too precious and prestigious to be exposed to such uncertainty. McDonald's, for example, accounts for 5 per cent of Coca-Cola sales in the US and a similar proportion of its worldwide trade (Love, 1987: 4). Furthermore, unlike the at-home market, buyers for the away-from-home market often prefer to buy the whole range of soft drinks they require from a single supplier. This allows them to economize on the costs of carrying several competing brands, and strengthens their hand in negotiations with suppliers. For soft drink bottlers and their franchisor these accounts have several advantages: they shut-out competition; they provide access to high through-put outlets; and they ensure high visibility for the brand, especially among young consumers.

However, any national or even global deal (a status accorded to 'Select International Account' customers) between the Coca-Cola

Company and McDonald's was not binding on each and every German franchisee, any one of whom could refuse to supply McDonald's outlets in its territory on these terms. This could jeopardize the entire account, as the Company's ability to supply and service McDonald's on a national basis (the key criterion set by many national customers) could be denied by a single franchisee. A means to protect the McDonald's account from such a threat was developed in the mid-1980s. It also provided an indication of the shape of things to come in the way that the Company now deals with its bottlers' largest customers. But in order to understand this development, one first needs to appreciate the method by which Coca-Cola is predominantly supplied in the away-from-home market.

In addition to being sold in glass bottles, plastic bottles and cans, the Coca-Cola range is dispensed. This form of distribution is particularly prevalent in the away-from-home market through chains such as McDonald's. Dispensing takes one of two forms: pre-mix, and post-mix. Supplies of pre-mix are in the standard carbonated form except that the packs (usually metal canisters) are larger, and the drink is dispensed directly into the cup or glass. Post-mix, on the other hand, is syrup supplied to the outlet in either the form of 'bag-in-box', metal canister or plastic jar. The post-mix syrup is automatically mixed with chilled carbonated water at the point of sale, using a dispensing unit. Units often have four or more separate taps linked to an equivalent number of syrup containers. Pre-mix is gradually being replaced by post-mix as this reduces the need for storage space and provides a more convenient means of serving a large number of chilled drinks.

As with additions to Coca-Cola's product range and brand extensions, bottlers were granted rights to produce and distribute syrup for post-mix units within their territory (or distribution rights only, with syrup supplied either by Company-owned plants or by franchised plants operating on the basis of a toll filling agreement). However, these rights did *not* include syrup supplied in the form of bag-in-box.

During the mid-1980s, McDonald's heightened pressure on the Coca-Cola Company for a price reduction. In forming its response, the Company feared that McDonald's might introduce its own-label cola (as it had in the UK), if bottlers delayed reducing prices or some simply refused to do so.[18] By agreeing to supply McDonald's with syrup bag-in-box the Company was able to deal directly with McDonald's, side-stepping the need for bottler approval, and thereby avoiding a possible loss of sales. In the words of a franchisee, 'they [the Company] cut us out, but still expected us to service McDonald's outlets on terms they'd agreed' (field notes). Nevertheless, bottlers could have been cut out altogether if McDonald's had decided to supply each of their outlets centrally, as they do for most of their other products.

The McDonald's episode is instructive of retailer concentration. On the one hand, the retailers to whom bottlers were selling were acquiring more and more buying power – purchasing decisions were becoming centralized, their orders were growing in size, chains were expanding nationally and their own-label products were becoming more acceptable. On the other hand, bottlers' sovereignty to decide the terms and conditions on which they sold the Coca-Cola range remained unbroken, and the network's decision points continued to be fragmented. Despite its national/global image, the franchise structure denied the Coca-Cola Company the power to negotiate with national account customers. Potentially at least, this put some of the largest accounts at risk, and as a consequence jeopardized concentrate sales from which the final product is made.

RESHAPING THE FRANCHISE STRUCTURE

The franchise structure of 100 or so bottlers, which had served both the Coca-Cola Company and its franchisees so well during its formative years in Germany, was beginning to hinder rather than help future growth. The Company's own revenue was derived entirely from sales of concentrate to the bottler. The Company therefore 'had a near-absolute interest in volume growth, and in keeping retail prices low in order to stimulate further sales of concentrate' (Monopolies and Mergers Commission, 1991: 122). The lower the cost of production, the greater the proportion of the wholesale margin available for non-price marketing, such as promotions, displays, technical sales aids and so on, which also stimulate sales. The German franchise structure, as of the mid-1980s, was making the goal of low-cost production increasingly difficult to achieve: small territories were unable to generate sufficient sales to support 'state-of-the-art' production facilities; capacity utilization was low (few operated round-the-clock production); too many products and packages were purchased from authorized suppliers instead of being produced and packaged in-house; for many family-owned and run bottlers profits were secondary; and the mechanisms through which negotiations with large retailers took place were cumbersome. In each of these ways, bottlers were operating in order to maximize their own profits (or other considerations), but not those of the franchisor. In addition, large national retailing chains were beginning to wield their buying power by refusing to recognize bottlers' territorial boundaries and instead seeking better terms and conditions of supply nationwide. Moreover, the closure of small retail outlets lengthened the distances those who drank soft drinks had to travel to points of purchase, thereby heightening the importance of investment in technical sales aids such as coin-vendors. Without changes to the original franchise structure, competitive brands would have been able to expand their footholds in the market, franchisees would have been squeezed, and would have eventually gone out of business.

The first moves to restructure the bottling network can be traced as far back as the late 1960s. They took two forms: encouraging bottlers to compare their cost structures with others in the network in the hope that economies would be made (through a system known as Bottler Cost Comparison); and encouraging bottlers to merge to form larger, more economic units. In the US, the Coca-Cola Company set up the Bottler Consolidation Department in 1967 for the same purpose (Katz, 1978: 90). However, their success was gradual rather than dramatic: in the US, bottlers declined from 900 in 1968 to about 600 by 1980, while in Germany their number declined only marginally from 123 to 105 (see Figure 6.3). Moreover, giving advice on cost efficiencies served to 'patch-up wobbly bottlers, instead of killing them outright' (Coca-Cola GmbH executive, field notes). In both countries consolidation was 'voluntary', although more so in the case of the US where franchisees had perpetual contracts.[19]

However, the bare figures do not tell the full story; they do not record the Company's more interventionist stance, especially in the US. There, in the 1980s, the Company became active in buying and selling the areas of franchisees who wished to sell-up. These were then sold to franchisees who were seeking to expand, were financially secure and had a long-term interest in the business. During the period 1978–1990, for example, 82 per cent of US volume changed hands, and 145 per cent changed hands more than once. Yet the decline in the number of franchised bottlers in the US was relatively gradual compared with the experience of the German network during the same period. In Germany, since the mid-1980s, the number of franchised bottlers has fallen more steeply. Instead of waiting for (or encouraging) franchisees to sell at a time of their choosing, the Company was able to force the pace of German change as the 'second round' of 20-year bottling contracts awarded after the Second World War approached expiry (contracts were for ten years with a further ten years renewal option – initially issued in the 1940s/1950s and then again in the 1960s/1970s).

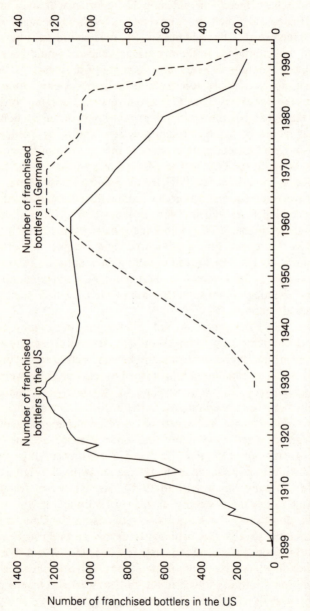

Figure 6.3 Number of franchised Coca-Cola bottlers in Germany and the United States, 1899–1992

Note:
This figure plots the recorded number of franchised bottlers; for some years the number of franchisees is not available.
Source: Archives, Coca-Cola GmbH, Essen and the Coca-Cola Company, Atlanta.

Data sheet for Figure 6.3

Year	1899	1900	1901	1902	1903	1904	1905	1906	1907	1908	1909	1910	1911	1912
No of US franchisees	1	4	13	45	77	123	241	201	268	290	374	493	611	691
No of German franchisees														

Year	1913	1914	1915	1916	1917	1918	1919	1920	1921	1922	1923	1924	1925	1926
No of US franchisees	504	562	636	948	1020	948	1069	1095	1115	1123	1142	1186	1203	1221
No of German franchisees														

Year	1927	1928	1929	1930	1931	1932	1933	1934	1935	1936	1937	1938	1939	1940
No of US franchisees	1228	1263	1235	1225	1191	1176	1161	1134	1101	1087	1071	1064	1058	1054
No of German franchisees			1	1	1							27		

Year	1941	1942	1943	1944	1945	1946	1947	1948	1949	1950	1951	1952	1953	1954
No of US franchisees	1051	1062	1050	1052										
No of German franchisees														96

Year	1955	1956	1957	1958	1959	1960	1961	1962	1963	1964	1965	1966	1967	1968
No of US franchisees			1100				1100							900
No of German franchisees								123	123			123	123	123

Year	1969	1970	1971	1972	1973	1974	1975	1976	1977	1978	1979	1980	1981	1982
No of US franchisees		860						690		637		600		
No of German franchisees	123	123	120	117	114	111	111	107	105	105	105	105	104	104

Year	1983	1984	1985	1986	1987	1988	1989	1990	1991	1992	1993
No of US franchisees				215					145		
No of German franchisees	104	102	98	81	68	65	64	37			14

Three factors were particularly important in the reshaped franchise structure which emerged in Germany: (1) the consolidation of production through mergers and buy-outs; (2) contractual changes designed to ensure that economies made are re-invested in generating further sales; and (3) the creation of a central sales company with the power and authority to negotiate with bottlers' largest customers. Each of these factors is considered in turn.

Consolidation of production

Although by 1988 the number of German bottlers had been whittled down to 65 (see Figure 6.4), something more drastic was being considered by Company executives. The plan was for the Coca-Cola Company to take a 35 per cent interest in a pan-German bottler,[20] with the remaining interest being split among existing bottlers (*New York Times*, 14 March 1988). This single bottler would then be able to produce the entire Coca-Cola range using 10–20 of the most up-to-date production units, maintain round-the-clock production, and set prices and marketing programmes for the whole of Germany. The plan was rejected by bottlers largely on the grounds that it would convert all of them from owner-managers to minority shareholders overnight.

In seeking an alternative solution, Coca-Cola GmbH and the Franchisees' Association commissioned an independent study of production and distribution arrangements in Germany (known as the Weihenstephan Study). Its brief was to report on where best to locate production plants and distribution depots, and how many of them there would be, if Germany was a virgin territory to Coca-Cola. The resulting map identified 14 production centres and 19 warehouses as the optimum mix. Just to approach this ideal, franchisees would have to merge or buy each other out, and then rationalize their production and distribution facilities. Coca-Cola GmbH made it clear that only those willing to move in this direction would be awarded a new contract. Discussions also took place between Coca-Cola GmbH and the Franchisees' Association on the contents of the new contract.

As soon as it became known that rationalization was favoured, all but tangible investments (e.g. coolers, coin-vendors, etc.) were postponed by many small bottlers: 'some bottlers almost struck, they stopped investment and started to invest outside the system' (Coca-Cola GmbH executive, field notes). Even so, the unexpired franchise of a small bottler continued to be worth much more to a nearby large bottler than to the small bottler actually holding it. A large, neighbouring bottler with under-utilized capacity could supply the small territory more

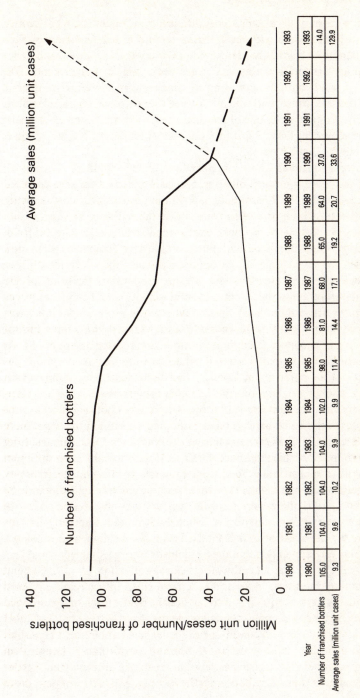

Year	1980	1981	1982	1983	1984	1985	1986	1987	1988	1989	1990	1991	1992	1993
Number of franchised bottlers	105.0	104.0	104.0	104.0	102.0	98.0	81.0	68.0	65.0	64.0	37.0			14.0
Average sales (million unit cases)	9.3	9.6	10.2	9.9	9.9	11.4	14.4	17.1	19.2	20.7	33.6			129.9

Figure 6.4 Number of franchised Coca-Cola bottlers and their average sales in Germany, 1980–1990

Source: Archives, Coca-Cola GmbH, Essen.

cheaply (even with higher transportation costs) than the local bottler, but could not do so without breaking territorial exclusivity. However, the chances of a small bottler having their contract renewed, and hence retaining territorial exclusivity, were becoming, at best, remote. The days of small bottlers unwilling to change were therefore numbered. Nevertheless, those who sold out left the Coca-Cola network as wealthy citizens. For example, one of the former small bottlers interviewed sold his franchise for DM2.3 million (equivalent to about £800,000); others sold out for much more.

However, in areas where large bottlers rubbed shoulders with smaller ones, the process of consolidation had been going on for several years. As a result, the 1980–90 period saw 42 mergers or take-overs between franchisees, which served to concentrate the majority of Coca-Cola's business in Germany in fewer and fewer hands (see Figure 6.5). For example, the Nürenberg and Fürstenfeldbruck franchises each now account for seven times the proportion of sales they accounted for in 1980. Both have closed some of the production facilities of the neighbouring areas they acquired, choosing to supply their enlarged territories from their most up-to-date plant. Lower production costs allowed profit margins to increase and widened the scope for the servicing of accounts through promotions, advertising and so on. In any case, the basis for greater sales was laid (see Figure 6.6).

Yet not all parts of the country had bottlers who were financially strong enough to buy outright neighbouring franchise areas. Here, mergers were the preferred solution, with bottlers holding shares in the merged entity. Even arrangements stopping short of full merger were permitted, as long as certain binding commitments and legal structures were adopted. In this situation, the Coca-Cola Company gave the rights to bottle and distribute Coca-Cola products to a company in which several bottlers had a stake (known as a Franchise Carrier Company; by the end of 1991 there were ten). Its territory was enlarged to cover the previously exclusive territories which each bottler member held (see Figure 6.7). In addition to the standard franchise agreement (see below), the Company demanded that the Franchise Carrier Company should set out, and stick to, a timetable for the centralization of its members' production facilities, marketing departments, information systems, administration structures, and so on. For the distribution of the product, bottler members become distribution-only franchisees, but are committed to the terms and conditions of the franchise agreement signed by the Franchise Carrier Company. Specific performance targets, for example, govern their distribution rights. Anyone failing to reach these targets within their distribution territories can lose their rights to do so

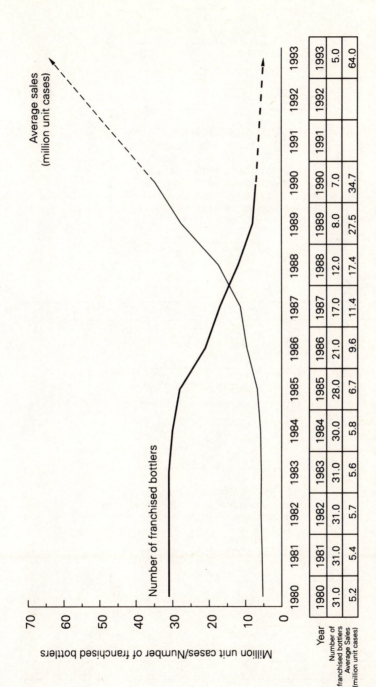

Year	1980	1981	1982	1983	1984	1985	1986	1987	1988	1989	1990	1991	1992	1993
Number of franchised bottlers	31.0	31.0	31.0	31.0	30.0	28.0	21.0	17.0	12.0	8.0	7.0			5.0
Average Sales (million unit cases)	5.2	5.4	5.7	5.6	5.8	6.7	9.6	11.4	17.4	27.5	34.7			64.0

Figure 6.5 Number of franchised Coca-Cola bottlers accounting for 50 per cent of total sales and their average sales in Germany, 1980–1990

Source: Archives, Coca-Cola, GmbH, Essen.

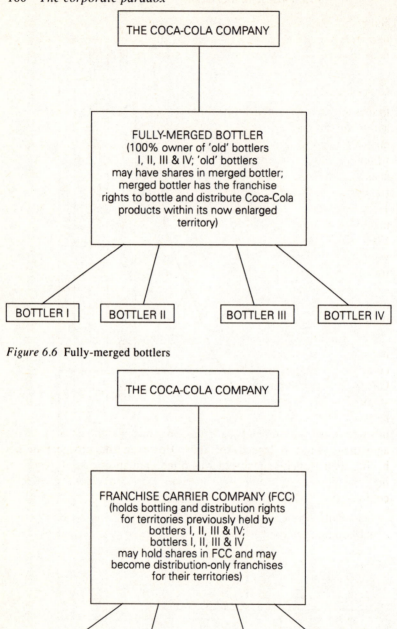

Figure 6.6 **Fully-merged bottlers**

Figure 6.7 **Franchise carrier company**

and be bought out from the Franchise Carrier Company by other members. As protection against both, targets (sales or investment, see below) need to be met even if this means reducing their own profits to do so.

Contractual changes

Franchise contracts are written normally by franchisors, for franchisors, and offered on a take-it-or-leave it basis to franchisees. It is therefore not surprising to find that franchise contracts impose certain controls which are designed, primarily, to serve the interests of the franchisor ahead of those of the franchisee. In this the Coca-Cola Company's franchise contracts are no different to many others (Chapter 4; Kessler, 1957; Macaulay, 1973; Beale, Harris and Sharpe, 1989). However, many discussions concerning the new contract did take place with the Franchisees' Association and concessions were made; the Company wanted to reform *not* abolish the existing network. Nevertheless, a franchisor (whether they be a manufacturer of soft drink concentrates, a car manufacturer or an owner of a business format) wants franchisees to maximize volume (as measured by units or turnover) since from this their income is derived.

The articulation, and hence strength, of this control varies and, moreover, is subject to change (Chapter 5). A comparison of the early contracts governing the Coca-Cola Company's franchise relationship in Germany with the current one bears this out. Originally, franchisees simply undertook to make every effort and to employ all the means necessary to expand the volume of Coca-Cola products sold. In practice, this commitment had little force during the currency of the agreement, since it lacked specifics. However, the prospect of not having their franchise renewed was often enough to push franchisees into the pursuit of loss-making activities towards the end of their contracts. For example, a former bottler recalled that:

> Coca-Cola [the Company] pressurized us to increase sales through marketing, special offers, promotions etc. We bowed to this pressure because we always had in the back of our mind the fact that our contract would come up for renewal. In the end, we were working more and more towards Coca-Cola's [the Company's] goal of increasing sales than our own profit goals.

(field notes)

The current contract, on the other hand, gives franchisees precise annual sales and investment targets, with the penalty of termination should *both not be met* at the end of a five-year period (15 years being the full contractual term).

The sales target commits franchisees to grow 2 per cent faster than the market for soft drink sales in their area. In addition, those whose sales per head fall below the network average have to grow at a faster rate still (the supplement rises in stages to 2 per cent). The annual minimum investment target is similarly specific. It is set at DM4.00 per head and linked to the sales increase required to meet minimum sales obligations (it is also adjusted for inflation). So for every case the bottler has to sell over and above its sales at the beginning of the agreement, a further DM0.60 investment is called for. With the exception of production, these investment obligations may be fulfilled in the following areas: advertising; sales promotions; market development; investments in technical sales aids such as coin-vendors, coolers, dispense units and so on; and the funding of rebate conditions for customers.

As planning tools to meet these *minimum* targets and to go beyond them (the requirement that franchisees 'make every effort and to employ all suitable means to develop and exploit the potential of the business' remains), a three-year plan and an annual working programme must be agreed with the Company. The former provides an overarching plan for the development of the business in terms of volume goals by product, package and trade channel, and the means to achieve these ends. The annual working programme provides more detail on the timing and financing of specific programmes: advertising; sales promotion; merchandising; the placement of technical sales aids; the introduction of new packages; and the servicing of accounts. Progress is assessed by the Coca-Cola Company monthly.

The bottling contracts governing the Coca-Cola Company's relationships in the US have also undergone change (see Table 6.2). However, the change has been more gradual on account of US bottling contracts existing in perpetuity. For example, only from 1986 (i.e. under the Master Bottler Contract) has the Company been able to set concentrate prices at its sole discretion, its advertising and marketing expenditures have become voluntary, and the Company and bottler must come to an agreement on an annual working programme setting out the bottler's plans for the forthcoming year. All of these elements existed in German contracts even before the introduction of the new contract.

However, the new German contract aims to go one step further. It aims to ensure that the gains made in production, occasioned by greater centralization, do not simply raise profits for the Company's, now much larger, German franchisees, but that, in addition, cost savings are reinvested in developing the market for Coca-Cola brands further, hence raising sales of concentrate and ensuring future growth.

Table 6.2 Evolution of Coca-Cola's bottling contract in the United States

Date	Event	Effect
1899	Parent Bottler Contract	Issued to Thomas and Whitehead for almost the entire US. Rights sold for $1. Sold territorial franchises to actual bottlers to whom they wholesaled Coca-Cola syrup. Parent bottlers bought Coca-Cola syrup at a fixed price which was then marked-up at 12.5c per gallon and resold to actual bottlers. By 1915 there were six parent bottlers.
1921	Consent Decree	The First World War reduced the supply of sugar and its price rose. The viability of the Company was threatened. Consent Decree meant: (1) price of syrup was fixed at $1.30 per gallon; (2) an additional 6c to be added for every 1c increase in price of sugar (above 7c per lb); and (3) contracts were valid in perpetuity.
1978	1978 Amendment	Syrup pricing formula changed. Calculated as product of Sugar and Base Elements. Sugar Element = average refiner prices (c/lb) × 5.663 (i.e. the historic per gallon yield of sugar in the manufacturing process). Base Element = $1.095 with an adjustment for inflation available if desired. Substitution of another sweetener allowable provided it yielded the same quality at a lower cost. Advertising expenditure by Company set at a minimum level of 8c per gallon of syrup sold provided bottler spends an equivalent amount. Marketing and merchandising programmes to be agreed – 8c per gallon of syrup sold acting as the floor. If no agreement, 4c per gallon spent according to the bottler's wishes, 4c per gallon according to the Company's. Advertising, marketing and merchandising minima adjusted according the Base Element. By 1987 97 per cent of US volume was supplied by 'amended' bottlers.
1983	1983 Amendment	Pricing formula for Diet Coke syrup. Price per gallon calculated as a product of Sweetener and Base Elements, both with ceilings adjusted for inflation ($0.80 and $2.80 respectively). Six per cent of Base Element is guaranteed to support Diet Coke advertising; 6 per cent is guaranteed to support Diet Coke marketing.
1986	Master Bottler Contract	A unifying contract for the Company's product range. Pricing at will; Annual Working Programme assessed quarterly – covers advertising, management and marketing plans; Company's contribution to advertising and marketing is made voluntary; failure to stick to Programme can offer grounds for termination or the repossession of a segment of the franchisee's territory. By 1991 72 per cent of US volume was supplied by bottlers operating under the Master Bottler Contract, 26 per cent were still operating under the 1978/1983 Amendments and 2 per cent were operating under the 1921 Consent Decree.

Source: contracts, amendments, explanatory documents supplied by and interviews conducted with Coca-Cola Company representatives.

Central sales company

One of the advantages to the Coca-Cola Company of establishing 'one bottler for Germany' would have been its ability to negotiate with, and offer a uniform set of prices and supply conditions to, customers with outlets previously located in more than one franchise territory. The existence of more than one franchisee gave each franchisee the right to veto any national agreement reached by negotiating committees which could either delay or even threaten the account. Despite the shrinking number of franchisees by the late 1980s, the accounts of Coca-Cola's largest customers – the national chains – continued to be exposed in this way.

Fearing the potential loss of their largest accounts in the face of mounting customer pressure, franchisees agreed to transfer their sales rights for large Key Account customers to a central sales company, Coca-Cola Deutschland Verkauf GmbH & Co. KG (hereafter referred to as CCDV) which became operational in March 1990. This is owned 50 per cent by Coca-Cola GmbH, 50 per cent by franchisees, and is supervised by a Board of four Coca-Cola GmbH appointed directors and four elected by Coca-Cola franchisees (votes initially weighted according to sales volume). The Supervisory Board determines the customers with whom CCDV will deal (as a rule of thumb, their outlets must be located in at least three German states and they must have a central purchasing department), and the *general* pricing and rebate conditions within which negotiations will take place. The inclusion or exclusion of certain customers from the Key Account list is decided by a simple majority, while for the pricing and supply conditions a majority of 6/8 is required. Currently, almost a half of total sales of Coca-Cola brands in Germany go through CCDV. Franchisees are still required to produce and distribute the Coca-Cola range of products and packages to Key Account customers within their territories, but only on the terms agreed by CCDV. Those who refuse to comply, lose territorial exclusivity for these accounts, and must therefore leave them to others to service.

In practice, CCDV can do something to tilt the balance between bottler and retailer in the bottler's favour. For example, in 1990 and 1991 CCDV was able to raise prices. However, the bargaining position of retailers remains strong on account of the competition for shelf space, access to high visibility outlets and the prospect (in the away-from-home market) of single sourcing. In fact, the operation of CCDV may simply mean that the conditions of supply are arrived at more quickly and national supply made more certain than in the past.

Safeguarding the sales of Coca-Cola brands to national account customers favours both bottler and the Coca-Cola Company alike. The costs of doing so, though, are unequally shared: the Company shoulders the costs of keener prices and more competitive conditions of supply which stronger and stronger retailers are able to demand *only* to the extent that it also acts as a bottler.[21] Indeed, CCDV provides an institutional device through which prices and conditions of supply can be enforced throughout the network. This is at little cost to the Company as a franchisor whose income is derived solely from the sale of concentrate to bottlers (although it pays 50 per cent of the costs of running CCDV).

CONCLUSION

Throughout the 1980s it became increasingly clear that Coca-Cola's franchise structure in Germany (as elsewhere) had outlived its usefulness. Small territories were preventing a low-cost production and distribution system being established, and the demands of large retailers for better terms and conditions of supply were becoming difficult to accommodate nationwide. Both problems were a product of a franchise structure which gave franchisees monopoly rights in the filling, packaging and sale of Coca-Cola's branded soft drinks within a small geographically defined area. While franchisees operated according to their own goals – profit maximization, the employment of family members, community status or whatever – these same considerations began to serve the interests of the Company – through the maximization of concentrate sales – less and less. As contracts approached renewal in the late 1980s, the Company flexed its hierarchical muscles by demanding changes. In the words of a franchisee:

> Although the conflict between franchisor and franchisee can be more precisely seen in theory than in practice, it became all too obvious during the process of restructuring. We were often told that we should consider ourselves as part of the Coca-Cola family, and that what was good for the Company was good for us. Yet Coca-Cola [the Company] owned everything of importance and was therefore able to call the shots.

(field notes)

As a result, a new generation of Coca-Cola franchisee has emerged. Today, there are fewer franchisees; but with larger territories they are able to support up-to-date, high capacity plants. Existing franchisees were given three options to produce these larger entities: either merge, buy each other out or create a franchise carrier company. Either way, franchisees must be committed to low cost, high volume production. Underpinning these production changes is a new contract designed to ensure that any economies made do not simply increase franchisee profits, but are also used to develop the market for Coca-Cola brands still further thereby reinforcing the products' 'Acceptability, Affordability and Availability' (known as the three As). Lastly, a central sales company was set up to deal with bottlers' largest customers, thereby ensuring that prices and terms of supply can be uniformly applied.

For the time being, the interests of franchisee and franchisor have been brought more into line. At present the emerging group of larger franchisees is committed to much larger production facilities, requiring a higher throughput to be economic. Sales, therefore, need to be higher, and investment in the market is the mechanism through which this is achieved. In the absence of a temporary coincidence of interests, however, the Coca-Cola Company's interests predominate. Sales and investment targets ensure that the Company's near absolute interest in volume growth (and hence sales of concentrate) takes precedence in guiding how Coca-Cola franchisees must operate if they wish to retain their franchise.

Although legally recognized as independent businesses, in practice the relationship between franchisor and franchisee is a close one. It consists of two inter-dependent elements. First, it is a market relationship through which franchisees either buy supplies of concentrate to make up the finished product, purchase cars/petrol from a manufacturer/oil company to sell on, and/or operate according to a tried and tested formula. Secondly, the market exchange itself is controlled and is subject to change – a range of contractual clauses govern the use to which these purchases are put. In other words, we really do need to look beyond the legal boundaries of the firm to gauge the true extent of a firm's power and control. As one franchisee put it, 'the cloak of the franchise system is often used to disguise the true situation of them [franchisors] calling all the major shots' (field notes). This includes reshaping the franchise structure to meet a changed commercial environment and underpin the organizational commitment to sales growth, first and last.

7   Conclusions

At one end of the scale is the independent retailer, exemplified by the general store or the corner grocery store. His [*sic*] independence is safeguarded: the manufacturer or wholesaler from whom he [*sic*] buys is only one of many possible sources supplying him [*sic*] with the goods he [*sic*] sells for resale. At the other end of the scale is the agent who may be a branch or subsidiary of the manufacturer. The franchised dealer occupies a position between the two extremes.

(Kessler, 1957: 1135)

The question which prompted this book is: who is in control of what, why and how in the franchise relationship? This is a variation of a theme at the heart of a large and still growing body of literature which explores how and why the capitalist firm came to dominate the industrialized world. Simply put, two opposing camps can be identified. On the one hand, there are those who believe that capitalist factories grew on account of their being able to seize for their owners two aspects of workers' control over the production process: control over the product; and control over the work process (e.g. Braverman, 1974; Marglin, 1974). Braverman refers to the separation of work tasks from one another, not on the grounds of efficiency, but as the means by which capitalists were able to carve out a place for themselves that they would not otherwise have had: 'without specialization, the capitalist had no essential role to play in the production process' (Braverman, 1974: 70). Marglin refers to the gathering of workers under one roof, which allows the employer to supervise and monitor the work of workers, thereby coercing more labour from them than would be possible if work were performed elsewhere. Set against this view are those promulgated by New Institutionalist economists (led by Williamson, various). Their argument is that organizational forms are determined by the quest for the most efficient. All transactions incur costs in the act of carrying them out.

These can arise at various stages – before, during and after the exchange has been consummated. As a rule, conducting an exchange within the administrative unit of the firm rather than the market takes place whenever the latter is associated with relatively high transaction costs.

Despite holding quite contrary views, the originators of each approach erected their theories to explain historical events dating back to the Industrial Revolution. More recent events have put a serious question mark over their present-day validity. Theories designed to account for the continued presence of hierarchical forms of work organization over apparently 'boss-free' enterprises such as co-operatives, self-employed contractors and franchisees have been thrown into confusion by the growth of these apparently autonomous forms of work. It is against this background that this book was researched and written.

A study of franchising was chosen because its promoters make much of the apparent 'boss-free' environment it creates for its franchisees, in terms of their dealings with the parent franchisor, if not with those whom they employ. Often heralded as a 'chance to be your own boss', 'an opportunity to mind your own business' and so forth, franchisors commonly use notions of independence to recruit franchisees. Because franchisees trade as legally independent businesses the implication is that the network cannot be considered to be a single hierarchical structure, but instead consists of several smaller hierarchies bound together by a common trade mark/idea/format. The book has therefore considered what ties the franchisor has over franchisees, why they are held and how these powers are exercised. To answer these questions several other matters have been addressed along the way. Why is franchising adopted, and by whom? What are its attractions, and to whom? What are the contractual parameters of the relationship? How is a contract made, and when is it used? What effect can a change in franchisor ownership have on how franchisees run their businesses? How does the franchise system respond to changes in the commercial environment they face? This chapter synthesizes the main argument of the book, while directing readers (particularly those who start by reading the conclusion!) to those chapters which tackle particular questions. The chapter then goes on to draw out some implications the book has for the specific study of franchising and the much wider issues surrounding reorganization of 'the firm'.

SYNTHESIZING THE ARGUMENT

It is common practice to regard employers as individuals. However, each employer is a registered company, whether operating on a self-employment, partnership or limited liability basis. Even so, an employer is regarded as a person in the eyes of the law. So, employers are held responsible under the principles of vicarious liability for the actions of their employees if they cause harm to others. Behind the legal persona of the limited liability company stand the shareholders who own it and the managers who manage it. The managers are those who, by virtue of the authority bestowed in them by the board of directors, legally represent and act in the interests of shareholders. Managers may or may not be shareholders themselves.

However, it is becoming harder to determine for whom one really works. Interlocking business relationships are at the heart of this confusion (subject of Chapter 1). For example, despite bearing a legally distinct label, wholly-owned subsidiaries are bound to their parents by ownership ties. In a typical large group there may be more than a hundred subsidiaries, or subsidiaries of subsidiaries, some held as far as five removes from the main board of directors, but still ultimately controlled by it (Haddon, 1983, quoted in Collins, 1990a). Similarly, holding a minority stake in a company may allow a minority shareholder sufficient leverage to determine its business behaviour in practice while absolving the shareholder from the actions of the company.[1] Provided there is a wide distribution of shares among other shareholders, a low propensity to vote and indifference among them, the largest minority shareholder can exercise control over the direction of the company with its minority stake. This shareholder may be yet another enterprise, and so the never-ending circle of connections may continue (Scott, 1986: 54–65). Firms can also be bound together by economic ties. For example, a core firm may surround itself with a ring of satellites which produce and supply components and distribute the finished products. The more economically dependent these satellites are, the greater the say the core firm has in how they operate. The McDonald's Corporation provides a good illustration of this in practice. McDonald's approves a handful of suppliers from whom its franchisees can order food, equipment and paper products for the running of their stores. The Corporation sets specifications and high quality standards which suppliers must meet.[2] As a result, most of McDonald's suppliers are heavily dependent on the Corporation for most, if not all, of their business (Love, 1987: 323–356). Franchisees are similarly dependent on McDonald's since their businesses are based on the intangible capital which McDonald's allows them to use. In other words, control need not be exercised by hierarchical authority alone. Less overt mechanisms can be deployed, which one cannot detect by simply identifying the legal boundaries of the firm. Franchising offers a classic illustration of this argument.

The dominant explanation for franchising is that provided by the New Institutionalist economists. For them, franchising represents the most 'efficient' organizational form of business, since only the most 'efficient' survive. The book takes issue with this interpretation (subject of Chapter 3). First, by securing greater effort from franchisees and their employees, franchisors can indeed increase their own revenues. However, this is not the same as increasing the level of output from the same quantity of inputs, since more output may simply be a reflection of more inputs. There are two competing concepts of 'efficiency' at work – one which takes account of everyone's interests and one which provides a justification for whatever organizational form is chosen from the point of view of those who decide. Secondly, without a concept of power, and an appreciation that franchisor and franchisee do not meet as equals, the New Institutionalists have no way of explaining how one concept of 'efficiency' takes precedence over the other. Thirdly, emphasis on cost comparison closes off the broader concept of efficiency from view.

The alternative explanation begins with the acknowledgement that the act of setting someone to work relies on seeking, at least in part, their co-operation and consent to perform a set of given tasks. This reliance can be reduced or increased by bestowing workers with limited or wide scope for autonomy in the way they carry out their allotted tasks (cf. Friedman, 1977, 1986). Franchising takes this to its extreme. Franchisees work for a profit instead of a wage, they have investments in the businesses they run and they are regarded as legally distinct from their franchisor. They therefore have incentives to work themselves and their workforces harder than they might otherwise do. While this may not necessarily be more efficient, in the sense of generating more outputs from a given set of inputs, it will give the franchisor the greatest benefit, in that it will drive up *their* revenues while pushing down on *their* costs. Franchising is adopted according to the latter criteria.

To understand why this is so, we must return to the basis on which franchisor and franchisee meet. The New Institutionalists assume they meet as equals. The book argues the contrary; the franchisee wants something from the franchisor more strongly than vice versa. The franchisor possesses a trade mark/product/idea/business format which the franchisee would like to use, while franchisees offer the money capital and their labour to set up an outlet. Just as employers recruit workers, franchisors recruit franchisees. The difference is that franchisees invest large sums of money in the purchase of the *physical* means of production (raw materials, plant, equipment), hire their own workforce (if appropriate) and operate as a legal distinct and separate entity from their franchisor. Nevertheless, they operate according to their franchisor's instructions and pay for the privilege. Payments are related to franchisee turnover by way of a percentage royalty on sales and/or the mark-up on supplies provided by the franchisor. The greater the franchisee's sales the greater the franchisor's revenue. Since franchisees make their living from the profits of their businesses, they have a tendency to work harder and longer (as well as ensuring that their workers, if any, do likewise) than they would if they were 'employed' on a traditional basis.

The analysis of the contractual ties which exist between franchisor and franchisee highlights where the balance of power really lies (subject of Chapter 4). Analysing what is included and what is left out of a franchise contract gives an indication of what makes franchising work. This may be summarized in three points. First, despite operating in the absence of someone looking over their shoulder, franchisees are required to operate within procedures laid down and often subject to unilateral change by the franchisor. Moreover, franchisees are sometimes committed to adhere to franchisor-set performance targets, and, in any case, to give the aim of the franchisor (turnover maximization) primacy in the running of the business. Secondly, while they appropriate the profits (and losses) of the business, they do so only after they have made turnover-related payments to their franchisor. Thirdly, although franchisees buy or lease much of the physical business apparatus, some parts remain in the hands of the franchisor, and some have franchisor-imposed restrictions on their use both during and after the currency of the agreement. Furthermore, franchisees have no ownership rights in the intangible business assets – they simply 'borrow' the business idea, trading name and/or format.

Nevertheless, there is no such thing as a standard franchise contract. To capture some of these variations, a 'soft'–'hard' continuum of contracts can be constructed. This suggests that some franchise systems are more tightly controlled by their franchisors than others. However, the specification of legal clauses and their use may not always coincide. There are several intervening factors. A franchisor's desire for and customer expectation of uniformity will make the franchisor less tolerant of maverick franchisees who do not follow the operations manual to the letter than a situation where uniformity is of lesser import. Franchisors are also unlikely to turn a blind eye to other contract violations (such as falling short of turnover targets, non-payment of royalties) and more likely to refuse to renew contacts, where the demand for franchised products/services is buoyant and there are plenty of suitable franchise candidates waiting for a franchise. Also, contractual powers to limit the use by a former franchisee of a franchisor's 'know-how' and any tangible assets in which it has a 'stake' are likely to be vigorously deployed.

What can happen when circumstances beyond franchisees' control change is the subject of Chapters 5 and 6. The franchisor may change hands, and the new owners may have a different idea of how the business should be run. At its extreme, a new contract may be issued. This may seek to tighten the relationship so as to give the franchisor what it considers an adequate return on its investment. Franchisees will have the choice to either accept or reject these conditions, but like workers facing new owners they will unable to carry on as before.

The commercial environment which franchisees face may change. It may open up opportunities for expansion with which a franchise system, as then constructed, may find it difficult to cope. Franchisees may no longer have the appetite for growth, they may be too small to deliver low cost products and their customers may be purchasing the same products (at different prices) across several franchise territories. The prospect of greater total sales (and hence higher franchisor revenues) may prompt the franchisor to overhaul of the entire franchise set-up. Fewer, but larger, franchisees may be better able to deliver lower cost products, thereby freeing more resources for longer-term investments in the business and reducing the number of franchisees with whom national customers have to deal. Existing franchisees may be offered a choice: either go along with the changes or else leave the network. This has been at the heart of the changes which have recently taken place in the Coca-Cola Company's franchise system in Germany. Indeed, similar developments have taken place in the way the Coca-Cola Company does business worldwide (subject of Chapter 6).

Contrary to the rhetoric which so often accompanies the mention of franchising, this book argues that franchisees operate businesses which are neither independent nor subsidiaries of another company. They can more aptly be considered to be 'betwixt and between' these two extremes (as in the quotation at the top of this chapter).[3] This has a number of implications for the study of franchising and for the study of business organization more generally.

DRAWING OUT SOME IMPLICATIONS FOR THE STUDY OF FRANCHISING

The argument of this book has several implications for the study of franchising, and in particular how we seek to understand issues which arise in practice. These can be summarized under three headings: pressures to organize franchisee associations; franchisees' personnel policies and practices; and franchising as viewed by labour law. Each reflects the ambiguous nature of the franchisee's status: sometimes acting and responding more like employees, while at other times resembling their rhetorical identity as independent businesses.

Pressures to organize franchisee associations

Although in the eyes of the law employer and worker are free and equal parties to the employment contract, 'there is usually no comparison between the consequences for an employer if an employee terminates the contract of employment and those which will ensue for an employee if he [*sic*] is dismissed' (Donovan Report, 1968: 142). Much of people's lives are tied up with their work. Their incomes and prospects for the future are founded on the expectation that their jobs will continue. Many friendships are made at work, and one's social standing in the community often derives from one's job. This is even more true for franchisees. Franchisees often risk their life savings in taking up a franchise and put many of their possessions (especially their houses) on the line. Their role as an employer of others (particularly if a relatively large employer in a local community, e.g. Coca-Cola bottlers in the early days) can bestow significant political and economic influence. All this is at risk if the franchise is lost.

The *raison d'être* for trade union organization of workers is as a means to redress the balance of power between employers and workers. The guiding principle of the collective organization is the notion that 'united we stand, divided we fall'. In other words, an attack against one member is considered an attack against all. Given the book's argument that franchisees have similarities as well as differences with employees, have collective organizations of franchisees been formed to represent franchisees' interests against those of franchisors'? The short answer appears to be: yes and no.

Attempts to organize franchisees have to overcome several large obstacles. First, franchisees are recruited on a take-it-or-leave-it basis. There is little, if any, room for negotiation about the terms of the relationship, which then generally last for 5, 10 or 15 years. Consequently, there are no annual negotiations around which to build support. Second, franchisees are often spread far and wide. There may be little opportunity to meet to discuss common problems and concerns. Third, franchisees may be too busy making their businesses work to be able to take time out meeting others in the same boat. Fourth, forming an association of franchisees cuts across franchisees' *feelings* of independence by acknowledging their reliance on others. A group of people for whom the status of 'independent' entrepreneurs is an ideal worthy of realization cannot easily discard the image of their being in partnership with their franchisor. These factors, coupled with franchisors' preference to deal with franchisees on a individual basis, have served to dilute the pressures to organize franchisee associations.[4] Some franchisors have sought to head off the formation of hostile franchisee associations by setting up franchisor–franchisee joint consultation committees. These can be variously organized: representatives can either be elected or appointed to serve and the committees can be nationally or regionally based. Their role is to act as a two-way communication channel, thereby alerting the franchisor to any issues which might prove contentious as well as providing a forum for suggestions to be discussed. Nevertheless, joint consultation committees are unlikely to satisfy the demands of franchisees if changes which will have a far-reaching effect on their businesses look likely to be carried out.

A common threat can provide the catalyst for the organization of franchisees. However, timing and the extent of the threat will affect the degree to which a group identity develops. For instance, modest changes to the contract instituted as and when franchisees' contracts come up for renewal are unlikely to provoke much of a reaction. If, on the other hand, the change is far-reaching (e.g. raising royalties and changing the way franchisees run their businesses, as in Chapter 5) and/ or the franchisor chooses to introduce it for all franchisees at the same time, then the conditions for a collective response are much more conducive.

Several examples serve to illustrate this point in practice. By the early 1970s, six national brewers had emerged from a large number of family-run small and medium-sized brewers which were the mainstay of the brewing business in the UK 20 years before. Then, it could be argued that 'a brewing business is a colony of houses; to close one is to abandon a member of the colony and so the strong support the weak' (Seldon, 1953: 43). However, since the 1970s brewers have had to re-evaluate the basis of the brewery–tenant relationship as financial pressures have tightened and as they have become a more important determinant of brewery behaviour. The break with the 'colonial' style of this relationship can be dated from the early 1970s, when tenants began to form associations to protect themselves against the brewers' demands for higher rents and the possibility that the most profitable pubs would be taken back as brewery-managed ones.[5] The growth of this collective consciousness challenged 'the general theory that the tenant [franchisee] could not do anything much about anything because the brewer had the last word' (*Morning Advertiser*, 16 July 1971, quoted in Hawkins, 1972: 37).

Collectivism has also taken root, albeit briefly, within McDonald's network of franchisees in the US. The number of units owned and operated by McDonald's rose from 9 per cent in 1968 to 31 per cent in 1975. Franchisees who wanted to remain within the system began to express concern that McDonald's might not continue to be committed to franchising, and that their contracts would not be renewed when they fell due (many were up for renewal in the mid-1970s). In addition, franchisees were anxious that the expansion of the number of Mc-Donald's stores would adversely affect the sales and profits of existing stores. Indeed, an executive of the McDonald's Corporation has been quoted as saying that 30 per cent of all new stores at that time had some measurable impact on the sales of nearby stores, and that 5 per cent of these stores reduced the profits of nearby stores (Love, 1987: 385). Against this background the McDonald's Operators' Association (MOA) was formed in 1975.

However, many of the issues on which MOA was founded evaporated shortly after its formation. McDonald's reduced the proportion of outlets it owned – to around one-quarter today – and it formalized its rewrite policy so as to make clear what needed to be achieved to be considered a renewable franchisee. The MOA's strength was further sapped by the establishment of the National Operators' Advisory Board (NOAB) and the appointment of an Ombudsman for dispute resolution. The NOAB is composed of two franchisees from each region, elected by the operators. Its brief is to examine and discuss all policies affecting the relationship between franchisees and McDonald's. Although its role is purely advisory, NOAB's opinions cannot be easily ignored. Disputes between McDonald's and a franchisee are referred to an Ombudsman, first set up in 1975. The Ombudsman consists of an operator, who is similarly placed in terms of size, age and history to the complainant, and a McDonald's representative. The dispute is reviewed and a report compiled with the aim of reaching a conciliated settlement. Against this background the pressures for independent franchisee representation waned, and with it the MOA was effectively disbanded in 1977.[6]

More recently, franchisees have shown their mettle in exercising influence on decisions made at the corporate (franchisor) level. For example, in the late 1980s the Pillsbury Corporation proposed spinning off its Burger King chain into a debt-laden company in a bid to thwart a takeover attempt by Grand Metropolitan, the UK drinks and food group. Three years previously Burger King franchisees in the US had banded together to form an association (at that time 5,200 of its 5,900 outlets worldwide were located in the US). The proposed spin-off prompted Burger King franchisees to use their newfound clout. The franchisees were opposed to the spin-off because they feared the debt would result in reduced support and endanger the chain in an economic downturn. While not endorsing Grand Metropolitan's bid for the chain, the hostility of the franchisees' association to the proposed spin-off raised the possibility of franchisees withholding royalties or otherwise wreaking havoc with Pillsbury's cash flow. This almost certainly made the banks loath to finance the spin-off, and as a result the franchisees' vote of no confidence may effectively have scotched Pillsbury's plan for staying independent. Grand Metropolitan took over Pillsbury in late 1988 (*Wall Street Journal*, 29 November 1988; *New York Times*, 4 December 1988; *Wall Street Journal*, 22 February 1989).

Franchisees have sometimes had a successful impact on who they want to lead the chain. For example, the replacement of Manpower's chief – the temporary employment agency chain – by the executive chairman of Blue Arrow – the UK employment agency group – provoked a hostile reaction from the Association of Manpower Franchisees in the US. This followed Blue Arrow's takeover of Manpower in September 1987. The enlarged Blue Arrow generated 35 per cent of its profits from the US, almost entirely from Manpower. The franchisees played a key role, contributing an estimated 60 per cent of Manpower's annual revenue. The Association passed a vote of no confidence in the new management and vowed to make efforts to unseat certain members. Its scope for action was, however, limited. They could leave Manpower, but they could not legally compete against it for two years (cf. Chapter 4). They could pay their franchise fees into a third party account and take Blue Arrow to court. This would be a lengthy and costly procedure, and in any case franchisees would be hard pressed to make the case that Blue Arrow had damaged their businesses. Nevertheless, the strength of feeling franchisees expressed seemed to be sufficient for Blue Arrow's board of directors to reverse their earlier decision. The franchisees by expressing their grievances collectively had got their way (*Sunday Times*, 18 December 1988; *Financial Times*, 21 December 1988; *Financial Times*, 14 January 1989).

The establishment of a collective identity among franchisees has, nonetheless, been patchy and largely confined to associations within rather than across chains. Even when such an identity has emerged it has often petered out once the threat has been extinguished. Moreover, the label 'trade union' is often vehemently shunned whenever the forces of collectivism are engaged, since this would sit uncomfortably with notions of 'being one's own boss'. For example, the Dyno-Rod

Franchisees' Association ends its articles of association with the following: 'the Association shall not support . . . any regulation, restriction or condition which if an object of the Association would make it a Trade Union' (quoted from *Labour Research*, 1986: 20).[7] Indeed, franchisees' associations have sometimes been formed as a result of franchisee groupings set up to fight unionization drives among their employees (Luxenberg, 1985: 267–268). The fortunes of franchisee associations, their influence and strength seem to be bound up with the ambiguous position of franchisee members – sometimes taking on more of an appearance which resembles independent entrepreneurs, sometimes acting more like workers.

Franchisees' personnel policies and practices

In terms of franchisee's personnel policies and practices, franchisors claim that these are franchisees' responsibilities (Stanworth *et al.*, 1986: 241). However, there may be circumstances in which franchisors intervene in the affairs of their franchisees on account of their industrial relations policies and practices. This would seem to cast some doubt over claims that franchisees act entirely on their own account in these matters. Moreover, the franchise system itself affects, albeit indirectly, what franchisees do in this area.

Despite taking a stand-off position with regard to the terms and conditions on which franchisees engage their own workers, if they employ anyone, controversial decisions in this area can eventually bring franchisor intervention. This was most visible in the case of an episode involving the Coca-Cola Company and one of its three franchised bottlers in Guatemala during the period 1976–1985. In short, the bottler who held the franchise rights for Guatemala's capital city and surrounding areas, Embotelladora Guatemalteca SA (EGSA), was engaged in a battle to thwart the unionization of its bottling facility throughout the period. An attempt to dismiss trade unionists from the plant in 1976 was followed by an occupation, with EGSA eventually backing down. However, other tactics were deployed against the union. New workers were employed on the condition that they would not join the trade union, they were paid higher wages, staff associations were set up by the company, a dozen or more companies were established to divide the union's organizing activities and there were reports of physical violence and intimidation against activists (Tobis, 1977; Gatehouse and Reyes, 1987: 6–8).

By the late 1970s these events were raised by the Interfaith Centre for Corporate Responsibility (ICCR) at the Coca-Cola Company's Annual

General Meeting. By using its rights as a shareholder, the ICCR submitted a resolution in December 1978 which called on the Company to insert a code of conduct for labour relations into its franchise contracts. This was defeated. The Company claimed that it could do nothing until the franchise contract came to an end, since the franchisee had not committed a breach. The contract was not due to expire until October 1981.

By now, the Guatemalan trade union representing the franchisees' workers had contacted the Geneva-based International Union of Food and Allied Workers' Associations (IUF). International support began to be mobilized during 1980. There were production stoppages at Coca-Cola plants in Finland (25–28 April), New Zealand (29 May) and Sweden (one week in late April). Stoppages were threatened in Canada, Mexico, the Federal Republic of Germany, Norway and Britain (Gatehouse and Reyes, 1987: 14–18). Also consumer boycotts began. The Coca-Cola Company responded by negotiating with the IUF. An agreement was reached whereby the franchise owner was bought out and replaced with new owners, the trade union was recognized, and the staff association was dissolved. The new owners took over in September 1980.

However, this provided the EGSA workers with only a temporary reprieve. During 1983, sales and production from the plant began to decline sharply, and the products of the other two Coca-Cola plants in Guatemala began to be sold within EGSA's franchise territories. On 20 February 1984, EGSA was declared bankrupt and the plant was closed. The workers occupied the plant and called once again for international support. This was once again forthcoming. On 7 May production stopped at 13 different Coca-Cola bottling and canning plants in Norway. In Italy, several short stoppages occurred at Coca-Cola plants while workers met to hear reports on the situation in Guatemala. Austrian unions wrote to their local management threatening action. In Mexico, ten different bottling plants held solidarity strikes for three days each on a rotating basis, while in Sweden a full production and sales stoppage was staged lasting for three days. Further plans were in the pipeline: a week-long production, sales and distribution stoppage in Norway; an indefinite stoppage in Denmark; and a national boycott campaign in the US led by IUF affiliates, church groups and consumer associations.

Before these plans were put into practice a solution was reached in May 1984. The Coca-Cola Company agreed to sell EGSA to a 'reputable' buyer and to prevent the two non-union Coca-Cola plants in Guatemala from poaching EGSA's sales territory; it guaranteed that the new owners would recognize the trade union and the existing bargaining agreement; it also guaranteed to employ and pay the surviving 350 workers (96 had taken the offer of redundancy) until the plant re-opened; lastly, the plant would re-open with all 350 employees and no-one would be laid off unless sales failed to reach an agreed target within 60 days. In the event, it took seven months to find a buyer. All the terms of the original agreement were kept apart from the initial staffing levels – only 265 workers were re-employed, but a further 52 former employees were taken on shortly after as production and sales grew (Gatehouse and Reyes, 1987: 31–33).

This episode has a number of implications. First, it provides a rare example of a multinational company negotiating with an international federation of national trade unions. Second, by so doing it was negotiating with a federation which represented franchisees' workers as well as company ones. This carried the implication that it was responsible for those who worked for franchisees as well as for those who worked directly for the Company. Third, although franchising allows franchisors to remain unimplicated and untarnished by the actions of their franchisees, there can come a time when this ceases to be the case. In such a circumstance, the franchisor may actively intervene to protect its corporate image by putting mild pressure on the franchisee to change tack or else replace them with a franchisee that will.

Also the very nature of the franchise system is likely to have an indirect bearing on franchisees' personnel policies and practices. This is likely to operate in two ways. First, attempts by the franchisees' workers to unionize will inevitably stop short of the entire chain, thereby insulating franchisees from each other's industrial relations policies and practices. The printers' union, the National Graphical Association (NGA) now part of the Graphical Paper and Media Union, for example, successfully organized three Prontaprint shops in the Liverpool area in early 1985. Following two weeks of picketing, an agreement was reached: one of the NGA's recruits dismissed shortly after joining the union was reinstated, an additional seven days' holiday was agreed, trade union rates – on a phased basis over 18 months – and recognition for the NGA over future vacancies and negotiating rights were also conceded. The agreement, though, stopped short of establishing a closed shop (*Print*, October 1985; *Printing World*, 23 October 1985). The franchise structure makes each franchisee formally an employer of other workers, if appropriate. This therefore requires that workers' unions negotiate with each franchisee rather than with the owners of the chain.

Secondly, the franchise relationship has a knock-on effect in terms of franchisees' treatment of those (if any) they employ. The clearest consequence of franchising in this regard is cost minimization, and that of wages, in particular. Other cost savings are more likely to be at the expense of business standards, and hence are effectively outlawed by the franchisor's policing role. Forcing wages down is a far quicker way for franchisees to raise profits without having to share the benefits with their franchisor as they would if turnover were to rise. Unfamiliarity with the sector itself is also likely to mean that franchisees unconsciously disregard employment 'norms' and practices. Empirical support for this contention can be found in a comparison of the terms and conditions of work found to prevail in a survey of franchised and non-franchised high street printers in the East Midlands (Felstead, 1988). The survey found that those who worked for franchisees were more likely to be young, government-sponsored (i.e. YTS), women workers in receipt of payment levels and non-pay benefits (such as holiday pay) substantially below those paid by the industry's more traditional employers (Goffee and Scase, 1982). This is corroborated by a survey of American fast food restaurants which indicates that, despite the common characteristics that employees of company-owned and franchised restaurants exhibit, wages and especially fringe benefits (paid holidays, sick leave, uniform allowance, free meals, etc.) are greater for workers employed by company-owned stores than for those employed by franchisees. Furthermore, the tenure-earning profile is steeper at company-owned restaurants than those run under franchise ownership (Krueger, 1991; Katz and Krueger, 1992: 11). For the one-person franchise these substantive consequences remain, but take the form of 'hidden', and often unpaid, family labour 'helping out' whenever needed (cf. homeworking).

Franchisees largely conduct industrial relations as they see fit. However, franchisors will draw the line on policies and practices which tarnish the chain's image, thereby threatening sales. The franchise arrangement will also have a bearing on the terms and conditions franchisees offer to those who work for them. Trade union organization, for example, is likely to face the obstacle of recruiting and negotiating on behalf of small, dispersed pockets of workers employed by different employers (franchisees) although part of the same chain. Substantively, too, the urge to make a profit is likely to reduce the pay and conditions on which franchisees recruit their workers.

Franchising as viewed by labour law

Although franchises carry the label of legally independent businesses, labour law has on occasions challenged the validity of this characterization of how franchisees operate. Instead, the ambiguity of their position has not only been recognized, but on the balance of probabilities they have sometimes been relabelled as employees. These type of cases have been most prevalent in the more tightly regulated labour markets of Germany, Denmark and the Netherlands than in the less regulated ones of the UK and the US (*Der Spiegel*, 2 April 1990; Kneppers-Heynert, 1992).

For example, the Danish Watchmakers', Opticians' and Assistants' Union recently challenged Synoptik, a Danish chain of opticians, for circumventing legally binding national agreements reached between it and the Danish Employers' Association following the setting up of franchised outlets (Arendorff, 1986). On arbitration, the finding was that the terms and conditions of the franchise agreement were so similar to those of an employment contract that Synoptik's 'franchise' arrangements must be subject to the agreement reached between the trade union and the employers' association.

Similarly, Germany's works council legislation requires that workers have a say in the decisions their company takes on social issues; on questions of staff utilization, such as short-time or overtime work; and on questions of personnel, such as hiring, dismissal, redeployment and training (cf. Lane, 1989: 226–239). The legislation requires that co-determination on these issues takes place wherever entrepreneurial power of direction is concretely exhibited and exercised (Buschbeck-Bülow, 1989). In the franchise context, it could be argued that this would require the organization of works councils at the level of the franchisor not the level of the franchisee. Once again, though, this comes down to how independent franchisees really are. Where franchisees' independence has been considered too narrow, German courts have been ready to sustain claims that works councils for franchisees' employees should be organized at the level of the franchisor. They have even sustained claims that works councils should represent 'franchisees' there too (Schulz, 1988; Buschbeck-Bülow, 1989).

While the number of these cases is small (and limited to a few countries), they do reflect the argument that franchisees are neither fully in control of their 'own' businesses nor are they fully controlled. They also, no doubt, reflect the fact that redress to labour as opposed to commercial law offers disgruntled franchisees with relatively meagre levels of compensation if successful. Nevertheless, these cases serve to warn franchisors against seeking too tight a relationship with their franchisees; to do so, puts at risk the legally independent label under which their franchisees trade.

DRAWING OUT SOME WIDER IMPLICATIONS

The argument of this book has some wider implications beyond the world of franchising. These bring us full circle, since they relate to the question posed at the beginning of this book: where should one draw the boundaries of the firm? First, by offering an analysis of who controls what, why and how, the nature of the bonds between franchisor and franchisee have been thoroughly examined for the first time. Mechanisms of control remain in the hands of franchisors, which allow them to shape and reshape how franchisees do business. All of this is in spite of the fact that franchisees remain legally independent of the franchisor, invest their own money in the business and possibly employ others in the process of doing business. The implication this carries for the concept of the firm is far-reaching. It implies that some firms have the ability to wield power over others despite appearances to the contrary. Traditionally, economists have treated 'the firm' as a readily identifiable entity, yet this book has pointed out that such a label may bear little relationship to how businesses operate in practice. Similarly, whether a person is in one class or another matters a great deal to sociologists who seek to understand how social actors relate to one another. The finding that apparently independent entrepreneurs are answerable to others in the way they run their businesses cautions against bestowing them with unambiguously capitalist credentials. Indeed, there may be times when their actions reveal their contradictory social status. This book has also added to the case law evidence which suggests that there is no clear-cut answer to the question: what is and what is not a firm? Yet labour law continues to be based on the premise that there is.

Second, the declining importance of the large firm may be more apparent than real, with the locus of strategic control remaining firmly rooted with those who co-ordinate the activities of apparently autonomous centres of work (Cowling and Sugden, 1987: 11–16). Claims that the long-run trend of capital concentration and centralization has been reversed are premature, as are those which associate the rising number of the self-employed and small business owners with an 'enterprise culture'. Instead, we are witnessing the process of capital metaphorphosis in which firms are bonded together by less visible ties than before.

Much research effort has already been expended uncovering who owns whom (Zeitlin, 1974; Francis, 1980; Scott, 1986). This has found that minority stakes held in companies are often sufficient to steer a company this way or that. Modern businesses are just as much owner-controlled as in the past; all that has changed is their owner's identity (namely other companies), and the shrinking stake necessary for the exertion of control. This book suggests that franchising allows the same result to be achieved without holding a single share in the franchisee's business. In this sense, franchising simply represents the continuation of trends first identified by Berle and Means 60 years ago:

> Economic power, in terms of control over physical assets, is apparently responding to a centripetal force, tending more and more to concentrate . . . At the same time, beneficial ownership is centrifugal, tending to divide and sub-divide, to split into ever smaller units . . . In other words, ownership continually becomes more dispersed; the power formerly joined to it becomes increasingly concentrated.
>
> (Berle and Means, 1932: 9)

There is, though, one important difference: in the case of franchising, economic power is exercised not by *directly* owning and controlling the physical assets of doing business, but by controlling the use to which the intangible assets, such as the trade mark/idea/format, are put.

Defining 'the firm' as the means of co-ordinating production without using market exchange excludes any analysis of the many market exchanges which firms themselves co-ordinate and control. Many have made this oversight. Yet the world can rarely be understood in terms of dichotomies – as markets *or* hierarchies. Relationships can take on the trappings of both. The franchise relationship is possibly the most stark example of this paradox. Even so, the elements of market and hierarchy do not vie with each other on equal terms. The most important decisions remain in the hands of the franchisor and those made by the franchisee are confined within strict boundaries. This enables elements of hierarchy to be created, arranged and maintained through what looks at first sight to be the market mechanism. Yet only by looking beyond the legal institution of the firm and its apparently market-based inter-firm relationships can one fully appreciate who controls what, why and how. An assessment of the nature of inter-firm relationships is the key to such an investigation. By focusing on one specific form of business relationship – franchising – this book has provided a start in that direction. It has also exploded the myth that what you do not own you cannot control. Both the approach and the message prompts us to look at the apparent break-up of today's large corporations afresh and to ask more probing questions about who is really in control of what, why and how.

Appendix I

Franchise opportunities by business category, United Kingdom

Building services

A & B Window Centres
A1 Damproofing
A1 Hygiena Rod
Adamos
Alpine Windows
Bath Doctor (The)
Bath Wizard (The)
Bathcare
Brick-Tie Services
Britannic Windows
British Damp & Timber Preservation
Cash 'N' Carry Window Centres
Cico
Complete Weed Control
Countrywide Interior Landscapes
Creteprint
Crimecure
Culligan
Cupboard Love
Dampcure-Woodcure /30
Decordoors
Dyno-Electrics
Dyno-Locks
Dyno-Plumbing
Dyno-Rod
Ensave
Evvacote
Fersina Windows
1st Call
Garage Door Associates
Garage Door Company (The)
Glastint
Global Building Maintenance
  Contracts

Graffiti Management
Graham Sclater Services
Gun-point
Inliner
Insublind
Jet-Rod
Lakeside Security Shutters
Leadstyle
Lockmasters Mobile
Marley Paving
Master Thatchers
Metro Rod
Mixamate
Mortar Mason
Newlook Bath Services
Pass & Co
Perennia Conservatories
Presscrete Paving
Rainstopper
Re-Nu
Replacement Kitchen Door Company
  (The)
Selections by Conestoga
Servowarm
Stained Glass Overlay
Stanair Industrial Door Services
Stately Conservatories
Stoneage
Texas Homecare Installations
Transform Solid Wood Replacement
  Doors
Uticolor
Ventrolla
Victoriana Conservatories
Vinyl Master
Weed Man

Catering and hotels

Ashbys
Banana Fritz
Baskin-Robbins
Bewleys
Big Bite
Blue Berry's Brasserie
Burger King
Burger Star
Captain Toni's Pizza
Catermat Fresh Drinks
Choice Hotels International
Climat de France
Coffeeman Management
Dial-A-Dino's
Dixy Fried Chicken
Domino's Pizza
Don Millers
Dunkin' Donuts
Fatty Arbuckles
Favorite Fried Chicken
Gino's Dial-A-Pizza
Gourmet Pizza Co (The)
Grandma Batty's
Harry Ramsden's
Ho-Lee-Chow
Hoggies
Holiday Inn
Indian Cavalry Club (The)
Kansas Fried Chicken
Kentucky Fried Chicken
Krogab
Master Brew
Manhattan Pizza Company
McDonald's
Merryweathers
Mister Donut
Morley's
Mr Cod
Olivers
Pancake Place
Pennywhackers
Perfect Pizza
Pierre Victoire
Pizza Express
Poppins
Snappy Tomato Pizza
Sprint Pizza
Spud-U-Like
Super Sandwich Company (The)
Telephone Pizza Company
Tickle Manor Tea Room
Toasty Kitchens
Trading Post
Wimpy
Winstons Pizza

Cleaning services

Chem-Dry Southern Services
Chem-Dry Midlands Services
Chem-Dry Northern Services
Chores
Coverall of London
Dial-A-Char
Maids (The)
Minster Cleaning Services
Mister Kool's
Molly Maid
Odd-Jobs
PAS Clean
Poppies
Rainbow
Safeclean
ServiceMaster (carpet cleaning)
ServiceMaster (contract cleaning)
ServiceMaster (home cleaning)
Square 1 Cleaning Services

Commercial and industrial services

Accounting Centre (The)
Advend
Anicare
ASC Group
CES
Codon Alloys
Credit Exchange (The)
Focus MicroSystems
Fonehire
Giltsharp
Great Adventure Game (The)
Hanging Basket
High Level Photography
Instant Image
Laser Sporting Leisure
Local Post
M & B Marquees
Mastersharp
Modular Marquees

National Vacuum Cleaner Services
Nationwide Investigations
OTSS Business Centres
Pirtek
Powerclean
Profiles Business Bureau
Real Estate Signs
Recognition Express
Red Letters
Rivermist Business Services
Sign Shop (The)
Small Business Advisory Centres
Somerford Claims Association
Stockcheck
Time and Place Marketing Services
Traders Lines
Trustock Valuers
UKAS
Val-U-Pak
VDU Techclean Services
Wedding Guide (The)
Winster Hoesman
Wrights Living Interiors

Distribution, wholesaling and manufacturing

Alpine Soft Drinks
Autela
Bread Roll Company (The)
Car Paint
Charnwood Surgical
Chemical Express
Coca-Cola
Cookie Coach Company (The)
Dairy Crest
Dinkum Dog
Direct Salon Services
Durex Vending
Flower Express
MAC Tools
Motabitz
Northern Dairies
Original Poster Company (The)
Peneni
Snap-On-Tools
Spaceage Plastics
Trafalgar Cleaning Chemicals
Trust Parts
Unigate Dairies

Domestic and personal servcies

Allied Dunbar
Busy Bees
Careline
Cavendish Gee
Chancellors
Cinderella
Country Cousins
Devonshire Nursing Agency
Dimples
DIY Homeseller
First Impressions
HDC Clinic
Home Will Services
Homebuyers Advice Centre (The)
House of Colour
Ideal Ironing Service
Jet Doctor International
Just Wills
Kids' Place
Kidz
Kwik-Strip
Lawn Ranger and Pronto (The)
National Will
Peter Pan Nannies
Premier Wills
Roman Spa Hydromassage
Safe Hands
Safeway Motoring School
ServiceMaster (furnishing repairs)
Spice
Splashdance
Squires
St Christopher's Private Ambulance
Sweat-Box
Tinies
Trimline
Tumble Tots
2-to-9 Club (The)
William Green Financial Services
Wimbledon Nannies Worldwide

Employment agencies and training Services

Alfred Marks
Ashfield Personnel
Driver Hire-Workforce
EPC
Future Training Services

Lambourn Court International
Maindate
Masterclass Recruitment Training
  Consultancy
Onsite Training
Priority Management
Profile Plus
Roevin
Travail
Wetherby Training Services

**Estate agents and business transfer
  agents**

Agencies No 1
Balmforth & Partners
Britannia Business Sales
Century 21
Chancellors
Chancery Business Sales
Choices Home Sales
Cornerstone
Country Business Sales
Country Properties
Countrywide Business Transfer
Donald Storrie
Everett Mason & Furby
International Property Centres
Property Sales Partnership
Quest Estates International
RSBS Group (The)
Seekers
Town & Country Property Services
Whitegates Estate Agency

Parcel, courier, taxi, etc. services

Amtrak
Apollo Dispatch
Brewer & Turnbull
Business Post
Captain Cargo
City Link
Duty Driver
G-Force Couriers
Intacab
Interlink Express Courier Parcels
Ladycabs
Leopard Express
Nextday
Panic Link
Sameday

TNT Parcel Office
WPS Express

Quick printing and graphic design

AlphaGraphics
EuroSpeedy Printing Centres
Kalamazoo Ink
Kall-Kwik Printing
PDC Copyprint
PIP Printing
Print Designs
Prontaprint

Retailing

Alan Paul Hairdresssing
Apollo Window Blinds
Applewoods
Athena
Baratt Officentres
Barry M Shop (The)
Beanfreaks
Bellina
Betterware
Blinkers
Body and Face Place (The)
Body Shop (The)
Bodyline
Bow Bangles
Bow Bells Bridal Hire
Bride at Home
Bumpsadaisy
Capricci
Captain OM Watts
Cenoura
Cinderella Designer Gowns
Circle C
Circle K
City Cycles
Clarks Shoes
Clothesline
Colour Counsellors
Compleat Cookshop
Compleat Engraver (The)
Computerland
Coppernob
Copy Cats
Creative Crystal
Crown Optical Centre
Cullens
Dancewear

Das Haar
Dash
Decorating Den (Scotland)
Decorating Den (South West)
Descamps
Dollond & Aitchison
Dutch Blooms
Education Through Theatre
Fantastic Sam's
Fastframe
Fentre
Flower Barrow Company (The)
Flower Stop
Folio
Frame Factory (The)
Francesco Group
Freewheel
GBC Buildings for Leisure
Golf Galore
Goodebodies Natural Beauty
Grooms Formal Hire
Hall of Names (The)
Hire-Rite Centres
Hiretech Hire Centres
Holland & Barrett
Home Choice Videos
Home Choose Carpets
I Can't Believe It's Yoghurt
In-Style Optical Centres
In-Toto
Jacadi
J F Lazartigue
Just for the Night
Knobs & Knockers
Kwik-Silver Print
Late Late Supershop (The)
Levi Shop (The)
Mag-it
Mainly Marines
Moviebank (The)
Muggins
Multiples
Murrays Fresh Foods
Nectar
Network Dry Cleaning
Nevada Bob
Nippers
Opel Kitchens
Open Fire Centres (The)
Original Art Shops (The)

Outside Inside
Pandel Tiles
Phone-In
Pineapple
Pronuptia de Paris
Robert Norfolk
Robin Hood Golf Centres
Rodier
Room Service
Rusts
Ryman
Saks
Schreiber Furniture
Scoop-A-Market
Segal
Shadow Blinds
Sharps Bedrooms
Shed Shop (The)
Shell
Singer Fashion Workshop
Snappy Snaps
Snips in Fashion
Soap Shop (The)
Society Interiors
Spadesbourne
Spar
Stefanel
Strachen Studio
Strap-On-Wristwear
Swinton Insurance
Talassio
Tandy
Thorntons
Tie Rack
Toni & Guy
Vantage Pharmacy
Video Cube
Votre Beauté
UniChem Chemist
Uniglobe
Websters Knitters Paradise
Wedding Secrets
Weigh and Save
Young's Formal Wear
Yves Rocher

Vehicle services

Arrow Car, Van & Truck Rental
Auto Armour
Auto Colormatch

Autosheen
Autotechnik
Avis Rent-A-Car
Budget Rent-A-Car
Bubbles
Car-A-Val
Cartech
Computa Tune
Countrywide Car Hire
Driveline
Electro Tune
Elephant Bleu
Fleetshield Services
Hertz
Highway Windscreens
Hometune
Jet Clean

Lucas Autocentres
Magic Windshields
Mobiletuning
Mr Clutch
National Car Cleaning Company
Novus Windscreen Repair
Practical Car & Van Rental
PVC Vendo
Roadside ReStart
Silver Shield Automotive Glazing
Stop-A-Thief
Supreme Car Valeting
Thrifty Car Rental
Tune-Up
Tyrefix
Vecta
Wash 'N' Wax

Source: Franchise World Directory 1992 (Franchise World Publications: London, 1991), pp. 21–26.

Appendix II

Franchise opportunities by business category, United States

Automotive products/services

Aamco Transmissions
ABT Service Centers
Acc-U-Tune & Brake
Action Auto
Aid Auto Stores
Al & Ed's Autosound
American Transmissions
Ammark
Appearance Reconditioning Co
Apple Polishing Systems
Atlas Automative Transmission
Auto Care Express
Auto One Accessories and Glass
Autospa
Auto Valet
Avis Service
BF Goodrich Company
Brako Systems
Big O Tire Services
Brake World Auto Centres
Cap-A Radiator Shops of America
Car Care International
Car-Matic Systems
Car-X Muffler Shops
Champion Auto Stores
Cleanco
Continental Transmission
  International
Cottman Transmission System
Detail Plus Car Appearance Centers
Dr Vinyl & Associates
Eaglespeed Oil and Lube
Econo Lube 'N' Tune
End-A-Flat

Endrust Industries
EPI
Fair Muffler Shops
Fantasy Coachworks
Firestone Tire & Rubber Company
  (The)
Gibraltar Transmissions
Goodyear Tire & Rubber Company
  (The)
Grease 'N' Go
Grease Monkey
Great Bear Auto Centers
Guaranteed Tune Up
Hollywood Auto Decor
House of Mufflers Enterprises
International Cooling Experts
  Systems
Interstate Automative Transmission
Jalco
Jiffiwash
Jiffy Lube
Johnny Rutherford Tune/ Lube
Kennedy Transmission
King Bear
Lee Myles Associates
Lubepro's
Lube Shop (The)
Maaco
Mad Hatter Muffler
Magic Franchise Systems
Malco Products
Mark I Auto Service Centers
McQuick's Oilube
Meineke Discount Muffler Shops
Merlin Muffler Shops
Mermaid Marketing

Nick's Systems
Midas
Mighty Distribution System of
  America
Milex of America
Ming of America
Miracle Auto Painting
Mobile Auto Trim
Morall Brake Centers
Motra
Mr Transmission
Muffler Crafters
National Car Care Centers
Novus Windscreen Repair and
  Scratch Removal
Oil Can Henry's
Oil Express National
Parts Plus
Pit Pros (The)
Plug Buggy
Precision Tune
Quick-O
Service Center
60 Minute Tune
Sparks Tune-Up
Speciality Lubrication
Speedee Oil Change & Tune-Up
Speedy Muffler King
Speedy Transmission Centers
Spot-Not Car Washes
Star Technology Windshield Repair
Stereo Workshop
Steve's Detailing
Sunshine Polishing Systems
Superperformance
Three Star Muffler
Tidy Car
Total Systems Technology
Tuff-Kote Dinol
Tuffy Associates
TuneOmize Tune-Up Centers
Tunex
Ultra Wash
USA Auto Appearance Centers
USA Fast Lube Systems
Victory Lane Quick Oil Change
Wash-O-Tel
Western Auto
Ziebart International

Auto/trailer rentals

Affordable Used Car Rental System
AIN Leasing Systems
Airways Rent A Car
American International Rent A Car
Amtralease
Atlantic Rent-A-Car
Avis Rent A Car
Budget Rent A Car
Dollar Rent A Car
Fancy Flivvers National Franchise
Freedom Rent-A-Car System
Hertz
Payless Car Rental
Mr Rent A Car, Mr Lease A Car
Practical Used Car Rental
Rent-A-Dent Car Rental Systems
Rent-A-Wreck of America
Thrifty Rent-A-Car System
Ugly Duckling Rent-A-System
U-Save Auto Rental of America

Beauty salons/supplies

Americuts
Barbers, Hairstyling for Men and
  Women (The)
Command Performance
Cost Cutters Family Care Shops
Eash Hair
Elan Hair Design
Fantastic Sam's, The Original
  Family Haircutters
First Choice Haircutters
First Place
Great Clips
Great Expectations Precision
  Haircutters
Haircrafters
Haircuts
Hair Performers
Joan M Cable's La Femmina Beauty
  Salons
Lord's & Lady's Hair Salons
Magicuts
Mane Event (The)
Mantrap Professional Hair Salons
Poppers Family Hair Care Center
Pro-Cuts

Rainy Day People
Supercuts
Third Dimension Cuts

Business aids and services

A Night With The Stars
A-Script
Adam Group
Advantage Payroll
Agvise
Air Brook Limousine
Allan & Partners
American Advertising Distributors
American Business Associates
American Heritage Agency
Ameristar
ANA
An International World of Weddings
ASI Sign Systems
Associated Air Freight
Banacom Instant Signs
Barter Exchange
Best Resume Service
Binex-Automated Business Systems
H & R Block
Bread Box (The)
Brooker One
Building Inspector of America (The)
Business America Associates
Business Consultants of America
Business Digest
Buying and Dining Guide
Buy Low Enterprises
Cam-Tel Productions
Caring Live-Ins
Certified Capital Correspondent
Convenience Money Centers
Check-X-Change
Chroma Copy
Closettec
Closet-Tier
Colbrin Aircraft Exchange
Communications World
Comprehensive Accounting
Compufund National Mortgage
   Network
Concept III
Corporate Finance Associates
Corporate Investment Business
   Brokers

Correct Credit Co of Howell
Credit Clinic
Cycle Service Messengers
Data Destruction Services
Debit One
Deliverex
Development Services
Dial One
Dixon Commercial Investigators
Dynamic Air Freight
Eastern Union
Econotax
EKW Systems (Edwin K Williams
   & Co)
Extended Service of America
Financial Transaction
Focus On Bingo Magazine
Focus On Homes Magazine
Franchise Architects – Consultants
   for Franchising (The)
Franchise Network USA
Franchise Store (The)
Franklin Traffic Service
Future Search Management
Gascard Club
General Business Services
Go-Video
Headquarters Companies (The)
Heimer Inspectors
Homecall
Homes & Land Publishing
Homewatch
Housemaster of America
Incotax Systems
Informerific
International Mergers and
   Acquisitions
K & O Publishing
K & W Computerized Tax Service
Kelly's Liquidations
Letter Writer (The)
Management Center (The)
Management Reports & Services
Mail Boxes Etc USA
Mail Sort
Marcoin
McTaggart Mortgage Assistance
   Centers
Medical Insura Form Service
Mel Jackson

Mifax Service and Systems
Million Air Interlink
Money Concepts International
Money Mailer
Mortgage Service Associates
Motivational Systems
Mr Sign
Muzak
Namco Systems
National Housing Inspections
National Tenant Network
Nationwide Income Tax Service
  Company
Needle In A Haystack Audio Video
  Service Center
Office Alternative
Office (The)
Packaging Know-How and Gift
  Shipping
Packaging Store (The)
Padgett Business Services
Pennysaver
Pension Assistance Through Hicks
Petro Brokerage & Service
Peyron Associates
Pilot Air Freight
Pinnacle 1 International
PNS
Pony Mailbox and Business Center
Prime-PM (The)
Princeton Energy Partners
Priority Management Systems
Proforma
Property Damage Appraisers
Property Inspection Service
Protocol Message Management
  Centers
Proventure
Realty Counsel Brokerage
  Management
Recognition Express
Reliable Business Systems
Room-Mate Referral Service Centers
Sandy Hook Scientific
Sara Care
Sav-Pac – The Money Saver
Selectra-Date
Signery Corporation (The)
Sign Express
Sign Stop

SMI International
SNC Telecom Problem Solvers
Sound Tracks Recording Studio
Southwest Promotional
Stork News of America
Stuffit Company
Super Coups
Tax Man
Tax Offices of America
TBC Business Brokers
Tender Sender Venture
Tote-A-Shower
Transformation Technologies
Trimark
Triple Check Tax Service
TV Facts
TV Focus
TV News
TV Scene
TV Tempo
TWP Enterprises
UBI Business Brokers
Voice Enterprises
VR Business Brokers
Western Appraisers

Campgrounds

Kamp Dakota
Kampgrounds of America
Yogi Bear's Jellystone Park

Children's Stores/Furniture/ Products

Baby's Room USA
Bellini Juvenille Designer
  Furniture
Lewis of London
Peppermint Fudge
Pregnant Inc For Babies Only

Clothing/shoes

Allison's Place
Athlete's Foot Marketing Associates
Athletic Attic Marketing
Bags & Shoes
Bencone Outlet Center
Canterbury of New Zealand
Cherokee
Fleet Feet
Formal Wear Service

Gingiss
Hats in the Belfry
Jilene
Just Pants
Kiddie Kobbler (The)
Lady Madonna Management
Lanz
Mark-It Stores (The)
Mode O'Day Company
New York City Shoes
President Tuxedo
Sally Wallace Brides Shop
Second Sole
Sox Appeal
Sportique
Sports Fantasy Marketing
T-Shirts Plus
Tyler's Country Clothes
Wild Tops

**Construction/remodelling –
materials/services**

ABC Seamless
Acrysyl International
Add-Ventures of America
American Leak Detection
Archadeck Wooden Patio Decks
Bathcrest
Bath Genie
B-Dry System
California Closet
Captain Glides
Chimney Relining
Closettec
College Pro Painters
Drain Doctor (The)
Easi-Set Industries
Eldorado Stone
Eureka Log Homes
Facelifters
Firedex
Flex-Shield
Four Seasons Greenhouses, Design
   and Remodelling Center
GNU Services
Heritage Log Homes
Hydroflo System Basement
   Waterproofing
K-Krete
Kitchen Savers

Lavastone
Linc International (The)
Lindal Cedar Homes
Magnum Piering
Master Remodellers National
Miracle Method
Mister Renovator
Mr Build
Natural Log Homes
New England Log Homes
Northern Products Log Homes
Novus Plate Glass Repair
Paul W Davis Systems
Perma Ceram Enterprises
Perma-Glaze
Perma-Jack
Porcelain Match & Glaze Company
   of America
Porcelite
Redi-Strip Co
Ryan Homes
Screenmobile (The)
Service America
Smokey Mountain Log Homes
Speed Fab-Crete
SPR International Bathtub
   Refinishing
Surface Specialists
Timbermill Storage Barns
Wall Fill Worldwide
Windows of Opportunities (The)

Cosmetics/toiletries

Aloette
Caswell-Massey
'i' Natural Cosmetics Nutrient
   Cosmetic, LTC
Judith Sans
Key West Fragrance & Cosmetic
   Factory
Suzanne Morel Cosmetics & Skin Care
Syd Simons Cosmetics

Dental centres

American Dental Council
Dental Health Services
Dental Power
Dwight Systems
Jonathan Dental
Nu-Dimensions Dental Services

Drug stores

Drug Castle
Drug Emporium
Health Mart
Le$-On Retail Systems
Medicap Pharmacies
Medicine Shoppe
Snyder Drug Stores

Educational products/services

Barbizon International
Better Birth Foundation
Carole Riggs Studios (The)
Child Enrichment Centers
College Centers of Southern
    California
Creative Training and Motivational
    Services
Echols International Travel and
    Hotel Schools
ELS International
Gymboree
Huntington Learning Centers
Institute of Reading Development
John Robert Powers Finishing,
    Modelling & Career School World
    Headquarters
Kinderdance
Mac Tay Aquatics
Model Merchandising International
Perkins Fit By Five
Personal Computer Learning Centers
    of America
Playful Parenting
Playorena
Primary Prep Pre-Schools
Sandler Systems
Sexton Educational Centers
Sportastiks
Sylvan Learning
Tegeler Time Day Care System
Teller Training Distributors
Travel Trade School (The)
USA Travel Schools
Weist-Barron

Employment services

AAA Employment
Adia Personnel Services

Atlantic Personnel Service Systems
Auntie Fay
Bailey Employment System
Baker & Baker Employment Service
Bryant Bureau
Business & Professional Consultants
Career Employment Services
Cosmopolitan Care
Dennis & Dennis Personnel Service
Division 10 Personnel Service
Dunhill Office Personnel
Dunhill Personnel System
Employers Overload
Express Services
Five Star Temporaries
F-O-R-T-U-N-E
Gerotoga Enterprises
Gilbert Lane Personnel Service
Hayes Personnel Services
Heritage Personnel Systems
HRI Services
Intellidex Contrac
JOBS
Lloyd Personnel Consultants
Management Recruiters International
Murphy Group (The)
Norrell Temporary Services
Olsten Corporation (The)
Parker Page Associates
Personnel Pool of America
Place Mart
Regional Network of Personnel
    Consultants
Retail Recruiters International/
    Spectra Professional Search
Romac & Associates
Roth Young Personnel Service
Sales Consultants International
Sanford Rose Associates
    International
Snelling and Snelling
Sourcenet International
Temporaries
Tempositions
Thank Goodness I've Found . . .
    TGIF
Time Services
Todays Temporary
Transworld Temporaries
TRC Temporary Services

Uniforce Temporary Personnel
Uni/Search
Western Temporary Services

Equipment/rentals

A to Z Rental Centers
Adventurent/Club Nautico
Apparelmaster
Associated Video Hut
Grand Rental Station
Home Call Mobile Video Libraries
Major Video
Mr Movies
Nation-wide General Rental Centers
PCR Personal Computer Rentals
Remco Franchise Development
Renappli of America
Rental Centers USA
Sounds Easy
Taylor Rental
United Rent-All
Yard Cards
ZM Video Rental

Food – donuts

Bosa
Dawn Donut
Dixie Cream Flour Company
Donut Mole (The)
Donut Inn
Donutland
Donut Maker
Donuts Galore
Donuts 'n' Coffee
Dunkin' Donuts of America
Foster's Donuts
Honey Fluff Donuts
Jolly Pirate Donut Shops
Mister Donut of America
Southern Maid Donut Flour
   Company
Spudnuts
Tastee Donuts
Whole Donut Franchise Systems
   (The)
Winchell's Donut House

Food – grocery/speciality stores

All My Muffins
Alpen Pantry

American Bulk Food
Atantic Concessions
Atlantic Richfield
Augie's
Balboa Baking
Barnie's Coffee & Tea Company
Blue Chip Cookies
Le Croissant Shop
Boardwalk
Bread Basket (The)
Breaktime
Bulk International
Buns Master Bakery Systems
Cheese Shop International
Chez Chocolat
Cinnamon Sam's
Coffee Beanery (The)
Coffee Merchant (The)
Coffee Mill (The)
Coffee, Tea & Thee
Colonial Village Meat Market
Convenient Food Mart
Cookie Bin (The)
Cookie Factory of America
Cookie Store (The)
Country Biscuits
Dairy Mart Convenience Stores
Dial-A-Gift
Food-N-Fuel
Laura
Giuliano's Delicatesssen & Bakery
Glass Oven Bakery
Gloria Jean's Coffee Bean Shop
Grandma Love's Cookies and
   Company
Great Earth Vitamin Stores
Great Harvest
Great San Francisco Seafood Co
   (The)
Heavenly Ham
Hickory Farms of Ohio
In 'n' Out Food Stores
International Aromas
Jo-Ann's Nut/House
JR Foodmart
Katie McGuire's Olde Fashioned Pie
   Shoppe
Kid's Korner Fresh Pizza
Li'l Peach Convenience Food Stores
Mr Dunderbak

Mrs Powells Delicious Cinnamon
  Rolls
Neal's Cookies
T F M Co
Original Great American Chocolate
  Chip Cookie Company (The)
Papa Aldo's
Papa John's
Saucy's Pizza
Sav-A Step Food Mart
Southland Corporation (The)
Swiss Colony Stores
Tidbit Alley
T J Cinnamons
White Hen Pantry
Wyoming Alaska Company
Zaro's America's Home Bakery
Zip Food Stores

**Foods – ice cream/yoghurt/candy/
popcorn/beverages**

Baskin-Robbins
Ben & Jerry's Homemade
Bresler's 33 Flavors
Brigham's
Californian Yoghurt Company (The)
Carberry's Homemade Ice Cream
Carter's Nuts
Carvel
Chipwich a la Carte of California
Creative Corn Company
Custom Leasing Co
Davie's Ice Cream Shoppes
Dipper Dan Ice Cream Shoppes &
  Sweet Shoppes for the
  Connoisseur
Double Rainbow
Emack and Bolio's Ice Cream and
  Ice Cream Cakes
Ernie's Wine & Liquor
Foremost Sales Promotions
Frosty Factory
Frusden Gladse
Fudge Co (The)
Gaston's
J L Franklin & Co
Gelato Classico
Gorin's Homemade Ice Cream and
  Sandwiches
Great Midwestern Ice Cream Co (The)

Hardin Group (The)
Heidi's Frozen Yozhurt Shoppes
I Can't Believe It's Yoghurt
Ice Cream Churn
I Love Yoghurt
Island Snow Hawaii
J Higby's Yoghurt Treat Shoppes
Kara Signature Chocolates
Karmelkorn Shoppes
Kilwins Chocolates
Larry's Olde Fashioned Ice Cream
  Parlors
Marble Slab Creamery
M G M Liquor Warehouse
Mister Softee
Nielsen's Frozen Custard
Old Uncle Gaylord's
Peanut Shack of America (The)
Perkits Yoghurt
Phanny'Phudge Emphoriums
Popcorn Parlour
Real Rich Systems
Rocky Mountain Chocolate Factory
Steve's Homemade Ice Cream
Sweetcreams
Swensen's Ice Cream Company
TCBY Enterprises
Topsy's Shoppes
Tra-Hans Candies
Tropical Yoghurt
Truffles Chocolatier
Twistee Treat
Vic's Corn Popper
Whirla Whip Systems
White Mountain Creamery
Wizard Ice Cream & Confectionery
  Shoppe
Zack's Famous Frozen Yoghurt

Foods – pancake/waffle/pretzel

Elmer's Pancake & Steak House
International House of Pancakes
  Restaurants
Le Peep Restaurants
Mary Belle Restaurants
Pancake Cottage Family
  Restauarants
Perkins Restaurants
Vicorp Restaurants
Waffletown USA

Foods – restaurants/drive-ins/ carry-outs

A & W Restaurants
Across the Street Restaurants of America
All American Hero
Allen's Subs International
All-V's
Al's Bar BQ
Andy's of America
Appetito's
Applebee's
Arby's
Arthur Treacher's
Aunt Chilotta Systems
Aurellio's Pizza
Becalls Cafe
Bagel Nosh
Baldinos Giant Jersey Subs
Barbacoa
Barro's Pizza
Bash Riprock's Restaurants
Beefy's
Ben Franks
Benihana of Tokyo
Big Boy Family Restaurants
Big Cheese Pizza
Big Ed's Hamburgers
Boardwalk Fries
Bobby Rubino's USA
Bo-James Saloon
Bojangles' of America
Bonanza Restaurants
Bowincal
Boy Blue of America
Boz Hot Dogs
Bread & Company
Bridgeman's Restaurant
Browns Chicken
Bubba's Breakaway
Bun N Burger
Burger Baron
Burger King
Buscemi's
California Smoothie
Callahan's International
Captain D's
Carbone's Pizza
Carl Karcher Enterprises
Casa Lupita Restaurants
Cassano's
Castleburger
Catfish Shak
Catfish Stations of America
Cheese Villa
Chelsea Street Pub
Chicago's Pizza
Chicken Delight of Canada
Chicken Unlimited
Chili Great Chili
Chowder Pot
Church's Fried Chicken
Circles International Natural Foods
Cluck In A Bucket
Cock of the Walk
Colonel Lee's
Cooker Concepts
Country Kitchen
Cousins Kitchen
Cousins Submarine Sandwich Shop
Cozzoli Pizza
Crusty's Pizza
Cucos
Dairy Belle Freeze Development
Dairy Cheer Stores
Dairy Isle
Dairy Sweet
Daly
Damon's
Danver's
Del Taco Mexican Cafe
Diamond Dave's Taco Co
Dietworks of America
Dog N Subs Restaurants
Domino's Pizza
Dosanko
Druther's
Everything Yoghurt
Randall
Famous Recipe
Fat Boy's Bar-B-Q
Fatburger
Flap Jack Shack
Fletcher's Industries
Fluky
Fosters Freeze
Four Star Pizza
Fox's Pizza Den
Frankie's

Frenchy's
Fuddruckers
Fuzzy's
Giff's Sub Shop
Giordano's
Godfather's Pizza
Golden Bird Fried Chicken
Golden Chicken
Golden Corral
Golden Fried Chicken of America
Golden Skillet
Gold Star Chili
Good Earth
Grandy's
Great Gyros (The)
Greenstreets National
Happy Joe's Pizza & Ice Cream
   Parlors
Happy Steak Companies
Hardee's
Hartz Krispy Chicken
House of Yakitori Japanese
   Restaurants
Hubb's Pub
Huddle House
Hungry Hobo (The)
International Blimpie
International Dairy Queen
International Short Stop
International Yoghurt Company
Italo's Pizza Shop
Jack In The Box Foodmaker
Jake's
Jerry's Sub Shop
Jimboy's Tacos
Jo Ann's Chili Bordello
Johnny Rockets
Joyce's Submarine Sandwiches
Jreck Subs
JR's Hot Dogs
J Systems
K-Bob's
Ken's Pizza
Kettle Restaurants
Kentucky Fried Chicken
Koor's Systems
Lamppost Pizza
Landis Food Services
Larosa's
Lifestyle Restaurants

Little Big Men
Little Caesar
Little King
London Fish 'N' Chips
Long John Silver's
Losurdo
Love's Wood Pit Barbeque
   Restaurants
Macayo Mexican Restaurants
Mahan's Taco Inn
Maid-Rite Products
Marco's
Maverick Family Steak House
Mazzio's Pizza
McDonald's
McFaddin Ventures
Melvin's
Milton's Pizza House
Minsky's Pizza
Minute Man of America
Mountain Mike's Pizza
Mr Burger
Mr Chicken National
Mr Gatti's
Mr Jims Pizzeria
Mr Philly
Mr Steak
Nathan's Famous
New Meiji
New Orleans' Famous Fried
   Chicken of America
Noble Roman's
North's
Nugget Restaurants
Numero Uno
O! Deli
Olde World Cheese Shop (The)
Olga's Kitchen
Omaha Steakshops
Onion Crock (The)
Orange Bowl
Original Wiener Works (The)
O'Toole's
Pacific Tastee Freez
Pantera's
Paris Croissant Northeast
Pasquale Food Company
Pasta House (The)
Penguin Point
Pepe's

Peter Piper Pizza
Pewter Mug (The)
Pewter Pot
Philadelphia Steak & Sub Company
Pietro's Pizza Parlors
Pioneer Take Out
Pizza Chalet
Pizza Inn
Pizza Man 'He Delivers'
Pizza Pit
Pizza Rack
Plush Pippin Restaurants
Po Folks
Ponderosa
Pony Express Pizza
Popeyes Famous Fried Chicken &
   Biscuits
Port of Subs
Primo
Pub Dennis
Pudgies Pizza
Ranelli
Rax Restaurants
Red Robin
Ritzy's America's Favorites
Rocky Rococo
Roma
Round Table
Royal Guard Fish & Chips
Mariott
SAF California/Lettuce
   Patch
Salad Bar (The)
Samuri Sam Jr
Sbarro
Schlotzsky's
Scotto
Seafood America
Sea Gallery Stores
Sergio's
Shakey's
Showbiz Pizza Time
Sir Beef
Sirloin Stockade
Sir Pizza
Sizzler Steak-Seafood-Salad
Skinny Haven
Skipper's
Skyline Chili
Sonic Industries

Sonny's Real Pit Bar-B-Q
Soup and Salad
Steak Escape (The)
Stewart's Restaurants
Stuckey's
Stuft Pizza
Sub & Stuff Sandwich Shops
Sub Station II
Subway
Taco Bell
Taco Casa
Taco Del Sol
Taco Grande
Taco Hut
Taco John's
Taco Maker (The)
Taco Mayo
Taco Tico
Taco Time
Tark
Tastee Freez
Texas Tom's
Tippy's Taco House
Toodle House Restaurants
Togo's Eatery
Tubby's Sub Shops
2 for 1 Pizza
Uncle Tom's Pizza & Pasta
   Family Restaurant
Uno Restaurants
Vista
Ward's
WCF of America
Wendy's
Western Sizzlin Steak House
Western Steer-Mom 'N' Pop's
Westside Deli
Whataburger
Wiener King
Wienschnitzel
Winners
Yankee Noddle Dandy
Your Pizza Shops
Yummy Yoghurt
Zab's Development

General Merchandising Stores

Ben Franklin Stores
Coast to Coast Stores

Health aids/services

American Health & Diet Company
American Physical Rehabilitation
  Network
Beta Osteoporosis Diagnostic
  Centers of America
Body Beautiful Boutique
Claflin Home Health Centers
Concept 90 Personal Fitness
  Stores
Contempo Women's Workout
Corporate Chiropractic Services
Diet Center
Fortunate Life Weight Loss Centers
Heath Care Recruiters
Health Clubs of America
Health Force
Homecare Helping Hand
Informed
Jazzercise
Jeneal International Skin Correction
  and Health Centers
Lean Line
Life Time Medical Nursing Services
Medical Networks
Med-Way Medical Weight
  Management
National Health Enhancement
Nu-Concept Body Wrap
Nursefinders
Nutra Bolic Weight Reduction
Nutri/System
Omni Health
Optimum Health Systems
Our Weigh
Physicians Weight Loss Centers
Pregnagym
Respond First Aid
Slender Center
Sutter Medical Management
Thermographic Medical Associates
Thin Life Centers
TLC Nursing
Toning & Tanning Centers
Total Lifestyle
United Surgical Centers
Victory
Weigh To Go
Women At Large

Hearing systems

Miracle-Ear

Home furnishings/furniture – retail/repair/services

Abbey Carpet Company
Americlean
Amity, Quality, Restoration Systems
Carpet Beauty
Carpeteria
Carpet Town
Center Third Mattress Stores
Chem-Clean Furniture Restoration
  Center
Chem-Dry Carpet Cleaning
Cleanmark
Decorating Den
Dip 'N' Strip
Duraclean
Expressions
Fabri-Zone
Floor To Ceiling Store (The)
G Fried Carpetland
Groundwater
Guarantee System
Hillside Bedding
Howard Kaplan's French Country
  Store
Indoor Magic
International Home Marketing
John Simmons Gift
King Koil Sleep
Langenwalter-Harris Chemical Co
Laura's Draperies & Bedspreads
  Showrooms
Modernistic Carpet Cleaning
Murphy Beds of California
Naked Furniture
Nettle Creek
Off-Track Bedding
Professional Carpet Systems
Rainbow International Carpet
  Dyeing and Cleaning Company
Recroom Shoppe of Omaha
Repele
Scandia Down
Siesta Sleep
Slumberland
Spring Crest

Stanley Steemer
Steamatic
Storehouse
United Consumers Club
Wallpapers To Go
Wash On Wheels – Vac II
WFO
Window Works
Workbench

Insurance

America One
ISU International
Pridemark
Systems VII

Laundries, dry cleaning services

A Cleaner World
Bruck Distributing
Cache Cleaners
Clean 'N' Press
Coit Drapery & Carpet Cleaners
Dryclean – USA
Duds 'N' Suds
Golden Touch Cleaners
His and Hers Ironing Service
London Equipment
Martin
Wash-Bowl

Lawn and garden supplies/ services

Barefoot Grass Lawn Service
Chemlawn Services
Green Care Lawn Service
Johnson Hydro Seeding
Lawn Doctor
Lawn Specialties
Liqui-Green Lawn Care
Nitro-Green
ServiceMaster Lawn Care
Spring-Green Lawn Care
Super Lawns

Maid services/home cleaning/ party serving

Classy Maids USA
Daisy Fresh
Day's Ease
Dial-A-Maid

Domesticaide
Maiday Services
Maids (The)
Maids-On-Call
McMaid
Merry Maids
Metrol Maid Housekeeping
Mini Maid
Molly Maid
ServiceMaster Residential and
   Commercial
Servopro
Wright-Way Cleaning

Maintenance – cleaning/sanitation, services/supplies

All-Bright
Americorp
Cheman Manufacturing
Chem-Mark
Cleanserv
Clentech-Acoustic Clean
Coustic-Glo
Highland's Maintenance
Jani-King
Jani-Master
Lien Chemical Company
Mr Maintenance
Mr Rooter
National Maintenance Contractors
OK Services
Protech Restoration
Roof-Vac
Roto-Rooter
Sparkle Wash
Super Management
US Rooter
Value Line Maintenance
Wash On Wheels Indoor
Wash On Wheels – Wow
Western Vinyl Repair
West Sanitation

Hotels, motels

America's Best Inns
AmericInn
Clubhouse Inns of America
Compri Hotel
Days Inns of America
Econo Lodges of America

Family Inns of America
Forte Hotels of America
Forte Hotels International
Friendship Inns
Hampton Inn
Ha'penny Inns of America
Hilton Inns
Holiday Inns
Master Hosts Inns
Midway Hospitality
Prime Rate
Comfort Inns, Quality Inns
Ramada Inns
Red Carpet Inn
Residence Inn Company (The)
Scottish Inns
Sheraton Inns
Super 8 Motels
Tourway Inns of America
Treadway Inns
Woodfin Suites

Optical products/services

American Vision Centers
DOC Optics
First Optometry Eye Care Centers
Nuvision
Pearle Vision Centers
Site For Sore Eyes Opticians
Texas State Optical (TSO)

Paint and decorating supplies

Davis Paint

Pet shops

Docktor Pet Centers
Dog 'N' Cat Pet Centers of America
Lick Your Chops
Petland
Pets Are Inn

Printing

AIC International
AlphaGraphics Printshops for the
   Future
American Speedy Printing Centers
American Wholesale
   Thermographers
Business Card Express

Business Cards Overnight
Business Cards Tomorrow
Franklin's Copy Service
Ink Well (The)
Instant Copy
Insty-Prints
Kwik-Kopy
Minuteman Press International
(PIP) Postal Instant Press
Printmasters
Printnet Laser Printing Centers
Print Shack
Pronto Printer
Quik Print
Sir Speedy
Stop & Go Printing
Transamerica Printing

Real estate

Art Feller Auction and Real Estate
   Company
Norred Real Estate
Better Homes and Gardens Real
   Estate Service
Better Homes Realty
Century 21 Real Estate
Coast To Coast Properties
Cormeal
Earl Keim
Electronic Realty Associates
Financial Partners
Gallery of Homes
Golden Rule Realty of America
Help-U-Sell
Her Real Estate
Home Master Realty
Homeowners Concept
Hometrend
Iowa Realty
Key Associates
Real Estate One
Realty Executives
Realty 500
Realty World
Red Carpet Real Estate
Re/Max
Rental Solutions
Ski & Shore Michagan
State Wide Real Estate

Recreation/entertainment/travel services/supplies

Air & Steamship Travel
Ask Mr Foster Associates
Batting Range Pro
Championship Miniature Golf
Cinema 'N' Drafthouse
Corner Pockets of America
Cruise Holidays
Cruise Shoppes America
Cruises Only
Cue Ball Family Pool Courses
Empress Travel
Fugazy
Fun Services
Go-Kart Track
Golf Players
Grand Slam USA Academy
International Tours
Lomma
Mini-Golf
Pay N Play Racquetball of America
Photon Entertainment
Putt-Putt Golf Courses of America
Putt-R-Golf
Travel Agents International
Travel All
Travel Professionals
Travel Travel
Uniglobe Travel

Retailing – art supplies/frames

Art Management
Creative World
Deck The Walls
Frame And Save
Frame World
Great Frame Up (The)
Ringgold (The)

Retailing – computer sales/services

Computerland
Computerland Renaissance
Computers Unlimited of Wisconsin
Connecting Point of America
Entré Computer Centers
Inacomp Computer Centers
Microage Computer Stores
Richard Young

SAC Distributors
Software Centers
Step-Saver Data
Today's Computers Business Centers
Valcom

Retailing – florist

Affordable Love
Amlings
Bunning The Florist
Conroy's Florists
Flowerama of America
Omalley's Flowers
She's Flowers
Silk Plants Etc
Wesley Berry Flowers

Retailing – not elsewhere classified

Adele's
Adventureland Video
Agway
American Fast Photo and Camera
Animation Station
Annie's Book Stop
Applause Video
Armchair Sailor
Balloon-Age
Bath & A-Half
Bathique
Blind Designs
Book Rack Management
Bowl and Board
Box Shoppe (The)
Budget Tapes & Records
Butterfields Development
CameraAmerica
Celluland
Chad's Rainbow
Cleaning Ideas
Colonel Video
Compact Disc Warehouse
Cook's Corner
Copy Mat
Create-A-Book
C-3 Management
Curtis Mathes
Delphi Stained Glass Centers
Descamps
Dollar Discount Stores
Fan Fair

Freidman
Gallery 1 Affordable Art
Goodwill Candle & Incense
Hammett's Learning World
Happi-Bather
Happi-Cook
Happi-Names
Heritage Clock and Brassmiths
Heroes World Centers
House of Watch Bands (The)
Incredible Machine (The)
Intile Designs
Island Water Sports
Jet Photo
Just Baskets
Just Chairs
Just Closets
Kits Cameras
Jabirotope
Lemstone Book Branch
Little Professor Book Centers
Loeschhorn's For Runners
Mehta Holdings
Miss Bojangles
Mobility Center
Moto Photo
Movies and More
Mr Locksmithy Convenience Centers
Namesakes Personalized Gifts
National Video
Neighborhood Video & 1-Hour
   Photo Center
Nevada Bob's Pro Shops
Pak Mail Centers of America
Palmer Video
Perfumery (The)
Pinch a Penny
POP America
Pro Golf of America
Pro Image (The)
Project Mulitiplication
Radio Shack
Receptions Plus
Re-Sell-It Shops
Ruslan Discount Petmart
Science Shop (The)
Silver Screen Video
Software City
Space Options
Sport-About

Sporting Life
Sporting Life (The)
Sport Shacks
Standard Tile Supply
Tinder Box (The)
USA Doraco
Varnet
Video Biz
Video Data Services
Video Exchange (The)
Video Update
Video USA
Video Village
Wedding Bell Bridal Boutiques
   (WEBB)
Wee Win Toys and Accessories
West Coast Video
Wicks 'N' Sticks
Wide World of Maps
Wild Birds Unlimited
Willian Ernest Brown
World Bazaar
Yerushalmi

Security systems

Chambers Franchised Security
   Systems
Dictograph Security Systems
Dynamark Security Centers
Security Alliance (The)
Sonitrol

Swimming pools

California Pools
Caribbean Clear

Tools, hardware

Ad A Boy Tool Rental
Imperial Hammer
Mac Tools
Tool Shack
Vulcan Tools

Vending

Ford Gum & Machine Company
Mechanical Servants
Servapure
United Snacks of America
Westrock Vending

226 *The corporate paradox*

Water conditioning

Culligan
Rainsoft Water
Watercare

Miscellaneous wholesale and service businesses

Addhair Technologies
Ads & Types Express
All-State Welding and Industrial
Almost Heaven Hot Tubs
Armoloy Corporation (The)
Armor Shield
Balloon Bouquets
Bavarian Wax Art
Chemstation
Composil North America
Crown Trophy
Datagas
Fire Defense Centers
Fire Protection USA
Foliage Design
Fridfix Refrigeration
Great Expectations Creative

Management
Green Keepers
Hair Associates
Heel Quik
Machinery Wholesalers
Meistergram
Mid Continent Systems
Oxygen Therapy Institute
Qual Krom
Redi National Pest Eliminators
Sports Section Photography (The)
Stained Glass Overlay
Starving Students
Stellarvision
Sunanque Island Tanning
Suddenly Sun & Firm
Tempaco
Together Dating Service
New Business Investment
United Air Specialists
United Dignity
United Worth Hydrochem
Video Shuttle
Watsco
Your Attic

Source: Franchise Opportunities Handbook (United States Department of Commerce, International Trade Administration and Minority Business Development Agency: Washington DC, 1988), pp. iii–xv.

Appendix III

Franchise opportunities by business category, Australia

Automotive services

Alan Jones Pit-Stop
Autogas Conversions
Berklee Australia Exhaust Centres
Bob Jane T-Marts
Bumpa T Bumpa
Complete Windscreens
Fast Fit
Fluidrive Automatic Transmissions
Frantz Filters
Glass Technology
Windscreen Repairs
Hometune
Midas Muffler
Natrad Auto Cooling Service Centres
New Life Vinyl & Leather Service
Peddlers Suspension
Posh Wash
Pro-Axle
Resin-Weld Windscreen Repairs
Scotch-Line
Spectrum Tint-A-Car
Speedy Muffler & Brake Shop
Stripe Master
Thermotek Autospray Painting
Tidy Car
Tyremag Retread Centres
Ultra Tune
VIP Car Care
Ziebart Car Improvement Specialists

Automotive service stations

Ampol
BP Australia
Caltex Oil (Australia)
Mobil Team Pak
Shell (including Auto Care Car Spa,
   Shell Shop, Truckers Diners)

Building services and improvements

Aussie Master Maintenance
Action Clean Air
Alarmtec
Award Winning Kitchens
Bathroom International
Clearspan Building Systems
Creative Wardrobe Company
Dial-A-Security Door
Edgeworks
Fersina Windows
Floor Safety Service
Hicks for Homes
Interline
Just Pergolas
Ladybird Skylights
Limelite Skylights
Metro Tiles
Miracle Method of ANZ
Mister Green
Network Pool & Spa Services
Pebble-Tex
Roseville Electrics
Safe Tzone
Secur-A-Jamb
Simply Skylights
Slatex
Sol-Ace Professional Window
   Tinting
Solar Mesh

Solar Pergola
Spa World
Spectrum Solar Film Products
Spinner's Team of Tradesmen
Stained Glass Overlay
Steelbond
Trowelcraft
Weekend Kitchens
Worldwide Refinishing Systems

Business services

ABC Tools
AusWide Communications
Chemex Chemicals
Compressed Air Service
Enzed the Hose Doctor
Garaquip Sales
Hannaford Seedmaster Services
Hitechnology Metal Recyclers
Mini-Tankers
Mogy Tools
Pirtek Hose Service Centres
Quik Kleen Parts Washers
Vat Man Fat-Filtering Systems

Domestic and maintenance services

Above All Ceiling Cleaning
Aussie's Angels
Bizzi Beez Residential Cleaning
Chem-Dry
Cleaning Wizard (The)
Dial-an-Angel
Drytron Carpet Drycleaning
Dumpers Handibin
Elite Maintenance Service
Jim's Mowing
Plastic Fix
Rainbow International
Rapport Cleaning Service
Rotaclean
Rub, Scrub 'n' Sparkle
Total Building Maintenance
VIP Lawnmowing Service

Education, training and self-development

Auseco
Australian Academy of Tai Chi
Australian Learning Academy
Fred Astaire Dance Studios

Gymbaroo
Gymbaree
Helen O'Grady Children's Drama
   Academy
Hospitality Training Group
Improved Communications Skills
Kip McGrath Education Centres
Knitwit
Pam Arnold Centre (The)
Professional Home Tutors

Food – confectionery

Baskins-Robbins Ice Cream
Californian Yoghurt Co
Carvel Ice Cream
Great Australian Ice Creamery
Health Licks Creamy Yoghurt
Lolly Pops
Mr Whippy
Mrs Fudge
New Zealand Natural
Royal Copenhagen Ice Cream
Snoopy's Ice Cream Parlours/Food
   Bistros
Wendy's Supa Sundaes

Food – convenience stores

7-Eleven
Ampol Road Pantry
Clancy's Food Stores
Ezy Plus Convenience Stores
Food Plus
Nightbowl Convenience Stores
Shell Circle K Stores

Food – fast food, take-away

Casa Del Gelato
Chicken Treat/Big Rooster
Donut King
Grandma Lee's
Happy Muffin (The)
Hot Dogs of the World
Kentucky Fried Chicken
McDonald's Restaurants
Muffin Break
Pure & Natural
Schwob's Swiss
Smokarama
Subway Restaurants

Food – home delivery

Associated Home Delivery
Aussie Chopsticks
Australian Spit Roast Professionals
Captain Dial-A-Pizza
Dial-A-Bottlestop
Domino's Pizza
Eagle Boy's Dial-A-Pizza
Pizza Haven
Pizza on Wheels

Food – restaurants

Barnacle Bill
Bar Roma Cafe (The)
Captain America's Hamburger
Heaven
Capt'n Bream Seafoods
Carlos Murphy Mexican Restaurant
Earth 'n' Sea Family Restaurants
Lone Star Cantina
Pancakes Restaurants
Pizza Hut Australia
Taco Bill

Food – retail

Bakers Delight
Banjo's Bakery
Brumby's
Cookie Man
Cut Price Deli
Gem Cakes & Pies
Lenard's Poultry Shop
Michel's Patisserie

Food services

Dinkum Dog
Discount Confectionery
Tri-Vend Coffee Service

Leisure services

Harvey World Travel
Pitch & Putt
Putt & Games Golf Courses
Timezone
Traveland
Zone 3 Laser Games

Management services

Abacus Bookkeeping Centre
Bookkeeping Network (The)
Count Financial
Dapiran Knight
Drake Personnel
Express Bookkeeping
Franchise Counselling Centre
Headstart Home Consult
Payless Bookkeeping Service

Miscellaneous

Chris Kaine Connections
Community Town Maps
Domain Security
Photo Ceramics
Plaster Funhouse
Recording Studios of Australia
Red Hot Parcel Taxis/Taxi Trucks/
Deliveries

Personal services – health and beauty

Advanced Hair Studio
Ashby & Martin
CiCi Beauty Centres/Schools
Get Smart Value Hairdressers
Just Cuts
Natural Health & Beauty Clinic
Nutri/System
Slender Image
Slym-Gym
Smokenders

Printing and publishing

Aall Graphics & Printing
About Me Books
Create-A-Book
Kwik-Copy Printing
Macaxis Professional Imaging Centre
Mr Copy's Colour Company
New Colour Process
Select Home Listings
Snap Printing
Teen Age News
This Week Tourist Guides

Real estate

Barry Plant Real Estate
Blackburn & Lockwood
Centry 21 Australia
Combined Real Estate
Elders Real Estate
L J Hooker
Laing & Simmons
Myles Pearce
Nationwide Realty
PRD Realty
Property Shop Real Estate Group
Raine & Horne
Richardson & Wrench
Stockdale & Leggo
Town & Country

Retailing – books and newspapers

Angus & Robertson
Collins Booksellers
Dymocks
Fleet Street Newsagencies

Retailing – clothing

Coco Kidz
Dobsons Menswear
Ivory Coast Travel and Safari
Just Socks
Just Ties
Knickers
Mainstream Clothing Co
Mariana Hardwick
Modular Fashions
Najee Australia
Opal Male Fashion
Rita Louise
Shark Attack
Shoee's Family Footwear
Speed's Shoes
Studio Jianni
Supermouse

Retailing – electrical goods

Beacon Lighting
Computerland
Godfreys
Harvey Norman
Tandy Electronics

Retailing – furniture

Bedpost
Bed Shed
Capt'n Snooze
Great Australian Sleep Centre
Just Storage
Oz Design
Pine Cottage
Posture Care Chairs
Sleeping Giant (The)
Sweader Furniture
Ultimate Waterbed Company (The)
Whitewood Warehouse

Retailing – general

Attunga
Aussie Disposals
Christopher Carl Co
Fantasy Lane
Fleet Street Business Supplies
Fletchers Fotographics
Framing Corner
Guitar Factory (The)
Having A Party
Life Time Trophies
Oz Camping & Disposals
Pets Paradise
Shades Shop
What's A Name

Retailing – gifts and toys

Apricot Flowers
Blues Jewellery
Copperart
Granny May's
House
Kenny's Cardiology
Kleins
Lost Forests
Mind Games
Riot Art & Craft
Send-A-Bear
Taka Jewel Box
Teddy & Friends
Whats New/Smokes 'n' Things

Retailing – hardware, etc.

Bristol Decorator Centres
Faraday & Kent
Hardex
Mad Barry's Home Improvement
   Centres

Retailing – soft furnishings

Carpet Call
Dollar Curtains
Decorating Den
Marrs Fabrics
Shademaster
Shades of Australia
Solomans Carpets

Retailing – sporting accessories

Action World
Got One Stores
Horseland
Sportsco

Vehicle rental

ABC Rent-A-Car
Avis Australia
Budget Rent-A-Car
Dollar Rent-A-Car
Handy Utes & Cars
Hertz Rent-A-Car
National Car Rental
Network Rentals
Rent-A-Ruffy Car Rentals
Thrifty Car Rental

Video hire

Atlantic Video
Focus Video
Lollypop Video
Showstopper Video
Tri-Star Video
Video Ezy

Source: The Directory of Australian Franchise Opportunities (Verdant: Hampton, Victoria, 1991), pp. 58–59.

Notes

1 BINDING 'FIRMS' TOGETHER

1 The growth in non-standard forms of employment, or atypical forms of work, has exposed a further weakness of labour law: its narrow conception of an 'employee'. This is based on a direct and continuous relationship with an employer, of an indeterminate duration and for a full working week. This therefore excludes a growing number of workers whose working relationship varies from the 'norm'. These variations have been summarized as where you work, when you work and how you work (Leighton, 1986). Thus, many workers are denied employee rights: part-time workers are excluded on account of the fragmentation of their working week; temporary workers because the length of their employment is fixed in advance; homeworkers because their work takes place beyond the physical boundaries of the firm; and subcontractors because the tangible products of their labour are purchased, not their labour time (Deakin, 1986; Rodgers and Rodgers, 1989).

2 In addition, some (e.g. Lane, 1991; Hilbert and Sperling, 1992) argue that the nature of inter-firm relationships are shaped by the social, institutional and political environment in which they are set.

3 The EC's statistical body – Eurostat – defines an enterprise as a 'legally autonomous unit under single management control, whereas an establishment is an operating unit under the control of an enterprise'.

4 Here 'small' refers to units employing less than 100 employees (i.e. the OECD definition). Although any figure is arbitrary (it was set at 200 by the *Bolton Report*; the European Commission uses the same bench-mark), it does provide a barometer with which to measure changes in organizational size (Bolton Report, 1971; Commission of the European Communities, 1990). Size alone, however, does not provide any analytical distinguishing marks (Curran, 1990; Rainnie, 1989).

5 Government figures show that during the period 1985–1989 firms employing fewer than 20 people created twice as many jobs as larger firms, despite their smaller share of the workforce (Department of Employment, 1991a: 1).

6 There is also an intermediate organizational form known as the 'matrix' organization. Under this arrangement there are both functional department heads (as in 'U-forms') and product heads (as in 'M-forms'). Each provides

leadership in their own area, with individuals responsible to the functional heads for the technical content of their work and to product heads for the provision of the product (Child, 1984: chapter 4).

7 This is reflected, for example, in The Coca-Cola Company's motto: 'Think Globally, Act Locally' (cf. Ohmae, 1989: 156–159).

8 The trend towards decentralized pay bargaining structures will therefore not bring in its wake pay wage settlements which reflect local labour demand and supply conditions (Brown and Walsh, 1991). They are more likely to reflect the performance of individual business units (Purcell and Ahlstrand, 1989: 409–410).

9 Although *Lee v. 1. Chung and 2. Shun Shing Construction and Engineering Co. Ltd* [1990] IRLR 236 PC has been interpreted as providing an antidote to this development (Pitt, 1990), the ruling was made with more than half an eye on the instrumental and practical concern of allowing an injured worker access to compensation.

10 Indeed recent advertising slogans such as 'We'll give you work everyday. Not everyday work' (Kelly Temporary Services, London tube advert, June 1990) stress the continuing obligation on the part of the employment agency to provide work for its 'temporary' staff.

11 Morris and Imrie (1992) at first deny this claim (ibid: 81), but then appear to admit that 'Nissan used affiliates in which it has equity investments as a way of securing access . . . Nissan justify equity shares in a number of ways' (ibid: 167–168).

2 DEFINING WHAT FRANCHISING IS

1 Some of today's well-known franchisors use their ownership of the site to collect revenues as a franchisor *and* a landlord. For example, McDonald's collects rent from its US franchisees either as a fixed minimum monthly charge or 8.5 per cent (raised from 5 per cent in 1970) of turnover, whichever is the greater. A further 3 per cent of turnover is levied as a royalty (and another 4 per cent must be spent on advertising, usually channelled through the Operators' National Advisory Cooperative). It is estimated that the McDonald's Corporation earns about one-third of its net income from outlets it runs (these make up about one-quarter of the total number in the US), the rest comes from its franchised stores. About 90 per cent of that profit comes from its real estate rentals (Love, 1987: 159). It is thus not surprising to find the comment:

> What converted McDonald's into a money machine had nothing to do with Ray Kroc [the modern-day chain's founder] or the McDonald's brothers [the original founders] or even the popularity of McDonald's hamburgers, french fries, and milk shakes. Rather, McDonald's made its money on real estate. (Love, 1987: 152)

2 As a result, a key element of franchising is missing from some relationships which are sometimes referred to as franchises. The life insurance agent, for example, sells insurance policies to clients and is rewarded with a commission on each policy sold. Money changes hands in the *opposite direction* to that which typifies the franchise relationship: from the life insurance company to agents rather than vice versa (Douds, 1976).

3 The European Franchise Federation (EFF) was founded in September 1972.

It comprises the national franchise associations established throughout Europe – Austria, Belgium, Denmark, the Federal Republic of Germany, France, Italy, the Netherlands, Portugal and the United Kingdom.

4 This typology was first put forward by the US Department of Commerce and used as a means of tracking the development of franchising since 1972. Each year it conducted an annual survey of US franchisors until 1989 when the US government decided to discontinue the publication. Since then, the survey has been conducted using the same methodology by the International Franchise Association Educational Foundation.

5 Other well-known users of multi-level selling are Amway, Mary Kay Cosmetics and Shaklee.

3 EXPLAINING HOW AND WHY FRANCHISING WORKS

1 Brickley and Dark (1987) cite interesting anecdotal evidence on the relationship between distance and monitoring costs as found in Ray Kroc's autobiography. In it, the McDonald's founder states:

> One thing I like about my house was that it was perched on a hill looking down on a McDonald's store in the main thoroughfare. I could pick up my binoculars and watch business in that store from my living room window. I drove the manager crazy when I told him about it. But he sure had one hell of a hard-working crew! (Kroc, 1977: 133)

2 The traditional argument for profit sharing schemes, and indeed an argument made for privatization (Leadbeater, 1987), is made along similar lines: to improve worker incentives by giving them a common goal with management. The more recent interest in these schemes, however, centres around the way in which profit sharing alters companies' employment strategies and, through this, changes the evolution of employment and inflation in the economy as a whole. According to this view, improvements in employee relations and incentives are a side benefit compared with the main change that would follow from the widespread adoption of profit sharing – which is to give the economy a much stronger tendency towards full employment (Weitzman, 1984; Wright, 1986; Holland, 1986).

3 On the basis of similar economic arguments the vertical restraints placed by some manufacturers on franchised dealers have been broadly upheld after government investigation (cf. Monopolies and Mergers Commission, 1982 on car parts; Monopolies and Mergers Commission, 1981 on Raleigh; Hay, 1985; Mathewson and Winter, 1985). However, while the literature on vertical restraints is useful in assessing the *competitive effects* of franchising, it is of little value in explaining *why* franchising might be preferred to full vertical integration.

4 In the case of *Israel Olivieri v. McDonald's Corporation* United States District Court Eastern District of New York [1988] a prospective franchisee participated in the training course for almost 3 years before being considered unsuitable to be offered a franchise.

5 Though not always. For example, evidence suggests that car suppliers actively seek out dealers with previous experience in the motor trade, if not actually selling cars then in the servicing and maintenance of them (Beale, Harris and Sharpe, 1989: 308; Monopolies and Mergers Commission,

1992a: 59). Other franchises such as Dyno-Plumbing, for example, look for plumbing credentials in potential franchisees. However, this is the exception rather than the rule.

6 According to a recent survey of small businesses the prime reason for incorporation is the protection it is thought to provide the owner's family home (Freedman and Godwin, 1991; *Financial Times*, 26 November 1991). However, over half the respondent companies had provided personal guarantees to the bank, so that their homes were not, in fact, protected.

7 For example, the results of the annual BFA/NatWest survey of franchising in the UK were reported as a 'franchise for job creation' (*Financial Times*, 21 January 1992).

8 A survey of fast food franchisees in the US found remarkably similar results: 68 per cent were not previously exposed to self-employment; and 36 per cent believed that without franchising they would not be in business (Ozanne and Hunt, 1971: 37–38).

9 A similar argument has been put forward for the increase in the UK's productivity record over the last decade (Nolan, 1988; Guest, 1990).

4 SETTING THE LEGAL CONTOURS OF FRANCHISING

1 Evidence of franchisees having to lodge non-returnable deposits before they even see the terms of the agreement have been recorded in the US (Ozanne and Hunt, 1971: 55, 259). However, since the Federal Trade Commission ruling of 1971 all franchisors, who sell or offer franchises for sale, are required by law to prepare a circular to prospective franchisees (not unlike a prospectus on a public offering of shares). It contains specific information under 22 separate headings. This includes a commercial profile of the franchisor, current and past litigation, bankruptcy record, the actual costs of set-up, the franchise agreement, projected earnings, a complete list of franchisees operating in the state and information on terminations, non-renewals and buy-backs over the preceding three-year period. This results in a bulky document – stretching to almost 150 pages in the case of the Fast Frame, a chain of picture framers, and McDonald's, the hamburger chain. In April 1991 a similar disclosure law came into force in France (known as the Loi Doubin law after its promoter). In the UK there is no legal requirement on franchisors to disclose any information on the past, current or expected performance of the network. Instead, the industry body – the British Franchise Association – voluntarily regulates the activities of its members (*Financial Times*, 6 July 1990).

2 According to a former McDonald's franchisee in the US:

> a prospective franchisee has the right to turn down at least one location and still remain at the top of the waiting list. More than one refusal and the franchisee is unlikely to get a franchise. McDonald's want operators who want to be operators, not operators who want to be operators at a particular location. (field notes)

3 Several car suppliers in the UK (e.g. Ford, Vauxhall, Rover, Mercedes, Volvo, Fiat, BMW) report that they have few 'open points' in their franchised dealer networks (Monopolies and Mergers Commission, 1992a: 60). Moreover, the great majority of dealers have just a single dealership

236 The corporate paradox

with some suppliers expressing a strong preference for sole traders owning one dealership (ibid: 61, 85). Some suppliers limit the number and location of dealerships held, and the maximum annual volume of sales of their new cars, by a single dealer or group. For example, Ford allows a maximum of eight dealerships (Monopolies and Mergers Commission, 1992b: 92). The purpose of these limitations is to limit the supplier's market vulnerability to dealers' actions or misfortunes, thereby limiting *its* dependence on any one dealer (Macaulay, 1973: 24).

4 MacKenna J at page 526 in *Ready Mixed Concrete (South East) Ltd v. Minister of Pensions and National Insurance* [1968] 2 QB 497.

5 The wholesale prices of new cars paid by dealers (franchisees) to their suppliers (franchisors) are usually expressed as list or recommended retail prices less a dealer's margin. Some agreements indicate that the recommended retail price is the maximum price at which the dealer may sell (Monopolies and Mergers Commission, 1992a: 83; Beale, Harris and Sharpe, 1989: 307). The major petrol wholesalers – Shell, Esso and BP – have similar agreements with their retailers regarding the supply of petrol (Monopolies and Mergers Commission, 1990: 367–373).

6 Contracts governing the relationship between car suppliers and their dealers carry sales targets for each model. These targets are generally set in consultation with the dealer. However, cases of the supplier imposing targets are not uncommon (Monopolies and Mergers Commission, 1992a: 65, 82).

7 Public house properties leased from Inntrepreneur, a division of Grand Metropolitan, set a minimum volume of beer which must be purchased from a nominated supplier each year. Compensation of £75 per barrel is payable on any shortfall (*Open Space – Over a Barrel*, BBC TV, 14 October 1991; company information).

8 More than 80% of car dealers have exclusive territories within which to work (Monopolies and Mergers Commission, 1992a: 63).

9 However, there is visible evidence that over the period 1975–1990 UK businesses have increasingly turned to ligitation as means to resolve their disputes (Vincent-Jones, 1991).

10 Cf. *Dayan v. McDonald's Corporation* [1984] North Eastern Reporter 958. McDonald's sent the complete 117 page Opinion to all its franchisees to underline its commitment to high standards of QSC.

11 Several car suppliers have introduced a 'customer satisfaction index' to monitor the performance of their dealers. If a dealership is given a below-average mark it may be prevented from expanding within or outside the existing chain. A low mark could also mean the withdrawal of the franchise (Monopolies and Mergers Commission, 1992a: 203).

12 While some early McDonald's franchisees were granted territories for metropolitan areas such as Washington DC, Cincinnati and Pittsburgh, the company began to cut down the area covered by a franchise. At first, franchisees were given an exclusive radial area of between one and two miles from the store. By 1969 the franchise had been reduced to the 'street address only'.

13 In order to be deemed 'expandable', a McDonald's franchise must average a 'B' grade on the quarterly restaurant assessments (see pp.119–120). Around 15% of stores are awarded 'A' grades, 15% get 'B' grades and the remainder attain grade 'C' or below.

14 The High Court also ruled in favour of Kentucky Fried Chicken (KFC) in its refusal to renew the contracts of five franchisees (operating seven units between them) once their contracts came to an end (a right to renew, provided certain conditions were met, was absent). The franchisees claimed that they had revamped their outlets at the company's request in the belief that they would be able to continue trading within the KFC network. The court ruled against the franchisees on the grounds that their agreements excluded liability for any oral promises made by KFC staff. However, KFC conceded in allowing these franchisees to continue trading as chicken take-aways and restaurants. Several other KFC franchisees who left the network (as a result of either non-renewal, termination for poor standards or voluntary departure) reached similar agreements, but with an additional undertaking that they would not open new outlets within three miles of existing KFC stores for a period of two years. The backbone of several rival chains consists of former KFC franchisees – Favorite Fried Chicken, Dixy Fried Chicken and Kansas Fried Chicken (*Franchise World*, March/May 1987; *Popular Food Service*, November 1986).

15 In the next issue of the *Yellow Pages* (published on a yearly basis) the Prontaprint advertisement suggested that customers contact the franchisor's corporate headquarters in Darlington for their nearest Prontaprint branch.

16 Another former Prontaprint franchisee began trading under a new name, Reliance Print, in May 1987. But following the High Court ruling against Laserprint (see text), Reliance Print quickly rejoined the Prontaprint chain (*Franchise World*, May–July 1987).

17 Cf. *Esso Petroleum Co. Ltd. v. Harper's Garage (Stourport) Ltd.* [1968] AC 269; *Office Overload Ltd. v. Gunn* [1977] FSR 39 CA; Aikin (1991).

18 In a series of 'tie-in' cases during the 1960s and 1970s in the US, rulings were consistently made against franchisors requiring their operators to purchase equipment and supplies from them on the grounds that it constituted an illegal conflict of interest (*Siegel v. Chicken Delight Inc.* [1971] Trade Cases 73,703). However, the courts ruled that selecting and controlling locations was an integral part of running a restaurant chain and that control of that function by the franchisor was natural and did not place the franchisor's financial interest in conflict with that of its franchisees (*Principe v. McDonald's Corporation* [1980] Trade Cases 76,960; Camp, 1981; Fischer, 1981).

19 This case also reached the national press, but for different reasons (*Observer*, 14 August 1988). During the dispute, franchisees' mail was redirected at the request of the franchisor to its head office in order to preserve the business and its reputation. However, Post Office procedure appeared to have been breached as franchisees did not receive a confirmation notice of redirection. Furthermore, while the franchisor might have had a claim on correspondence requiring the franchisee to carry out work or give an estimate under the franchisor's trade name, they had no claim whatsoever on correspondence with customers who were customers prior to the ending of the franchise agreement and who may well have owed money for outstanding work. The dispute over the ownership of mail was not resolved, the mail was therefore treated as undeliverable and returned to senders. However, some months later the application for redirection was dropped by the franchisor.

5 CHANGING FRANCHISOR OWNERSHIP AND ITS CONSEQUENCES

1 In order to protect the identity of the companies involved, pseudonyms are used throughout – Vehicle Dealers Limited refers to the new owners, CarCo to the franchise it bought and AutoCo to the break-away group of franchisees.

2 The engine tune includes examination and adjustment, where necessary, of the following:

   - engine condition
   - engine compressions
   - engine breathing systems
   - the starting circuit
   - the charging system
   - the ignition system, including timing
   - the carburation or fuel injection system
   - exhaust emission.

3 Faced with calls for greater regulation of the franchising industry, the British Franchise Association – a voluntary association of 130 franchise companies – has tightened the criteria for membership (*Financial Times*, 6 July 1990). Full members must submit to initial accreditation and re-accreditation on five criteria. First, they must demonstrate that their business is viable, by producing two years of recently audited accounts which show that the business is capable of being run at a profit and therefore capable of supporting a franchise network. Second, they must provide evidence that the operating units of the business can be successfully replicated. To meet this criteria they must produce one year's recently audited accounts showing the trading performance of a managed 'arm's length' pilot franchise, or a fully fledged pilot franchise, at least in line with the business plan set for it. Thirdly, a copy of the then current franchise agreement must be lodged with the Association for inspection by appointed franchisees. Fourthly, the franchisor must demonstrate that the offer documents present a full and realistic picture of the franchise proposition. Finally, the franchisor must provide a record of franchise openings, withdrawals and disputes (which required external intervention to resolve) together with evidence of the profitability of individual units and of the network as a whole over a two-year period (taken from BFA Membership Criteria, 1990).

4 For example, it was reported that several computer retail franchisees were given oral assurances that should their businesses turn sour, the franchisor would launch a 'lifeboat' operation to ensure that not a single store would close (*Sunday Times*, 18 January 1987). All 15 stores have since closed and the franchisor is no longer operating in the UK.

5 Product/trade mark franchises have experienced similar difficulties with territorial franchising. The Coca-Cola Company, for example, originally gave the bottling rights for practically all parts of the US (apart from New England, Texas and Mississippi) to Messrs Thomas and Whitehead in 1899. Both emerged as parent bottlers managing a tier of sub-bottlers below. This diluted the link between The Coca-Cola Company and the actual bottlers, but was only curtailed when the Company bought out Thomas in 1975 (see Chapter 6).

6 In the US, there are eight very strong independent franchisee associations within particular franchise systems (shown in brackets): International Pizza Hut Franchise Holders Association (Pizza Hut); FACT Association (Hertz); International Association of Holiday Inns (Holiday Inn); National Coalition of Associations of 7-Eleven Franchisees (7-Eleven); Association of Kentucky Fried Chicken Franchisees, Inc. (Kentucky Fried Chicken); Midas Muffler Dealers Association (Midas); Dairy Queen Operators Association (Dairy Queen); and Franchisee Associates (Ponderosa). There are approximately 20 others. Overall, it is estimated that there are no franchisee associations in over 90% of the franchised systems operating in the US (Fine, 1987).

7 Restrictive clauses may seek to cover too wide a geographical area, apply to customers with whom the former employee (franchisee) had no contact and prevent involvement with too broad a class of products. In these circumstances enforceability is most unlikely (*Clarke Sharp Co Ltd v. Soloman* [1921] TLR 176 CA; *Wessex Dairies Ltd v. Smith* [1935] 2 KB 80 CA; *The Marley Tile Co Ltd v. Johnson* [1982] IRLR 75 CA; *Office Angels Ltd v. Rainer-Thomas and O'Connor* [1991] IRLR 214 CA). But restrictive clauses are enforceable so long as they do *no more than* protect the employer's (franchisor's) legitimate interests – trade connections, goodwill as well as business methods and systems in the case of business format franchising (*1. Spafax Ltd v. Harrison 2. Spafax Ltd v. Taylor* [1980] IRLR 442 CA; *Scorer v. Seymour-Johns* [1966] All ER 347 CA). Indeed, in certain circumstances restrictive covenants are the most appropriate way of protecting an employer's (franchisor's) legitimate interests:

if [the managing director] is right in thinking that there are features in his process which can fairly be regarded as trade secrets and which his employees will inevitably carry away with them in their heads, then the proper way for the plaintiffs to protect themselves would be by extracting covenants from their employees restricting the field of their activity after they have left their employment. (Cross J in *Printers and Finishers Ltd v. Holloway* [1964] 3 All ER 731 at 736)

8 The importance of access to former customers was vividly illustrated by a recent dispute between Nissan UK – the distributor of Nissan vehicles until 31 December 1991 – and Nissan Motor GB – a wholly-owned Nissan distributor put in its place from 1 January 1992. The Driver and Vehicle Licensing Agency (DVLA) supplied the names and addresses of about 400,000 customers who had bought Nissan vehicles within the last six years to the new distributor. Although not a public register, the DVLA supplied the list on the grounds that it was sought 'solely to advise the keepers of Nissan vehicles of the position with regard to warranty following the withdrawal of the manufacturer's franchise from the previous distributor'. Nissan UK feared that it would be used for more overt marketing purposes, thereby devaluing one its few remaining assets and prejudicing its attempts to sell alternative makes of car (*Financial Times*, 31 January 1992).

9 However, there may be nothing elsewhere in the agreement that might allow the court to cut down wide words to words of more limited scope (*Commercial Plastics Ltd v. Vincent* [1964] 3 All ER 546). Browne LJ dissenting in *The Littlewoods Organisation Ltd v Harris* [1978] 1 All ER 1026 CA made the same point: construction can only take place if more

limiting and more specific references can be found elsewhere in the agreement – since no reference was made to the 'mail order business', Browne LJ argued that more limited constructions could not be made. The principle of construction does not operate in reverse; courts are reluctant to widen the scope of a restraining covenant by reference to some separate and additional interest which does not govern the covenant under scrutiny, but is specified elsewhere (*Office Angels Ltd v. Rainer-Thomas and O'Connor* [1991] IRLR 214 CA).

6 MANAGING A FRANCHISE IN A CHANGING COMMERCIAL ENVIRONMENT

1 Sales turnover across the entire network of 373 stores (308 of them franchised, the remainder company-owned) was reported to have dropped by 20 per cent as a result (*Popular Food Service*, June 1985). Some stores recorded declines of up to 35 per cent (*Popular Food Service*, March 1986).

2 For example, a franchisee spent £44,000 'repositioning' his two Kentucky Fried Chicken outlets only to be told one year after making this investment that his contract would not be renewed (*Frankirk Foods Ltd v. 1. Kentucky Fried Chicken (GB) Ltd 2. Kentucky Fried Chicken Ltd* (1986) High Court of Justice Chancery Division, unpublished).

3 Throughout this chapter 'Germany' before the Second World War refers to the German Empire, while after the Second World War it refers to the Federal Republic of Germany, before and after reunification on 3 October 1990. The former German Democratic Republic is currently supplied by a wholly-owned subsidiary of the Coca-Cola Company.

4 Ever since 1926 Coca-Cola has chosen to export concentrate rather than syrup to its overseas bottlers. This reduced shipping costs, and passed on the risks associated with fluctuating sugar prices to bottlers. Since 1978 American bottlers have been given the option to take concentrate or syrup; today about 98 per cent of US shipments are in the form of concentrate. While data on concentrate prices is not available, recent evidence given to the Monopolies and Mergers Commission in the UK suggests their magnitude (apart from Greece, the same concentrate prices apply throughout the European Community). Coca-Cola Schweppes Beverages, a joint venture company bottling Coca-Cola and Schweppes brands in the UK, reported that 19.3 per cent (£110.3 million) of its 1989 turnover was absorbed by concentrate payments. However, the marketing and advertising programmes these payments help to support varies as between franchisees (Monopolies and Mergers Commission, 1991: 77, 305–306).

5 When Coca-Cola was invented in 1886, it was sold as a syrup to soda fountains, who then added the carbonated water at the point of sale and sold it to customers (known today as post-mix). Although a few Coca-Cola bottlers did exist prior to 1899, it was only when Thomas and Whitehead were given the right to bottle and sell Coca-Cola anywhere in the US (with the exception of New England, Mississippi and Texas, where prior distribution agreements had already been made) that Coca-Cola bottlers became more widespread. Unable to build bottling plants of their own, Thomas and Whitehead became parent bottlers. Their prime activity ceased to be the bottling of Coca-Cola and became instead the franchising of

bottling territories to others to whom they sold Coca-Cola syrup. By 1915 there were six parent bottlers in the US. Today, there is none, with the last having been purchased in 1975 (Tedlow, 1990: 41–47, 390). Car manufacturers have also established a network of distribution points in a similar way: Nissan, for example, entered the UK in 1969 by granting a master franchise to a company which built a network of nearly 400 distributors, 230 of whom were legally independent (Beale, Harris and Sharpe, 1989). The Japanese motor manufacturer terminated the master franchise agreement on 31 December 1991 and has since set up its own network through a wholly-owned subsidiary (*Financial Times*, 28 December 1990; *Independent on Sunday*, 30 December 1990; *Financial Times*, 1 August 1991).

6 Towards the end of 1929 a total of 44 plants had been franchised throughout Europe, all of whom produced mineral water as well (Archives, The Coca-Cola Company, Atlanta). Today, there are 190 mineral water producers in Germany; for most of whom soft drink production is marginal to their main activity (Sutton, 1991: 445).

7 Similar considerations have been advanced to explain the nature of the relationship between car manufacturers and dealers in the UK (Beale, Harris and Sharpe, 1989).

8 My interviews revealed that this might have been the case in only two instances.

9 In those days, a case of Coca-Cola referred to 24 6.5 fluid ounce bottles. Nowadays, a unit case refers to 24 servings of 8 fluid ounces.

10 A bottling line has the following components:

water treatment;
syrup room;
bottling line with:
– bottle washer/rinser (for returnables)
– proportioner, including carbonization system
– filler allied with a closing machine
– ancillary systems such as case packers/unpackers, palletizers/de-palletizers, etc.

11 A substitute beverage was born out of this shortage – Fanta. By the end of the war, sales of Fanta had reached half the level achieved by Coca-Cola at the outbreak of war (Archives, The Coca-Cola Company, Atlanta).

12 As a rule of thumb, the minimum investment requirement at the time stood at $1.00 (DM4.00) per inhabitant. But with the lack of capital in Germany immediately after the war, an exception was made.

13 After the Second World War the 200 ml (0.2 litre) bottle became the standard metric equivalent of the 6.5 fluid ounce bottle.

14 Pepsi-Cola introduced a 12 fluid ounce package as far back as 1935 in the US. This was used as the basis of a competitive advertising campaign aired on US radio networks in the late 1930s. The following verse became the first jingle aired on radio: Pepsi-Cola hits the spot, Twelve full ounces that's a lot, Twice as much for a nickel too, Pepsi-Cola is the drink for you (Tedlow, 1990: 90).

15 Initially, canners were awarded a ten year contract for the supply of a guaranteed volume of cans. Today, the length of the contract has been shortened to five years and the guaranteed volume of sales has been replaced by a cost-plus pricing formula (i.e. a requirements contract which fixes the

price in advance, but does not commit the purchaser to any fixed number of purchases, cf. Macaulay, 1973: 19).

16 A recent survey found that one-third of UK retail food sales are made up of own-label products (*Financial Times*, 31 October 1991).

17 The Coca-Cola Company's franchise structure faces a similar concentration of buying power in other advanced industrial economies. For example, in the UK just 5 customers accounted for 21 per cent of total sales of Coca-Cola brands in 1989, 10 accounted for 40 per cent and the top 20 took 60 per cent (Monopolies and Mergers Commission, 1991: 108, 116, 156). Moreover, Coca-Cola's largest customers are becoming pan-European; in 1991 ten customers accounted for 17 per cent of the European sales of the Coca-Cola organization, and this is projected to rise to 28 per cent by 1994 (*Journey*, September 1991: 10).

18 All McDonald's restaurants in the UK carry the company's own-label range of carbonated drinks supplied by a dedicated manufacturer (Monopolies and Mergers Commission, 1991: 243).

19 The original franchise contracts in the US obliged the Coca-Cola Company to sell syrup (i.e. concentrate plus sugar) at a fixed price. However, the First World War reduced the supply of sugar and its price rose. The bottlers agreed to give the company price relief via a formula which linked a proportion of the syrup price to movements in the cost of refined sugar. In return, bottlers were granted a contract in perpetuity (this was given as part of a Consent Decree agreed in 1921). In 1978 the syrup pricing formula was changed. Its main effect was to allow the previously fixed element to rise in line with inflation. In return, the Company guaranteed minimum levels of advertising and marketing expenditure related to the volume of syrup it sold to each franchisee. In 1983 an amendment set out the pricing formula governing the supply of Diet Coke syrup to its bottlers (cf. Table 6.2). Not all franchisees signed the 1978 and 1983 amendments. In fact, 30 'unamended' bottlers successfully challenged the legality of the Coca-Cola Company's refusal to pass on the savings made by substituting high-fructose corn syrup to sweeten Coca-Cola in place of sucrose to those unwilling to amend their 1921-style contracts. A US court ordered the Coca-Cola Company to refund the price difference for the period during which these bottlers were supplied with high-fructose corn syrup sweetened Coca-Cola syrup (1980–1987) (*Atlanta Constitution*, 2 July 1991). A second case involving many of those involved in the above, sought to extend the case to the pricing of Diet Coke syrup. The bottlers argued that the artificial sweetener used cost much less than sugar, yet the Company was charging them even more for Diet Coke syrup than it was for Coca-Cola syrup. The argument that Diet Coke should be linked to the 1921 Consent Decree was rejected on the grounds that it was a different product not governed by the original contract (*Wall Street Journal*, 2 July 1991).

20 The Coca-Cola Company has taken up ownership positions in approximately 60 different bottling, canning and distribution operations around the world. Often this entails taking managerial responsibility for the operation, and where, as in many cases, the Company's equity falls short of 100 per cent ensuring that the dividend pay-out to shareholders is subject to its approval (*The Coca-Cola Company Annual Report 1990*: 30). In 1991 the Company estimated that it had equity stakes in those responsible for

generating 38 per cent of its worldwide volume. Thus ensuring that: 'By working closely with our bottlers to help increase retail sales, we are also boosting our concentrate sales' (*The Coca-Cola Company Annual Report 1991*: 37).

21 In the US, competitive sales and advertising campaigns between Pepsi-Cola and Coca-Cola (the 'Cola Wars') are having a similar effect. In the early 1980s, these were spearheaded by Pepsi's company-owned bottling territories (CoBo) through which about one-quarter of its US sales was generated. Their effect has been to drive prices downward, and although *total* soft drink sales have risen, the profits of small bottlers have fallen. Over the period 1988–1991, for example, 85 per cent of Coca-Cola bottlers either suffered falls in their absolute sales levels (60 per cent) or grew at less than the industry average (25 per cent). However, this was more than offset by the remainder; they grew faster than the industry as a whole and accounted for over 80 per cent of the Coca-Cola Company's US sales. Across the soft drink industry larger bottlers have bought out their weaker and much smaller neighbours, and franchisors have taken major equity positions in some of their largest bottlers. For example, by 1991 Pepsi-Cola was in direct control of about 60 per cent of its US sales, while Coca-Cola had a 44 per cent stake in a bottler which produced about 40 per cent of its sales. In addition, the Company held stakes in other US bottlers which accounted for a further 28 per cent of its US sales (Sculley, 1990: chapter 2, 149; *The Coca-Cola Company Annual Report 1991*: 36–37; interviews).

7 CONCLUSIONS

1 The distinction between outright ownership and being a shareholder was made clear in the Coca-Cola Company's submission to the Monopolies and Mergers Commission investigation into the supply of carbonated drinks in the UK. It owns a 49 per cent stake in the holding company which owns Coca-Cola Schweppes Beverages Ltd (CCSB), a joint venture formed with Cadbury Schweppes in 1987 for the bottling and sale of their respective brands. Although represented on the holding company's board, the Coca-Cola Company is not involved in the day-to-day running of CCSB, but is party to setting the parameters within which CCSB operates. For example, the shareholders' agreement provides that all CCSB's profits be distributed, subject to the proviso that CCSB retain funds necessary for the purposes of its business. These purposes are set out in the annual business plan and long-range plan, initiated and agreed by CCSB, in liaison with its shareholders. In fact, CCSB's working and fixed capital expenditure has been such that no distribution of profits has been made since CCSB was formed. This implies that CCSB's shareholders – the Coca-Cola Company and Cadbury Schweppes – are more interested in maximizing the volume of concentrates they sell than in receiving dividends on their shares. This inevitably affects the way CCSB acts, yet allows the minority shareholder to claim, with justification, that it does not have a controlling interest in the company. Thus, a finding, for instance, that a monopoly existed in favour of CCSB could be extended to the person controlling the monopolist (in this case Cadbury Schweppes), but could not be extended to minority shareholders or the monopolist's suppliers (Monopolies and Mergers Commission, 1991: 8–11, 109–110, 123–125).

2 When McDonald's opened its first store in the UK in 1974, none of the indigenous UK suppliers of kitchen equipment, food supplies or paper products were able to meet McDonald's quality standards. Initially, these supplies were imported from the US. But this increased costs and made them vulnerable to disruptions to supply. McDonald's therefore set about establishing a supply chain itself. Once this was in place, McDonald's began to sell off its interests in its suppliers (Love, 1987: 440–445; Transnationals Information Centre London, 1987: 7–8).

3 Indeed, this expression was used in one of the few cases which has focused on the franchise relationship (*Office Overload Ltd v. Gunn* [1977] FSR 39 CA).

4 Subtle pressures were applied against those franchisees who were seeking to organize a franchisee association within Taco Bell, a chain of Mexican fast food restaurants, in the US during the early 1980s (Luxenberg, 1985: 270). While the franchisor did not want to endanger its own profits by closing outlets down, the franchisor made it clear that troublemakers might not be permitted to open additional units, and that franchisees who refused to support the association would be rewarded with the right to buy additional franchises.

5 For example, in the summer of 1970 Watney Mann (now part of Courage) gave 80 of its tenants in the London area notice to quit with the intention of replacing them with salaried managers. Some of those disenfranchised had been notably successful in building up their trade and had reinvested a good deal of their profits in improving amenities. The notices were given without warning. This pricked the collective consciousness of tenants and a Watney Mann Tenants' Association was formed to strengthen the tenants' hands in opposing this and other developments. Facing this kind of opposition, Watneys offered compensation to dispossessed tenants and subsequently negotiated a 'tenants' charter' (Hawkins, 1972: 27). Similar tenants' associations were formed in each of the other five national brewery networks.

6 Having lost much of its constituency within the McDonald's organization, the MOA began to look elsewhere for support. In fact, it only survived by being subsumed within the National Franchisee Association which solicits franchisees across a range of franchise systems (Love, 1987: 404).

7 Nonetheless, some franchisees appear more amenable to traditional trade unions than others. For example, McGuire notes that:

> since many franchisees are so closely controlled by their dominant franchisor that the relationship strongly resembles the traditional employment relationship, it is not surprising that the franchisees who bear the strongest resemblance to the conventional employee – the single distributors – are often the subject of union organizational drives. (1971: 226)

The switch from managed milk rounds to franchised ones, for example, has reduced trade union membership as milk deliverers tend to drop their membership once they become self-employed. It is estimated that in 1978 200 rounds were operated on a franchised basis; by the end of the 1980s this had risen to 4,700 (Fulop, 1989). One might expect, though, these franchisees to be more recruitable by traditional trade unions than other franchisees such as fast food operators (*Financial Times*, 28 November 1988; *Financial Times*, 5 July 1991; *Independent on Sunday*, 18 August 1991).

Bibliography

Abell, M. (1989) *The Franchise Option: A Legal Guide*, Waterlow: London.

Ackroyd, S., Burrell, G., Hughes, M. and Whitaker, A. (1988) 'The Japanisation of British industry?', *Industrial Relations Journal*, vol. 19, no. 1, Spring, 11–23.

Aikin, O. (1991) 'Creating workable restraint clauses', *Personnel Management*, vol. 20, no. 10, 89–90.

Alchian, A. A. and Demsetz, H. (1972) 'Production, information costs and economic organization', *American Economic Review*, vol. 2, no. 5, December, 777–795.

Allen, S. and Wolkowitz, C. (1986) 'The control of women's labour: the case of homeworking', *Feminist Review*, no. 22, Spring, 25–51.

Allen, S. and Wolkowitz, C. (1987) *Homeworking: Myths and Realities*, Macmillan: London and Basingstoke.

Allen, S., Truman, C. and Wolkowitz, C. (1992) 'Home-based work: self-employment and small business', in Leighton, P. and Felstead, A. (eds) *The New Entrepreneurs: Self-Employment and Small Business in Europe*, Kogan Page: London.

Amin, A. (1991) 'Flexible specialization in Italy: myths and realities', in Pollert, A. (ed.) *Farewell to Flexibility?*, Blackwell: Oxford.

Amin, A. and Dietrich, M. (1990) 'From hierarchy to "hierarchy": the dynamics of contemporary restructuring in Europe', paper presented to the European Association for Evolutionary Political Economy, Florence, 15–17 November.

Arendorff, P. A. (1986) 'Denmark: franchising and employment contracts', *Journal of International Franchising and Distribution Law*, vol. 1, no. 2, December 1986, 97–98.

Atkinson, J. (1984) 'Manpower strategies for flexible organisations', *Personnel Management*, vol. 16, no. 8, August, 28–31.

Atkinson, J. (1985) 'Flexibility: planning for an uncertain future', *Manpower Policy and Practice*, vol. 1, Summer, 26–29.

Atkinson, J. and Meager, N. (1986) *Changing Working Patterns: How Companies Achieve Flexibility to Meet New Needs*, National Economic Development Office: London.

Bach, S. (1989) 'Too high a price to pay? A study of competitive tendering for domestic services in the NHS', Warwick Papers in Industrial Relations No. 25, University of Warwick: Coventry.

246   *The corporate paradox*

Bade, F.-J. (1983) 'Large corporations and regional development', *Regional Studies*, vol. 17, no. 5, 315–326.
Barrow, C. and Golzen, G. (1991) *Taking Up a Franchise*, Kogan Page: London.
Beale, H. and Dugdale, T. (1975) 'Contracts between businessmen: planning and the use of contractual remedies', *British Journal of Law and Society*, vol. 2, no. 1, Summer, 45–60.
Beale, H., Harris, D. and Sharpe, T. (1989) 'The distribution of cars: a complete contractual technique', in Harris D. and Tallon, D. (eds) *Contract Law Today: Anglo-French Comparisons*, Clarendon Press: Oxford.
Bechhofer, F. and Elliot, B. (1978) 'The voice of small business and the politics of survival', *Sociological Review*, vol. 26, no. 1, February, 57–88.
Belussi, F. (1987) 'Benetton: information technology in production and distribution: a case study of the innovative potential of traditional sectors', SPRU Occasional Paper Series No. 25, Science Policy Research Unit: Brighton.
Berg, M. (1984) 'The power of knowledge: comments on Marglin's "knowledge and power"', in Stephen, F. H. (ed.) *Firms, Organization and Labour: Approaches to the Economics of Work Organization*, Macmillan: London and Basingstoke.
Berle, A. A. and Means, G. C. (1932) *The Modern Corporation and Private Property*, Macmillan: New York.
Best, M. (1986) 'Strategic planning and industrial policy', *Local Economy*, no. 1, Spring, 65–77.
BFA/NatWest (1987) *Business Format Franchising in the United Kingdom*, Power Research Associates: London.
BFA/NatWest (1989) *The BFA/NatWest Franchise Survey 1989*, Power Research Associates: London.
Biggart, N. W. (1988a) *Charismatic Capitalism: Direct Selling Organizations in America*, University of Chicago Press: Chicago.
Biggart, N. W. (1988b) 'Charismatic capitalism: direct selling organizations in the United States and Asia', Graduate School of Management, University of California, Davis, unpublished mimeo, March.
Birch, D. L. (1979) *The Job Generation Process*, MIT Program on Neighborhood and Regional Change: Cambridge, Massachusetts.
Birkbeck, C. (1978) 'Self-employed proletarians in an informal factory: the case of Cali's garbage dump', *World Development*, vol. 6, no. 9/10, 1173–1185.
Blackburn, R. A. (1992) 'Small firms and subcontracting: what is it and where?', in Leighton, P. and Felstead, A. (eds) *The New Entrepreneurs: Self-Employment and Small Business in Europe*, Kogan Page: London.
Blackburn, R. A. and Curran, J. (1989) 'The future of the small firm: attitudes of young people to entrepreneurship', paper presented to the 12th UK Small Firms Policy and Research Conference, Thames Polytechnic, 23–25 November.
Bluestone, B. and Huff Stevenson, M. (1981) 'Industrial transformation and the evolution of dual labour markets: the case of retail trade in the United States', in Wilkinson, F. (ed.) *The Dynamics of Labour Market Segmentation*, Academic Press: London.
Bolton Report (1971) *Small Firms: Report of the Committee of Enquiry on Small Firms*, Cmnd 4811, HMSO: London.
Bowles, S. (1985) 'The production process in a competitive economy:

Walrasian, Neo-Hobbesian and Marxist models', *American Economic Review*, vol. 75, no. 1, March, 16–36.

Braverman, H. (1974) *Labor and Monopoly Capital: The Degradation of Work in the Twenthieth Century*, Monthly Review Press: New York.

Brickley, J. A. and Dark, F. H. (1987) 'The choice of organizational form: the case of franchising', *Journal of Financial Economics*, vol. 18, no. 2, June, 401–420.

Brickley, J.A., Dark, F.H. and Weisbach, M.S. (1989) 'The economic effects of franchise termination laws,' LSE Financial Markets Group Discussion Paper Series No. 67, London School of Economics: London.

Brickley, J. A., Dark, F. H. and Weisbach M. S. (1991) 'An agency perspective on franchising', *Financial Management*, vol. 20, no. 1, Spring, 27–35.

Brown, W. and Walsh, J. (1991) 'Pay determination in Britain in the 1980s; the anatomy of decentralization', *Oxford Review of Economic Policy*, vol. 7, no. 1, Spring, 44–59.

Burawoy, M. (1979) *Manufacturing Consent: Changes in the Labor Process Under Monopoly Capitalism*, University of Chicago Press: Chicago and London.

Burck, C. G. (1970) 'Franchising's troubled dream world', *Fortune*, March, 116–121, 148–152.

Burr, P., Burr, R. and Bartlett, P. (1975) 'Franchising and the ominous "buy-back" clause', *Journal of Small Business Management*, vol. 13, no. 4, 38–41.

Buschbeck-Bülow, B. (1989) 'Betriebverfassungsrechtliche Vertretung in Franchise-Systemen', *Betriebs-Berater*, vol. 5, 20 February, 352–354.

Camp, F. A. (1981) 'Antitrust franchising – Principe v. McDonald's Corporation – Big Mac attacks the Chicken Delight rule', *Journal of Corporation Law*, vol. 7, Fall, 137–156.

Campbell, D. and Harris, D. (1990) 'Flexibility in long-term contractual relationships: the testing of extra-legal strategies', paper presented to the 7th Annual Conference of the European Association for Law and Economics, Rome, September.

Caves, R. E. and Murphy II, W. F. (1976) 'Franchising: firms, markets and intangible assets', *Southern Economic Journal*, vol. 42, no. 4, April, 572–586.

Chandler, A. D. (1962) *Strategy and Structure: Chapters in the History of the Industrial Enterprise*, MIT Press: Cambridge, Massachusetts.

Chandler, A. D. (1977) *The Visible Hand: The Managerial Revolution in American Business*, Harvard University Press: Cambridge, Massachusetts.

Child, J. (1984) *Organization: A Guide to Problems and Practice*, Harper and Row: London.

Child, J. (1987) 'Information technology, organisation and the response to strategic challenges', paper presented to the 8th EGOS Colloquium, Antwerp.

Clutterbuck, C. (1985) 'Introduction' in Clutterbuck, C. (ed.) *New Patterns of Work*, Gower: Aldershot.

Coase, R. H. (1937) 'The nature of the firm', *Economica*, vol. 4, no. 16, November, 386–405.

Colling, T. and Ferner A. (1992) 'The limits to autonomy: devolution, line managers and industrial relations in privatized companies', *Journal of Management Studies*, vol. 29, no. 2, March, 209–227.

Collins, H. (1990a) 'Ascription of legal responsibility to groups in complex patterns of economic integration', *Modern Law Review*, vol. 53, no. 6, November, 731–744.

Collins, H. (1990b) 'Independent contractors and the challenge of vertical disintegration to employment protection laws', *Oxford Journal of Legal Studies*, vol. 10, no. 3, 353–380.

Commission of the European Communities (1990) *Enterprise in the European Community*, Office for Official Publications of the European Commmunities: Luxembourg.

Commons, J. R. (1934) *Institutional Economics*, University of Wisconsin Press: Madison.

Conservative Central Office (1992) *The Best Future for Britain: The Conservative Party Manifesto 1992*, Conservative Central Office: London.

Cowling, K. and Sugden, R. (1987) *Transnational Monopoly Capitalism*, Wheatsheaf: Brighton.

Creigh, S., Roberts, C., Gorman, A., and Sawyer, P. (1986) 'Self-employed in Britain: results from the Labour Force Surveys 1981–1984', *Employment Gazette*, vol. 94, no. 6, June, 153–194.

Cressey, P. and MacInnes, J. (1980) 'Voting for Ford: industrial democracy and the control of labour', *Capital and Class*, no. 11, Summer, 5–33.

Crowther, S. and Garrahan, P. (1988) 'Corporate power and the local economy', *Industrial Relations Journal*, vol. 19, no. 1, Spring, 51–59.

Curran, J. (1990) 'Re-thinking the economic structure: exploring the role of the small firm and self-employment in the British economy', *Work, Employment and Society*, Special Issue, May, 125–146.

Curran, J. and Burrows, R. (1988) 'Sociological research on service sector small businesses: some conceptual considerations', *Work, Employment and Society*, vol. 3, no. 4, December, 527–539.

Daly, M. and McCann, A. (1992) 'How many small firms?', *Employment Gazette*, vol. 100, no. 2, February, 47–51.

Daly, M., Campbell, M., Robson, G. and Gallagher, C. (1991) 'Job creation 1987–89: the contributions of small and large firms', *Employment Gazette*, vol. 99, no. 11, November, 589–596.

Deakin, S. (1986) 'Labour law and the developing employment relationship in the UK', *Cambridge Journal of Economics*, vol. 10, no. 3, September, 225–246.

Debreu, G. (1959) *Theory of Value*, Yale University Press: New Haven, Conn., and London.

Department of Employment (1991a) *Small Firms in Britain 1991*, Department of Employment: London.

Department of Employment (1991b) *Industrial Relations in the 1990s*, Cmnd 1602, HMSO: London.

Dickens, L. (1988) 'Falling through the net: employment change and worker protection', *Industrial Relations Journal*, vol. 19, no. 2, Summer, 139–153.

Dickens, P. and Savage, M. (1988) 'The Japanisation of British industry? Instances from a high growth area', *Industrial Relations Journal*, vol. 19, no. 1, Spring, 60–68.

Domberger, S. (1986) 'Economic regulation through franchise contracts', in Kay, J., Meyer, C. and Thompson, D. (eds) *Privatisation and Regulation: The UK Experience*, Clarendon Press: Oxford.

Domberger, S. and Middleton, J. (1985) 'Franchising in practice: the case of

Independent Television in the UK', *Fiscal Studies*, vol. 6, no. 1, February, 17–32.

Donovan Report (1968) *Royal Commission on Trade Unions abd Employers' Associations*, Cmnd 3623, HMSO: London.

Dore, R. (1987) *Taking Japan Seriously: A Confucian Perspective on Leading Economic Issues*, Athlone Press: London.

Dore, R. (1989) 'Where we are now: musings of an evolutionist', *Work, Employment and Society*, vol. 3, no. 4, December, 425–446.

Douds, H. J. (1976) 'The (non) franchising relationship of the life insurance agent', *Journal of Risk and Insurance*, vol. 43, September, 513–520.

Drago, R. (1986) 'Capitalism and efficiency: a review and appraisal of the recent discussion', *Review of Radical Political Economics*, vol. 18, no. 4, Winter, 71–92.

Drake, C. D. (1968) 'Wage-slave or entrepreneur?', *Modern Law Review*, vol. 31, July, 408–423.

Drucker, P. F. (1977) *Management*, Pan: London.

Drucker, P. F. (1990) 'The emerging theory of manufacturing', *Harvard Business Review*, vol. 68, May-June, 94–102.

Duncan, C. (1988) 'Why profit related pay will fail', *Industrial Relations Journal*, vol. 19, no. 3, Autumn, 186–200.

Dunne, J. P. (1988) 'The structure of service employment in the UK', in Barker, T. S. and Dunne, J. P. (eds) *The British Economy After Oil: Manufacturing or Services*, Croom Helm: London.

Dutfield, T. (1988) 'Franchising comes of age', *Employment Gazette*, vol. 96, no. 2, February, 70–74.

Eccles, R. G. (1981) 'The quasi-firm in the construction industry', *Journal of Economic Behavior and Organization*, vol. 2, 335–357.

Edens, F. N., Self, D. R. and Douglas, T. G., (1976) 'Franchisors describe the ideal franchise', *Journal of Small Business Management*, vol. 14, no. 3, July, 39–47.

Edwards, P. K. (1990) 'The politics of conflict and consent: how the labor contract really works', *Journal of Economic Behavior and Organization*, vol. 13, no. 1, 41–61.

Edwards, P. K. and Marginson, P. (1988) 'Trade unions, pay bargaining and industrial action', in Marginson, P., Edwards, P. K., Martin, R., Purcell, J. and Sisson, K. (eds) *Beyond the Workplace: Managing Industrial Relations in the Multi-Establishment Enterprise*, Blackwell: Oxford.

Edwards, R. (1979) *Contested Terrain: The Transformation of the Workplace in the Twentieth Century*, Heinemann: London.

Elbaum, B. and Wilkinson, F. (1979) 'Industrial relations and uneven development: a compartive study of the American and British steel industries', *Cambridge Journal of Economics*, vol. 3, no. 3, September, 275–303.

Employment Department (1992) *People, Jobs and Opportunity*, Cmnd 1810, HMSO: London.

Euromonitor (1987) *Franchising in the European Economy*, Euromonitor: London.

European Franchise Federation (1990) *European Code of Ethics for Franchising*, European Franchise Federation: Paris.

European Franchise Federation (1992) Figures supplied to the author on request (see Table 2.4), European Franchise Federation: Paris.

Evans, S. (1990) 'Free labour and economic performance: evidence from the construction industry', *Work, Employment and Society*, vol. 4, no. 2, June, 239–252.

Evans, S. and Lewis, R. (1989) 'Destructuring and deregulation in the construction industry', in Tailby, S. and Whitson, C. (eds) *Manufacturing Change: Industrial Relations and Restructuring*, Blackwell: Oxford.

Fama, E. F. and Jensen, M. C. (1983a) 'Agency problems and residual claims', *Journal of Law and Economics*, vol. 24, no. 2, June, 327–349.

Fama, E. F. and Jensen, M. C. (1983b) 'Separation of ownership and control', *Journal of Law and Economics*, vol. 24, no. 2, June, 301–325.

Felstead, A. (1988) 'Technological change, industrial relations and the small firm: a study of small printing firms', unpublished PhD, University of London.

Felstead, A. (1991a) 'Facing up to the fragility of "minding your own business" as a franchisee', in Curran, J. and Blackburn, R. A. (eds) *Paths of Enterprise: The Future of the Small Business*, Routledge: London.

Felstead, A. (1991b) 'Franchising: a testimony to the "enterprise economy" and economic restructuring in the 1980s?', in Pollert, A. (ed.) *Farewell to Flexibility?*, Blackwell: Oxford.

Felstead, A. (1991c) 'The social organization of the franchise: a case of "controlled self-employment"', *Work, Employment and Society*, vol. 5, no. 1, March, 37–57.

Felstead, A. (1992) 'Franchising, self-employment and the "enterprise culture": a UK perspective', in Leighton, P. and Felstead, A. (eds) *The New Entrepreneurs: Self-Employment and Small Business in Europe*, Kogan Page: London.

Ferner, A. (1989) 'Ten years of Thatcherism: changing industrial relations in British public enterprises', Warwick Papers in Industrial Relations No. 27, University of Warwick: Coventry.

Fine, T. H. (1987) 'What's happening in franchisee associations?', mimeo, Law Offices of Timothy H. Fine, San Francisco, California.

Fischer, K. J. (1981) 'Product separability in franchise tying arrangements: the Fourth Circuit's new rule', *Washington and Lee Law Review*, vol. 38, 1195–1210.

Fox, M. C. (1988) 'Kall-Kwik Printing (UK) Ltd. v. Baypress and others', *Journal of International Franchising and Distribution Law*, vol. 2, no. 3, March, 152.

Francis, A (1980) 'Families, firms and finance capital: the development of UK industrial firms with special reference to their ownership and control', *Sociology*, vol. 14, no.1, February, 1–27.

Francis, A. (1989) 'The structure of organisations', in Sisson, K. (ed.) *Personnel Management in Britain*, Blackwell: Oxford.

Francis, A., Turk, J. and Willman, P. (eds) (1983) *Power, Efficiency and Institutions*, Heinemann Educational Books: London.

Freedman, J. and Godwin, M. (1991) 'Legal form, tax and the micro business', paper presented to the 14th National Small Firms Policy and Research Conference, 20–22 November. United Kingdom Enterprise Management and Research Association: Stirling.

Freeman, R. and Medoff, J. L. (1984) *What Do Unions Do?*, Basic Books: New York.

Friedman, A. (1977) 'Responsible autonomy versus direct control over the labour process', *Capital and Class*, no. 1, Spring, 43–57.

Friedman, A. (1986) 'Developing the managerial strategies approach to the labour process', *Capital and Class*, no. 30, Winter, 97–124.

Fulop, C. (1989) 'The effect of changing channels of distribution in the market for liquid milk in the UK', paper presented to the Fifth International Conference on Distribution, Milan, 3–4 July.

Gatehouse, M. and Reyes, M. A. (1987) *Hard Labour, Soft Drink: Guatemalan Workers Take On Coca-Cola*, Latin American Bureau: London.

Gerry, C. (1985) 'The working class and small enterprises in the UK recession', in Redcliff, N. and Mingione, E. (eds) *Beyond Employment: Household, Gender and Subsistence*, Blackwell: Oxford.

Gerry, C. and Birkbeck, C. (1981) 'The petty commodity producer in Third World cities: petit-bourgeois or "disguised" proletarian?', in Bechhofer, F. and Elliot, B. (eds) *The Petite Bourgeoise: Comparative Studies of the Uneasy Stratum*, Macmillan: London and Basingstoke.

Giebelhaus, A. W. (1988) 'An early experiment in world-wide franchising strategy: the Coca-Cola Company abroad, 1901–1939', paper presented to the Economic and Historical Society, Toronto, Canada, 28 April.

GLC (1985) *London Industrial Strategy*, Greater London Council: London.

Goffee, R. and Scase, R. (1982) ' "Fraternalism" and "paternalism" as employer strategies in small firms', in Day, G. (ed.) *Diversity and Decomposition in the Labour Market*, Gower: Aldershot.

Gordon, D. M., Edwards, R. and Reich, M. (1982) *Segmented Work, Divided Workers: The Historical Transformation of Labor in the United States*, Cambridge University Press: Cambridge and New York.

Gordon, R. A. (1976) 'Rigor and relevance in a changing institutional setting', *American Economic Review*, vol. 66, no. 1, 1–14.

Gough, J. (1986) 'Industrial policy and socialist strategy: restructuring and the unity of the working class', *Capital and Class*, no. 29, Summer, 58–81.

Granovetter, M. (1984) 'Small is bountiful: labor markets and establishment size', *American Sociological Review*, vol. 49, no. 3, June, 323–334.

Green, F. (1988) 'Neoclassical and Marxian conceptions of production', *Cambridge Journal of Economics*, vol. 12, no. 3, September, 299–312.

Guest, D. E. (1990) 'Have British workers been working harder in Thatcher's Britain? A re-consideration of the concept of effort', *British Journal of Industrial Relations*, vol. 28, no. 3, 293–312.

Hadden, T. (1983) *The Control of Corporate Groups*, Institute of Advanced Legal Studies, University of London: London.

Hakim, C. (1989) 'New recruits to self-employment in the 1980s', *Employment Gazette*, vol. 97, no. 6, June, 286–297.

Hall, W. P. (1964) 'Franchising – new scope for an old technique', *Harvard Business Review*, January–February, vol. 42, no. 1, 60–72.

Handy, C. (1984) *The Future of Work: A Guide to Changing Society*, Oxford: Blackwell.

Hannah, L. (1976) *The Rise of the Corporate Economy: the British Experience*, Methuen: London.

Hanson, C. G. and Mather G. (1988) *Striking Out Strikes: Changing Employment Relations in the British Labour Market*, Hobart Paper 110, Institute of Economic Affairs: London.

Hawkins, K. (1972) 'Brewer-licensee relations: a case study in the growth of collective bargaining and white collar militancy', *Industrial Relations Journal*, vol. 3, no. 1, Spring, 23–39.

Hawkins, K. and Radcliffe, R. (1971) 'Competition in the brewing industry', *Journal of Industrial Economics*, vol. 20, no. 1, November, 20–41.

Hay, G. A. (1985) 'Vertical restraints', *Fiscal Studies*, vol. 6, no. 3, August, 37–50.

Hepple, B. A. (1986) 'Restructuring employment rights', *Industrial Law Journal*, vol. 15, no. 2, June, 69–83.

Higson, C. and Ornhial, A. (1985) 'Towards an economic analysis of franchising', Kingston Polytechnic, School of Economics and Politics, Discussion Paper in Political Economy, no. 53, March.

Hilbert, J. and Sperling, H.-J. (1992) 'The small firm: some West German evidence', in Leighton, P. and Felstead, A. (eds) *The New Entrepreneurs: Self-Employment and Small Business in Europe*, Kogan Page: London.

Hill, C. W. L. and Pickering, J. F. (1986) 'Divisionalisation, decentralisation, and performance of large United Kingdom companies', *Journal of Management Studies*, vol. 23, no. 1, January, 26–50.

Hill, S. (1991) 'Why Quality Circles failed, but Total Quality Management might succeed', *British Journal of Industrial Relations*, vol. 29, no. 4, December, 541–568.

Hirst, P. and Zeitlin, J. (1989) 'Introduction', in Hirst, P. and Zeitlin, J. (eds) *Reversing Industrial Decline? Industrial Structure and Policy in Britain and Her Competitors*, Berg: Oxford.

Hirst, P. and Zeitlin, J. (1991) 'Flexible specialisation versus post-Fordism: theory, evidence and policy implications', *Economy and Society*, vol. 20, no. 1, February, 1–56.

History Workshop Editorial Collective (1977) 'British economic history and the question of work', *History Workshop Journal*, issue 3, Spring, 1–4.

Hobsbawm, E. (1964) *Labouring Men*, Weidenfeld and Nicolson: London).

Holland, S. (1986) 'The wages of thin', *New Socialist*, no. 40, Summer, 22–23.

Holmes, J. (1986) 'The organisation and locational structure of production subcontrating', in Scott, A. J. and Storper, M. (eds) *Production, Work, Territory: The Geographical Anatomy of Industrial Capitalism*, Allen and Unwin: London.

Horne, J. (1992) 'The outbreak of conflict', *Franchise World*, no. 70, July–August, 36–37.

Hough, J. (1986) 'Power and authority and their consequences: a study of the relations between franchisors and franchisees', unpublished PhD thesis, Polytechnic of Central London.

Housden, J. (1976) 'Brewers and tenants: a changing relationship', *Hotel Catering and Institutional Management Association Review*, vol. 2, no. 1, Autumn, 5–23.

Housden, J. (1984) *Franchising and Other Business Relationships in Hotel and Catering Services*, Heinemann: London.

Hunt, S. D. (1972) 'The socioeconomic consequences of the franchise system of distribution', *Journal of Marketing*, vol. 36, July, 32–38.

Hunt, S. D. (1973) 'The trend towards company-operated units in franchise chains', *Journal of Retailing*, vol. 49, no. 2, Summer, 3–12.

Hyman, R. (1987) 'Strategy or structure? Capital, labour and control', *Work, Employment and Society*, vol. 1, no. 1, March, 25–55.

International Franchise Association Educational Foundation (1990) *Franchising in the Economy 1988–1990*, International Franchise Association Educational Foundation: Washington DC.

International Franchise Association Educational Foundation (1991) *Franchising in the Economy 1991*, International Franchise Association Educational Foundation: Washington DC.

Izraeli, D. (1972) *Franchising and the Total Distribution System*, Longman: London.

Jack, A. B. (1957) 'The channels of distribution for an innovation: the sewing machine industry in America, 1860–1865', *Explorations in Entrepreneurial History*, vol. 9, no. 1, February, 113–141.

Jensen, M. C. and Meckling, W. H. (1976) 'Theory of the firm: managerial behavior, agency costs and ownership structure', *Journal of Financial Economics*, vol. 3, no. 4, October, 305–360.

Justis, R. T. and Judd, R. (1986) 'Master franchising: a new look', *Journal of Small Business Management*, vol. 24, no. 3, July, 16–21.

Justis, R. T. and Judd, R. (1989) *Franchising*, South-Western Publishing: Cincinnati, Ohio.

Kahl, J. (1957) *The American Class Structure*, Rinehart: New York.

Katz, B. G. (1978) 'Territorial exclusivity in the soft drink industry', *Journal of Industrial Economics*, vol. 27, no. 7, September, 85–96.

Katz, L. F. and Krueger, A. (1992) 'The effect of the minimum wage on the fast food industry', National Bureau of Economic Research Working Paper No. 3997, February, NBER: Cambridge, Mass.

Kaufmann, P.J. (1988) 'Dunkin' Donuts: 1988 distributions strategies', Case Material, N-9–589–017, Rev. 11/88, Harvard Business School: Boston, Mass.

Kay, J. A. and Silberston, Z. A. (1984) 'The new industrial policy – privatisation and competition', *Midland Bank Review*, Spring, 8–16.

Kessler, F. (1957) 'Automobile dealer franchises: vertical integration by contract', *Yale Law Journal*, vol. 66, no. 8, July, 1135–1190.

Klein, B. and Saft, L. F. (1985) 'The law and economics of franchise tying contracts', *Journal of Law and Economics*, vol. 28, no. 2, May, 345–361.

Kneppers-Heynert, E. M. (1989) 'Why franchising?', paper presented to the Fifth International Conference on Distribution, Milan, 3–4 July.

Kneppers-Heynert, E. M. (1992) '"Hard" and "soft" franchising – legal classification: some Dutch evidence', in Leighton, P. and Felstead, A. (eds) *The New Entrepreneurs: Self-Employment and Small Business in Europe*, Kogan Page: London.

Knight, R. M. (1984) 'The independence of the franchise entrepreneur', *Journal of Small Business Management*, vol. 22, no. 2, April, 53–64.

Kroc, R. (1977) *Grinding it Out: The Making of McDonald's*, Contemporary Books: Chicago.

Krueger, A. (1991) 'Ownership, agency and wages: an examination of franchising in the fast food industry', *Quarterly Journal of Economics*, vol. 56, issue 1, February, 75–101.

Labour Research (1986) 'Franchising – who really benefits?', *Labour Research*, vol. 75, no. 8, August, 18–20.

Landes, D. S. (1986) 'What do bosses really do?', *Journal of Economic History*, vol. 66, no. 3, September, 585–623.

Lane, C. (1989) *Management and Labour in Europe: The Industrial Enterprise in Germany, Britain and France*, Edward Elgar: Aldershot.

Lane, C. (1991) 'Industrial reorganization in Europe: patterns of convergence and divergence in Germany, France and Britain', *Work, Employment and Society*, vol. 5, no. 4, 515–539.

Larner, R. (1977) 'The economics of territorial restrictions in the soft drink industry', *Antitrust Bulletin*, vol. 22, no. 1, Spring, 145–156.

Lazonick, W. (1979) 'Industrial relations and technical change: the case of the self-acting mule', *Cambridge Journal of Economics*, vol. 3, no. 3, September, 231–262.

Lazonick, W. (1981) 'Production relations, labor productivity and choice of technique: British and US cotton spinning', *Journal of Economic History*, vol. 41, no. 3, September, 491–516.

Leadbeater, C. (1987) 'The Sid in us all', *Marxism Today*, vol. 31, no. 1, January, 18–23.

Leighton, P. (1983) 'Employment and self-employment: some problems of law and practice', *Employment Gazette*, vol. 91, no. 5, May, 197–203.

Leighton, P. (1985) 'A narrowing and a widening of the categories of employment status', *Industrial Law Journal*, vol. 14, no. 1, March, 54–57.

Leighton, P. (1986) 'Marginal workers', in Lewis, R. (ed.) *Labour Law in Britain*, Blackwell: Oxford.

Leighton, P. and Doyle, B. (1982) 'The making and varying of contracts of employment', Department of Law Research Paper, The Polytechnic of North London.

Leighton, P. and Felstead A. (eds) (1992) *The New Entrepreneurs: Self-Employment and Small Business in Europe*, Kogan Page: London.

Levitt T. (1972) 'Production-line approach to service', *Harvard Business Review*, vol. 50, no. 5, September-October, 41–52.

Lewis, N. (1975) 'IBA programme contract awards', *Public Law*, Winter, 317–340.

Lewis, R. (1982) 'Contracts between businessmen: reform of the law of firm offers and an empirical study of tendering practices in the building industry', *Journal of Law and Society*, vol. 9, no. 2, Winter, 153–175.

Love, J. F. (1987) *McDonald's: Behind the Arches*, Bantam Press: London.

Loveman, G. and Sengenberger, W. (1990) 'Introduction: economic and social reorganisation in the small and medium-sized enterprise sector', in Sengenberger, W., Loveman, G. and Piore, M. J. (eds) *The Re-emergence of Small Enterprises: Industrial Restructuring in Industrialised Countries*, International Institute for Labour Studies: Geneva.

Lupton, T. (1963) *On the Shop Floor*, Pergamon: Oxford.

Luxenberg, S. (1985) *Roadside Empires: How the Chains Franchised America*, Viking Penguin: New York.

Macaulay, S. (1963) 'Non-contractual relations in business: a preliminary study', *American Sociological Review*, vol. 28, no. 1, 55–67.

Macaulay, S. (1973) 'The standardized contracts of United States automobile manufacturers', *International Encyclopaedia of Comparative Law*, vol. 7, chapter 3, 18–34.

McGuire, R. G. (1971) 'The labor law aspects of franchising', *Boston College Industrial and Commerical Law Review*, vol. 23, no. 2, December, 215–268.

MacInnes, J. (1987a) *Thatcherism at Work: Industrial Relations and Economic Change*, Open University Press: Milton Keynes.

MacInnes, J. (1987b) 'The question of flexibility', Research Paper Number 5, Department of Social and Economic Research, University of Glasgow, August.

McPherson, M. (1983) 'Efficiency and liberty in the productive enterprise: recent work in the economics of work organisation', *Philosophy and Public Affairs*, Fall, vol. 12, no. 4, 354–368.

Macrae, N. (1976) 'The coming entrepreneurial revolution: a survey', *The Economist*, 25 December, 41–65.

Maguire, M. (1986) 'Recruitment as a means of control', in Purcell, K., Wood, S., Watson, A., and Allen S., (eds) *The Changing Experience of Employment: Restructuring and Recession*, Macmillan: London.

Marginson, P. (1985) 'The multidimensional firm and control over the work process', *International Journal of Industrial Organization*, vol. 3, no. 1, March, 37–56.

Marginson, P. (1986a) 'How centralised is the management of industrial relations?', *Personnel Management*, vol. 18, no. 10, October, 53–57.

Marginson, P. (1986b) 'Labour and the modern corporation: mutual interest or control?' Warwick Papers on Industrial Relations No. 9, University of Warwick: Coventry.

Marginson, P. (1989) 'Employment flexibility in large companies: change and continuity', *Industrial Relations Journal*, vol. 20, no. 2, Summer, 101–109.

Marginson, P. and Sisson, K. (1988) 'The management of employees', in Marginson, P., Edwards, P. K., Martin, R., Purcell, J. and Sisson, K. (eds) *Beyond the Workplace: Managing Industrial Relations in the Multi-Establishment Enterprise*, Blackwell: Oxford.

Marginson, P., Edwards, P. K., Martin, R., Purcell, J. and Sisson, K. (1988a) (eds) *Beyond the Workplace: Managing Industrial Relations in the Multi-Establishment Enterprise*, Blackwell: Oxford.

Marginson, P., Edwards, P. K., Martin, R., Purcell, J. and Sisson, K. (1988b) 'Structure, strategy and choice', in Marginson, P., Edwards, P. K., Martin, R., Purcell, J. and Sisson, K. (eds) *Beyond the Workplace: Managing Industrial Relations in the Multi-Establishment Enterprise*, Blackwell: Oxford.

Marglin, S. A. (1974) 'What do bosses do? The origins and functions of hierarchy in capitalist production', *Review of Radical Political Economy*, vol. 6, no. 2, Summer, 60–112.

Marglin, S.A. (1984) 'Knowledge and power', in Stephen, F.H. (ed.) *Firms, Organization and Labour: Approaches to the Economics of Work Organization*, Macmillan: London.

Mathewson, G. F. and Winter, R. A. (1985) 'An economic theory of vertical restraints', *Rand Journal of Economics*, vol. 15, no. 1, Spring, 27–38.

Mendelsohn, M. (1985) *The Guide to Franchising*, Pergamon Press: Oxford.

Monopolies and Mergers Commission (1981) *Bicycles: A Report on the Application by TI Raleigh Industries Limited and TI Raleigh Limited of Certain Criteria for Determining Whether to Supply Bicycles to Retail Outlets*, HC 67, HMSO: London.

Monopolies and Mergers Commission (1982) *Car Parts: A Report on the Matter of the Existence or the Possible Existence of a Complex Monopoly Situation in Relation to the Wholesale Supply of Motor Car Parts in the United Kingdom*, HC 318, HMSO: London.

Monopolies and Mergers Commission (1989) *The Supply of Beer: A Report on the Supply of Beer for Retail Sale in the United Kingdom*, Cmnd 651, HMSO: London.

Monopolies and Mergers Commission (1990) *The Supply of Petrol: A Report on the Supply in the United Kingdom of Petrol by Wholesale*, Cmnd 972, HMSO: London.

Monopolies and Mergers Commission (1991) *Carbonated Drinks: A Report on the Supply by Manufacturers of Carbonated Drinks in the United Kingdom*, Cmnd 1625, HMSO: London.

Monopolies and Mergers Commission (1992a) *New Motor Cars: A Report on the Supply of New Motor Cars Within the United Kingdom, Volume 1*, Cmnd 1808, HMSO: London.

Monopolies and Mergers Commission (1992b) *New Motor Cars: A Report on the Supply of New Motor Cars Within the United Kingdom, Volume 2 – Appendices*, Cmnd 1808, HMSO: London.

Morris, J. (1988) 'The who, why and where of Japanese manufacturing investment in the UK', *Industrial Relations Journal*, vol. 19, no. 1, Spring, 31–40.

Morris, J. and Imrie, R. (1992) *Transforming Buyer–Supplier Relations: Japanese-Style Industrial Practices in a Western Context*, Macmillan: Basingstoke and London.

Murray, F. (1983) 'The decentralisation of production – the decline of the mass-collective worker?', *Capital and Class*, no. 19, Spring, 74–99.

Murray, F. (1987) 'Flexible specialisation in the "Third Italy"', *Capital and Class*, no. 33, Winter, 84–95.

Murray, R. (1985) 'Benetton Britain: the new economic order', *Marxism Today*, November, vol. 29, no. 11, 28–32.

Murray, R. (1988) 'Life after Henry (Ford)', *Marxism Today*, vol. 32, no. 10, October, 8–13.

Noble, D. F. (1978) 'Social choice in machine design: the case of automatically controlled machine tools, and a challenge for labour', *Politics and Society*, vol. 8, no. 3–4, 313–347.

Nolan, P. (1983) 'The firm and labour market behaviour', in Bain, G. S. (ed.) *Industrial Relations in Britain*, Blackwell: Oxford.

Nolan, P. (1988) 'Walking on water? Performance and industrial relations under Thatcher', *Industrial Relations Journal*, vol. 19, no. 1, Spring, 81–92.

Nolan, P. and Edwards, P.K. (1984) 'Homogenise, divide and rule: an essay on Segmented Work, Divided Workers', *Cambridge Journal of Economics*, vol. 8, no. 2, 197–215.

Nolan, P. and Marginson, P. (1990) 'Skating on thin ice? David Metcalf on trade unions and productivity', *British Journal of Industrial Relations*, vol. 28, no. 2, July, 227–247.

Nolan, P. and O'Donnell, K. (1987) 'Taming the market economy? A critical assessment of the GLC's experiment in restructuring for Labour', *Cambridge Journal of Economics*, vol. 11, no. 3, September, 251–263.

OECD (1985) *OECD Employment Outlook*, Organisation for Economic Co-operation and Development: Paris.

OECD (1986) *OECD Employment Outlook*, Organisation for Economic Co-operation and Development: Paris.

Ohmae, K. (1989) 'Managing in a borderless world', *Harvard Business Review*, vol. 67, no. 3, May–June, 152–161.

Oliver, N. and Wilkinson, B. (1988) *The Japanization of British Industry*, Blackwell: Oxford.

Oxenfeldt, A. R. and Kelly, A. O. (1968–69) 'Will successful franchise systems ultimately become wholly-owned chains?', *Journal of Retailing*, vol. 44, no. 4, Winter, 69–83.

Ozanne, U. B. and Hunt, S. D. (1971) *The Economic Effects of Franchising*, US Government Printing Department: Washington DC.

Paba, S. (1986) '"Brand-naming" as an entry strategy in the European white goods industry', *Cambridge Journal of Economics*, vol. 10, no. 4, December, 305–318.

Penn, R. (1991) 'Contemporary relationships between firms in a classic industrial locality', Social Change and Economic Life Initiative Working Paper 23, Nuffield College: Oxford.

Perrow, C. (1986) 'Economic theories of organization', *Theory and Society*, vol. 15, nos 1–2, 11–45.

Peters, T. J. and Waterman, R. H. (1982) *In Search of Excellence: Lessons from America's Best-Run Companies*, Harper and Row: New York.

Pfeffer, J. (1981) *Power in Organizations*, Pitman: Boston, Massachusetts.

Piore, M. J. and Sabel, C. F. (1984) *The Second Industrial Divide: Possibilities for Prosperity*, Basic Books: New York.

Pitt, G. (1990) 'Deciding who is an employee – fact or law?', *Industrial Law Journal*, vol. 19, no. 4, December, 252–254.

Pleijster, F. (1992) 'Towards full-scale business integration? The development of business co-operatives in Dutch retailing', in Leighton, P. and Felstead, A. (eds) *The New Entrepreneurs: Self-Employment and Small Business in Europe*, Kogan Page: London.

Pollert, A. (1988a) 'Dismantling flexibility', *Capital and Class*, no. 34, Spring, 42–75.

Pollert, A. (1988b) 'The "flexible firm": fixation or fact?', *Work, Employment and Society*, vol. 2, no. 3, September, 281–316.

Pollert, A. (ed.) (1991) *Farewell to Flexibility?*, Blackwell: Oxford.

PPITB and PIRA (1982) *Developments in Printing Technology – A Ten Year Forecast, Executive Summary*, PPITB and PIRA: Leatherhead.

Purcell, J. and Ahlstrand, B. (1989) 'Corporate strategy and the management of employee relations in the multi-divisional company', *British Journal of Industrial Relations*, vol. 27, no. 3, November, 396–417.

Pyke, F. (1988) 'Co-operative practices among small and medium-sized establishments', *Work, Employment and Society*, vol. 2, no. 3, September, 352–365.

Rainbird, H. (1991) 'The self-employed: small entrepreneurs or disguised wage labourers?', in Pollert, A. (ed.) *Farewell to Flexibility?*, Blackwell: Oxford.

Rainnie, A. (1984) 'Combined and uneven development in the clothing industry: the effects of competition and accumulation', *Capital and Class*, no. 22, Spring, 141–156.

Rainnie, A. (1989) *Industrial Relations in the Small Firm: Small Isn't Beautiful*, Routledge: London.

Rainnie, A. (1991) 'Just-In-Time, subcontracting and the small firm', *Work, Employment and Society*, vol. 5, no. 3, September, 353–375.

Ramsay, H. (1985) 'What is participation for? A critical evaluation of the "labour process" analysis of job reform', in Knights, D., Willmot, H. and

Collinson, D. (eds.) *Job Redesign: Critical Perspectives on the Labour Process*, Gower: Aldershot.

Ramsay, H., Hyman, J., Baddon, L., Hunter, L. and Leopold, J. (1990) 'Options for workers: owner or employee?', in Jenkins, G. and Poole, M. (eds) *New Forms of Ownership: Management and Employment*, Routledge: London.

Rehbinder, M. (1973) 'The automobile service station contract in the Federal Republic of Germany', *International Encyclopaedia of Comparative Law*, vol. 7, chapter 3, 35–45.

Richardson, G. B. (1972) 'The organisation of industry', *Economic Journal*, vol. 327, no. 82, September, 883–896.

Rodgers, G. and Rodgers, J. (1989) *Precarious Jobs in Labour Market Regulation: The Growth of Atypical Employment in Western Europe*, International Institute for Labour Studies: Geneva.

Rosenfield, C. R. (1970) *The Law of Franchising*, The Lawyers Co-operative Publishing Company: Rochester, NY.

Roy, D. (1953) 'Work satisfaction and social reward in quota achievement: an analysis of piecework incentive', *American Sociological Review*, vol. 18, no. 5, October, 507–514.

Rubery, J. (1988) 'Employers and the labour market', in Gallie, D. (ed.) *Employment in Britain*, Blackwell: Oxford.

Rubery, J. and Wilkinson, F. (1981) 'Outwork and segmented labour markets', in Wilkinson, F. (ed.) *The Dynamics of Labour Market Segmentation*, Academic Press: London.

Rubin, P. H. (1978) 'The theory of the firm and the structure of the franchise contract', *Journal of Law and Economics*, vol. 21, no. 1, April, 223–233.

Sabel, C. F. (1989) 'Flexible specialisation and the re-emergence of regional economies', in Hirst, P. and Zeitlin, J. (eds) *Reversing Industrial Decline? Industrial Structure and Policy in Britain and Her Competitors*, Berg: Oxford.

Sako, M. (1987) 'Buyer–Supplier relations in Britain: a case of Japanization?', paper presented to the conference on the Japanization of British Industry, UWIST, Cardiff, 17–18 September.

Sako, M. (1990) 'Buyer–supplier relationships and economic performance: evidence from Britain and Japan', unpublished PhD thesis, University of London.

Samuelson, P. (1957) 'Wage and interest: a modern discussion of Marxian economic models', *American Economic Review*, vol. 47, no. 6, December, 884–912.

Schulz, A. (1988) 'Germany: are franchisees salaried employees?', *Journal of International Franchising and Distribution Law*, vol. 2, no. 3, March, 149–150.

Scott, J. (1986) *Capitalist Property and Financial Power: A Comparative Study of Britain, the United States and Japan*, Wheatsheaf: Brighton.

Sculley, J. (1990) *Odyssey: Pepsi to Apple*, Fontana: London.

Seldon, A. (1953) 'The British brewing industry', *Lloyds Bank Review*, no. 30, October, 30–44.

Sharpe, T. (1983) 'The control of natural monopoly by franchising', paper presented to the Public Money seminar, Wolfson College, Oxford, 15 April.

Sheard, P. (1983) 'Auto-production systems in Japan: organisational and locational features', *Australian Geographical Studies*, vol. 21, no. 1, 49–68.

Shelton, J. P. (1967) 'Allocative efficiency vs "X-efficiency": comment', *American Economic Review*, vol. 57, no. 5, December, 1252–1258.

Sisson, K., Waddington, J. and Whitson, C. (1992) 'The structure of capital in the European Community: the implications for industrial relations', Warwick Papers in Industrial Relations, No. 28, University of Warwick: Coventry.

Smith, C. (1989) 'Flexible specialisation, automation and mass production', *Work, Employment and Society*, vol. 3, no. 2, June, 203–220.

Stanworth, J. (1988) 'Socio-economic factors in franchising', paper presented to the World-wide Economic Situations and Franchising Development Conference, Universita degli Studi di Pisa, 11–13 May.

Stanworth, J., Curran, J. and Hough, J. (1986) 'The franchised small enterprise: formal and operational dimensions of independence', in Curran, J, Stanworth, J. and Watkins, D. (eds) *The Survival of the Small Firm, Volume 1: The Economics of Survival and Entrepreneurship*, Gower Publishing: Aldershot.

Stanworth, J., Stanworth, C., Granger, B. and Blyth, S. (1989) 'Who becomes an entrepreneur?', *International Small Business Journal*, vol. 8, no. 1, October-December, 11–21.

Stanworth, J. and Smith, B. (1991) *The Barclays Guide to Franchising for the Small Business*, Blackwell: Oxford.

Stern, P. and Stanworth, J. (1988) 'The development of franchising in Britain', *National Westminster Quarterly Bank Review*, May, 38–48.

Stinchcombe, A. L. (1985) 'Contracts as hierarchical documents', in Stinchcombe, A. L. and Heimer, C. A. *Organizational Theory and Project Management: Administering Uncertainty in Norwegian Offshore Oil*, Norwegian University Press: Oslo.

Storey, D. J. and Johnson, S. (1987) *Job Generation and Labour Market Change*, Macmillan: Basingstoke and London.

Sturgess, B. (1983) 'The economics of cable television', *Economic Review*, no. 2, Autumn, 33–40.

Sutton, J. (1991) *Sunk Costs and Market Structure: Price Competition, Advertising, and the Evolution of Concentration*, MIT Press: Cambridge, Massachusetts and London.

Tedlow, R. S. (1990) *New and Improved: The Story of Mass Marketing in America*, Basic Books: New York.

Thompson, D. N. (1971) *Contractual Marketing Systems*, Heath: Lexington, Massachusetts.

Tobis, D. (1977) 'How Coca-Cola keeps its corporate image bubbly', *Business and Society Review*, no. 22, Summer, 71–74.

Transnationals Information Centre London (1987) *Working for Big Mac*, Transnationals Information Centre London: London.

Turnbull, P. (1986) 'The "Japanisation" of production and industrial relations at Lucas Electrical', *Industrial Relations Journal*, vol. 17, no. 3, Autumn, 193–206.

US Department of Commerce (1988) *Franchising in the Economy 1986–88*, US Department of Commerce: Washington DC.

Vaughn, C. L. (1979) *Franchising: Its Nature, Scope, Advantages and Development*, Lexington Books: Lexington, Mass.

Veljanovski, C. (1987) 'British cable and satellite television policies', *National Westminster Bank Quarterly Review*, November, 28–40.

Vincent-Jones, P. (1991) 'Contract litigation in England and Wales 1975–1990:

a transformation in business disputing?', mimeo, School of Financial Studies and Law, Shefffield City Polytechnic.

Walker, B. J. and Cross, J. (1989) 'A progress report on the scope of international expansion by US franchise systems', paper presented to the Society of Franchising Conference, Bal Habour, Florida, 29–31 January.

Watters, P. (1978) *Coca-Cola: An Illustrated History*, Doubleday and Company: New York.

Weitzman, M. (1984) *The Share Economy*, Harvard University Press: Cambridge, Mass.

Williamson, O. E. (1975) *Markets and Hierarchies*, The Free Press: New York.

Williamson, O. E. (1979) 'Transaction-cost economics: the governance of contractual relations', *Journal of Law and Economics*, vol. 22, no. 2, October, 233–261.

Williamson, O. E. (1980) 'The organization of work: a comparative institutional assessment', *Journal of Economic Behaviour and Organisation*, vol. 1, no. 1, March, 5–38.

Williamson, O. E. (1981a) 'The economics of organization: the transaction cost approach, *American Journal of Sociology*, vol. 87, no. 3, November, 548–577.

Williamson, O. E. (1981b) 'The modern corporation: origins, evolution, attributes', *Journal of Economic Literature*, vol. 19, December, 1537–1568.

Williamson, O. E. (1986) 'Economics and sociology: promoting a dialog', Yale School of Organization and Management, Working Paper Number 25, August.

Wood, S. J. (1991) 'Japanization and/or Toyotaism?', *Work, Employment and Society*, vol. 5, no. 4, December, 567–600.

Wright, E. O. (1976) 'Class boundaries in advanced capitalist societies', *New Left Review*, no. 98, July–August, 3–41.

Wright, E. O. (1978) *Class, Crisis and the State*, New Left Books: London.

Wright, V. (1986) 'Does profit sharing improve performance?', *Personnel Management*, November, 46–50.

Zeitlin, M. (1974) 'Corporate ownership and control: the large corporation and the capitalist class', *American Journal of Sociology*, vol. 79, no. 5, 1073–1119.

References to Law Reports

All ER	All England Law Reports
FSR	Fleet Street Reports
ICR	Industrial Cases Reports
IRLR	Industrial Relations Law Reports
KB	King's Bench Reports
STC	Simon's Tax Cases
TLR	Times Law Reports
QB	Queen's Bench Reports

References to Courts

CA	Court of Appeal
EAT	Employment Appeals Tribunal
HL	House of Lords
QBD	Queen's Bench Division (High Court)

Newspapers/Trade Journals

Atlanta Constitution
Business Franchise Magazine
Daily Mail
Der Spiegel
Financial Times
Franchise Magazine
Franchise World
Guardian
Independent
Independent on Sunday
Inplant and Instant Printer
International Business Week
Journey – The Magazine of the Coca-Cola Company
Morning Advertiser
Motor Trader
New York Times
Observer
Popular Food Service
Print
Printing World
The Grocer
The Sunday Times
Time
Wall Street Journal

Index

Note. Most references are to franchising in Britain, unless otherwise indicated.

CleanCo 81

cleaning services 49, 50; lists of 205, 222–3

clothing and textile firms 11, 23, 38, 51, 130–1; and law 122, 123, 127; lists of 213–14

clusters of franchises 65, 66, 122; craft-based firms 34–6

Clutterbuck, C. 22

Coase, R.H. 10, 61, 62

Coca-Cola 38; GmbH *see* Coca-Cola in Germany; law 108; and McDonald's 170–1; management 56–7, 240–3 (*see also* Coca Cola in Germany); motto 233; number of employees xi; operation 77; origins 41–2, 183, 193, 238, 240–1, 242; ownership 238; personnel policies 197–9; in USA 7, 9, 52, 165, 173–5, 182–3 (*see also* origins *above*)

Coca-Cola in Germany (Coca-Cola GmbH) 3–4, 7, 9, 159–86, 192, 198, 230; Coca-Cola Deutschland Verkauf GmbH and Co. KG (CCDV) 184–5; contradictions 159–60, 163–72; original franchise structure 160–3; reshaping franchise structure 172–85

Coca-Cola Schweppes Beverages (CCSB) 240, 243

coercion 73–4

coin-vendors 171, 173

collective identity *see* associations

Colling, T. 25

Collins, H. 12, 26, 33, 59, 70, 189

commercial environment, changing *see* Coca Cola in Germany

commercial and industrial services 50; list of 205–6

Commercial Plastics Ltd v. Vincent (1964) 156, 239

commerical and employment contracts, distinction between 93; *see also* contracts

Commons, J.R. 61

competition: foreign 25; and franchising 45–6; investigating *see* Monopolies and Mergers;

prohibited 111, 153–4

concentration, retail 160, 168–72

confidentiality of contracts 95

conflict of interests 78–9

consent 73–4

consolidation of production in Coca-Cola 176–81

Construction Industry Training Board v. Labour Force Ltd (1970) 29

construction/remodelling services 214

Continuous Stationery 131

contracts 28, 94–128, 191, 194, 235–7; and changing ownership 140, 143–7, 152–5; and Coca-Cola in Germany 181–3; making 93, 94–116; and operation 74, 77, 91; using 94, 116–28

'control' test 27–9

co-operation in inter-firm relationships 33–6; *see also* associations

'core' and 'periphery': employment 24, 26, 27–8, 62, 93, 98; firms 189

cosmetics and beauty aids services 131, 214; Body Shop 38, 51, 58, 120–1

costs: of selling business 113; *see also* advertising; capital investment; finance

Courage 244

courier services 51, 207

Cowling, K. 36, 202

craft-based firms, clusters of 34–6

Creigh, S. 27, 86

Cressey, P. 74

Cronin v. Customs and Excise Commissioners (1991) 29

Cross, Justice 55, 239

Crowther, S. 31, 33

Curran, J. 82, 86, 232

Curry, Mr Judge 120

Curtain Dream 131

Curtainz 131

customer sovereignty 34

Dairy Queen 239

Daly, M. 19, 20, 22